First Among Equals

CHIEF JUSTICES OF SOUTH AUSTRALIA
SINCE FEDERATION

JOHN BRAY LAW NETWORK BOOKS

History of the Independent Bar of South Australia
John Emerson

Hague's History of the Law in South Australia 1837-1867
Ralph Hague

Roma Mitchell: Glimpses of a Glorious Life
Anthology edited by Susan Magarey

A Portrait of John Bray
Anthology edited by Wilfrid Prest

available online through
www.jjemerson.com

First Among Equals

CHIEF JUSTICES OF SOUTH AUSTRALIA
SINCE FEDERATION

JOHN EMERSON

FOREWORD
BY
THE HON. J. J. DOYLE AC
CHIEF JUSTICE OF SOUTH AUSTRALIA

THE UNIVERSITY
OF ADELAIDE
BARR SMITH
PRESS

University of Adelaide Barr Smith Press
Barr Smith Library
University of Adelaide
South Australia
5005

Sale and distribution by Dr John Emerson Publishing Solutions Pty Ltd
PO Box 96
Belair, South Australia, 5052
www.jjemerson.com

First published 2006

Dust-jacket design by Chris Tonkin
Book design by John Emerson

The following institutions have kindly given permission to reproduce illustrations in this book: State Library of South Australia; Supreme Court Library of South Australia; Advertiser Newspapers.

Cataloguing-in-Publication-Data
Emerson, John James, 1960-
First Among Equals: Chief Justices of South Australia since Federation
/ John Emerson
p. cm
Includes bibliographical references and index.
ISBN 9780863968365 (hbk.)
1. South Australia. Supreme Court--History. 2. Judges--South Australa--Biography.
3. Judicial process--South Australia--History. 4. Appellate courts--South Australia--History. 5. Law--South Australia--History. 1. Title

Moys KL241.1.K2S
347/.9423/014--ds22
(AuCNLKIN)000040589241

Publication of this book was assisted by:
The Law Foundation of South Australia
The University of Adelaide
The John Bray Law Chapter of the University of Adelaide's Alumni Association
Law School, University of Adelaide

Printed and bound by IngramSpark worldwide

Foreword

BY THE HON J J DOYLE AC
CHIEF JUSTICE OF SOUTH AUSTRALIA

The system of government inherited by Australia's Commonwealth and State Governments is one that finds no need to define exhaustively by law the functions and powers of its principal institutions and offices.

Much of what is significant is left to be regulated by the common law, which can change over time, and by conventions and practices. When it is necessary or convenient to resort to statute law, as often as not the statute will deal with a mix of core and peripheral matters, still avoiding a complete and systematic treatment of the subject.

The contents of the Constitution of the Commonwealth and of the Constitution Act 1934 (SA) illustrate this point. Neither of them defines comprehensively the powers and functions of the three arms of government, the legislative, the executive and judiciary. They say relatively little about the principal offices that they assume or create. Sometimes provisions that one would expect to find in a constitution are found in other legislation.

This explains why the office of Chief Justice is one that lacks legal definition in our Constitution Act, and even in the Supreme Court Act 1935 (SA). Characteristically, the Constitution Act refers to the office of

Chief Justice only in provisions relating to the appointment of the Electoral Districts Boundaries Commission. It does not refer to the Supreme Court as such. In two short provisions it deals only with the tenure of the office of a judge, and with removal from office of a judge. The Supreme Court Act is not much more informative about the office of Chief Justice. Section 9A provides that the Chief Justice is "the principal judicial officer of the Court", and is "responsible for the administration of the Court". Part 6 gives the Chief Justice control over appointments to a number of administrative offices in the Court. Section 45 gives the Chief Justice power to direct at what "times and places" the Court will sit. Beyond that, little can be gleaned from the Supreme Court Act about the role of Chief Justice.

It is characteristic of our legal system that the law will, as in the case of South Australia, state the qualifications for the office, make some general statements about the powers of the office holder, and leave all else to be deduced from the manner in which the Court functions and from occasional glancing references in statute law to functions of a Chief Justice.

This comes as no surprise to one brought up in a common law system. The common law itself is a system of law the content of which must be deduced and identified from the manner in which the system operates, and from individual decisions.

Such systems have the advantage of flexibility. But with that comes a lack of systematic legal definition that surprises those familiar with other legal systems.

This lack of definition also gives rise to some difficulty in describing the office, and in identifying change in the manner in which it is discharged. The difficulty arises because so much depends on the practice of the office holder, and the manner in which the office is discharged from time to time. And these details are barely visible to those outside the system, because they are largely unrecorded.

Dr Emerson's study of the lives of the five Chief Justices who have held office since Federation is an attempt to remedy the lack of information about this office. Reflecting the point that I have made, he says:

> Because of the importance of personal interpretation of the role, the book is divided accordingly into chapters on each successive Chief Justice. This biographical structure acts as a foundation for a more socio-historical exploration of the way each Chief Justice dealt with

not only changing community expectations of justice but broader changes in society overall.

This approach puts each of the five office-holders firmly in the context of his (they were all men) time and place.

Not surprisingly, the chapters tell us as much about the history of the State, and about the relationship between judicial office and the administration of justice on the one hand, and the community on the other, as they do about the individual office-holders.

Between 1900, when Sir Samuel Way held office, and 1995, when the Hon LJ King AC retired, the law became increasingly pervasive in our society and, I believe, more complex.

Reflecting that, the five chapters reveal a gradual process through which the Chief Justice changed from being a leading actor in the life and affairs of the State, to an office holder whose working life (as Chief Justice) became the law and the work of the courts. It would not be practical, and probably not acceptable, for a Chief Justice to be engaged in the life of the State in the way in which earlier Chief Justices were.

The strength of Dr Emerson's approach to the subject is the way in which it reveals the role of Chief Justice, and the gradual change in that role, in its socio-historical aspect.

Inevitably, the book is unable to tell us how each of the five Chief Justices functioned within his Court, although some of that can be deduced. This kind of detail is lost in the past, because it would never have been recorded.

A point that Dr Emerson's treatment brings out is the manner in which the term of office of my predecessor, the Hon LJ King AC, serves as a marker in the changing nature of the office.

Changes in his time, largely initiated by him, resulted in the Chief Justice assuming a more significant role in the administration of the Supreme Court and of the other Courts of the State. They also resulted in him, more clearly than in the past, representing to the community the Courts and the administration of justice. There is a noticeable contrast between the exercise of the office in his time, and the exercise of the office in the past.

His tenure can be seen, I think, as marking the beginning of a new phase in the office of Chief Justice. It is a change which occurred, around about this time, throughout Australia. The Chief Justice began to be seen as representing the judicial arm of Government, and as responsible for the efficient and effective administration of justice in a way in which that office holder had not been previously so regarded.

The Honourable Dr JJ Bray AC, the predecessor of the Hon LJ King AC, bridged what we now see as an unwanted gap between the Courts and the community. The Hon LJ King AC continued on that path, but as well developed aspects of the role of Chief Justice that in earlier times had not been contemplated.

This book contains much of interest to the general reader, not only to those who are part of or linked to the legal profession. As well, through exposing the link between the administration of justice and the community, by describing the discharge of the office of Chief Justice, the book tells us a good deal about the life of our State and the administration of justice during the twentieth century.

J J Doyle
Chief Justice's Chambers
Adelaide, June 2006

Contents

Preface and Acknowledgments

Occasionally, historical books are written according to strict conventions, but I adopted the view during my doctoral thesis that material should dictate the form, not the reverse. Hopefully readers, particularly professional historians, will forgive me for this slightly idiosyncratic approach.

This means that each chapter in *First Among Equals* will vary in individual character as it follows an otherwise similar path. Sir Samuel Way, for example, left thousands of letters revealing strong opinions which gave his chapter a flavour that, for example, differs from Sir George Murray's, who revealed considerably less in the way of personal opinions in his correspondence.

The chapters also differ according to the photographs available. There are fewer for Sir Samuel Way, because photographic technology was still in its early days during his lifetime. In later periods, however, photographs existed but we found ourselves under the yoke of new copyright laws that have hardened under the Howard government. No longer can a photograph in copyright (after 1 January 1955) be published without specific permission from its copyright owner. Making "all attempts" at locating copyright owners is no longer enough, although unworkable restrictions such as these are already under review. In the chapter on

Dr Bray I was unable to locate copyright holders for many excellent photographs taken after the beginning of 1955, and held in the State Library of South Australia's archival collection, so I have compensated by publishing a relatively disproportionate number taken prior to that date.

But not only photographs have suffered from these recent laws. In the chapter on Sir George Murray I was unable to publish a one-page letter he wrote as a ten-year-old in 1874 because it had never been published. The fifty-years-after death rule (now increased to seventy in any account) did not apply since the letter had never been published. I am under the impression that generally I am a logical person and I remain completely unable to comprehend such a restriction. This law is under review too.

But I hope you will enjoy this book. I have attempted to maintain a conversational style and bring long-forgotten events to life as best one can. I found the lives of these Chief Justices fascinating and the background history of the developing South Australia held some surprises. I am hoping it will make a contribution to putting South Australia's history on the map. There is more to Australian history than Captain Cook and Ned Kelly.

The task of researching and writing this history required the kind assistance of many people. I should first thank the Hon. Justice Tom Gray who commissioned me to write it for the John Bray Law Chapter of the University of Adelaide's Alumni Association.

I needed a base and Kath McEvoy, the Dean of Law in 2002 offered me the most amazing environment an historian could hope for: the Law School's Staff Library. It will be the only period in my life when I benefit from funding cuts. The Staff Library had ceased being restocked around the mid-1990s and was falling into disuse as it grew increasingly out of date. But I was only interested in the period that ended then. There I spent over two years, surrounded by many of the old books and journals I needed, some dating back to the nineteenth century or further. The new Dean, Professor Paul Fairall, continued the Law School's support and found me an office when funds finally became available to transform the area into a 21st-century Moot Court.

I thank the Law Foundation under the Presidency of the Hon. Justice Margaret Nyland AM for awarding an initial grant so the research could begin. For the additional funding that enabled me to complete the book over the period it required, I thank former University of Adelaide interim Vice-Chancellor Professor Cliff Blake AO.

Michael Jacobs did a superb job editing not only the text but also the final layout.

The book would have been substantially lacking without help and advice from the following people: Michael Abbott QC, Sam Abbott, Angela Bentley, Peter Burdon, Sally Burgess, Hon. Clyde Cameron AO, Rob Cameron, the late Professor Alex Castles, Ray Choate, Dr Steven Churches, Pam Cleland, Anthony Crocker, Satish Dasan, Di Dawson, Garry Downs, Hon. John Doyle AC, John Edge, Hon. Bob Fisher QC, Caitlin Gill, Bruce Greenhalgh, Sandy Hancock, Lorna Hartwell, Patricia Hawke, Henry Heuzenroeder, Panita Hirunboot, Helen Horton, Hon. Sam Jacobs AO QC, Kate Jennings, Hon. Elliott Johnston AM QC, Dr John Keeler, Hon. Len King AC QC, Carolyn Lam, Mrs Sarah Lang, Hon. Christopher Legoe QC, Professor Horst Lücke, Professor Fred McDougall, Prue McKechnie, Professor James McWha, the late Professor Brian Medlin, Sue Milne, Rowan Mitchell, Hon. Robin Millhouse QC, the late Hon. Bob Mohr, Robyn Nagel, Master Peter Norman, Hon. Justice John Perry, Sharon Polkinghorne (*Advertiser*), Professor Wilfrid Prest, Margaret Priwer, Sandra Ross, Professor Tom Shapcott, Kym Tilbrook (*Advertiser*), Chris Tonkin, Mary Walters, Peter Ward, Allayne Webster and Sarah Wickham. I am also specially grateful to Prue McDonald, Anthony Laube and Joyce Garlick in the Reading Room of the State Library for their help. If I have inadvertently omitted anyone, I apologise.

J J Emerson
Law School
University of Adelaide
September 2006

ILLUSTRATIONS: KEY TO ABBREVIATIONS

Advertiser Newspapers Ltd	**Advertiser**
State Library of South Australia	**SLSA**
Supreme Court Library of South Australia	**SCLSA**

CHAPTER 1

Introduction

THE OFFICE OF CHIEF JUSTICE

The office of Chief Justice is part of the common law legal system that South Australia inherited from Great Britain. Yet the office predates even common law, established in the early thirteenth century by Henry II. It is the direct descendant of Norman customary law's "Chief Justiciar", brought to England in 1066 by William the Conqueror.[1]

After a thousand years little formal detail exists as to what the office entails. There is no modern-style "job description" listing the duties of the Chief Justice in the South Australian statutes, nor in those of England. As a result, the most important component of the office is without doubt the personality of the individual who fills it. This is why literature on Chief Justices tends to be as much biographical as historical. It is through the eyes of individual Chief Justices that we discover how they interpret the formal role of the office, and how well they adapt to the particular social and historical changes of their time.

What is the difference between the Chief Justice and other judges in the court? How is a Chief Justice chosen? Why would there be

---

1   John Campbell, *The Lives of the Chief Justices of England* p. 1.

differences between one Chief Justice and another? How do they know what to do the first day at work as Chief Justice?

The most obvious duty of the Chief Justice is to sit as a judge on trials and appeals. As a judge, she or he is equal to any other judge. Because the independence of Supreme Court judges in South Australia is protected by the Constitution, the Chief Justice cannot exert any influence over the judgment of another judge. The clear signs of this judicial independence are those Full Court appeal judgments when the Chief Justice is the dissenting judge. So it is not as a judge that a distinction between the Chief Justice and the other judges can be found. Nevertheless, Kenneth Umbreit found in his study of the Chief Justices of the United States that the Chief Justice can exert influence in subtle ways:

> He is the presiding officer both in the court room and in the conference room. As such, he has considerable control both over the course of the argument before the judges and over the course of the discussion among the judges. He can direct attention to a point or away from it more easily than any of his colleagues.[2]

This unofficial influence at the Full Court stage has perhaps grown increasingly important as the number of judges has grown. In a small court the Chief Justice may sit on as many trials as appeals. But as the court grows in size, so does the number of appeals, and the Chief Justice generally sits on the appeals rather than trials.

The key date in the history of the office of Chief Justice in South Australia is 1993. Before that date all the courts were under the administrative control of the Attorney-General. The Chief Justice fulfilled judicial and ceremonial functions, but had little say about the administration of the courts. The South Australian Courts Administration Act 1993 delineated the Chief Justice's administrative role as the presiding officer of the Courts Administration Council, which oversees all the courts in South Australia. The Chief Justice since then, therefore, has been the administrative head of the entire State's court system, not just the Supreme Court. The power of being head is that no proposal can be a decision of the Council unless the Chief Justice supports it.

---

2   Kenneth Bernard Umbreit, *Our Eleven Chief Justices*, p. xiii.

The formal qualifications of a Chief Justice are as indeterminate as the job description. The South Australian Supreme Court Act 1935 only distinguishes the Chief Justice from puisne (ordinary) justices or Masters by the length of time that they must have spent in legal practice to qualify for appointment:

> The Chief Justice must have been a practitioner of the court at least 15 years standing, or a Puisne Judge; a Puisne Judge must be a practitioner of the court of at least 10 years standing and a Master must be a practitioner of at least 7 years standing.[3]

It is crucial to understand then that without any clear delineation of duties, or of qualifications, a high degree of discretion is allowed both in the choosing of a Chief Justice and in the interpretation of what the office means. The person who makes the recommendations to Cabinet for judicial appointments is the Attorney-General. This means that each person appointed Chief Justice, even if not the first person asked, must conform to a large degree to the image that the incumbent Attorney-General has of the office of Chief Justice.

According to the English custom, the Attorney-General has also had the possibility of appointing himself. This has happened on one occasion in South Australia, and that was when Samuel Way recommended himself in 1876. This caused some controversy, which we discuss later, but Way proved more than just a good judge; under him the office of Chief Justice in South Australia became very prominent.

The legal system that South Australia inherited from England in 1836 was a mess. Six hundred years of evolution had produced parallel and conflicting court systems without clearly defined boundaries to their jurisdictions. Litigants could take a case all the way through to the House of Lords only to discover that from the very start they had chosen the wrong court. There were twenty-year waits in the Chancery Court for estates to be settled. The legal profession bickered about the duties to be carried out by its various divisions: barristers, solicitors, proctors, attorneys and scriveners overlapped in many areas.

Reform was in the air, pushed by writers and philosophers such as Jeremy Bentham, John Stuart Mill, Robert Owen, Thomas Arnold,

---

3   Supreme Court Act 1935, sections 8 and 9.

Thomas Carlyle, Charles Dickens and Mrs Gaskell. One of the city of Adelaide's streets is named after Jeremy Bentham. England had to wait for the Judicature Act of 1873 to get some relief, but South Australia, the new colony, benefited straight away. From the purely practical point of view, the new colony had not the population to support more than a single court system. Thus while England then had four primary court systems and four heads, the Chief Justice of the King's Bench, the Chief Justice of Common Pleas, the Chancellor of the Chancery Courts and the Chief Baron of the Exchequer, in the colony a single judge was appointed to satisfy their entire combined jurisdictions.

That judge was Sir John Jeffcott, but he was not South Australia's first Chief Justice. Jeffcott had been Chief Justice of Sierra Leone and the Gambia, in Africa, but the sole judge of the yet to be settled colony in Australia was not given that title – he was just the "Judge". Jeffcott arrived in South Australia in May 1837. He had been unable to travel on the Buffalo as creditors were waiting for him on the quay. As well as leaving unpaid debts behind him, he had also killed a man in a duel in Exeter. He was only forty-one, and therefore could have lived until the title of Chief Justice was introduced. But his life was as short as it was colourful, and he drowned in December 1837 at the mouth of the River Murray, on his way to Tasmania to see his fiancée.

He was temporarily replaced by Henry Jickling, a myopic eccentric who wore bright green glasses, until Charles Cooper arrived in 1839. Cooper was sole judge until 1850, when Dr George Crawford was appointed Second Judge. Crawford – who held a Bachelor of Arts, and both a Bachelor of Laws and Doctor of Laws from Trinity College, Dublin – unfortunately died two years later at just forty and was replaced by Benjamin Boothby. Around this period, according to Ralph Hague, the push began for the title of "Chief Justice":

> Although both Sir John Jeffcott and Sir Charles Cooper were from very early days frequently styled "Chief Justice", even in acts of parliament, the title was not legally created until 1856. Mr Justice Cooper had asked for it in 1844, without result. When Mr Justice Crawford was appointed, the judges were styled "First Judge" and "Second Judge". In 1853, Mr Justice Boothby, with an eye to his future prospects, recommended that the senior judge should be called Chief Justice and that his successor in that office should be

nominated thereto by the Crown. The title of Chief Justice, he said, was given to the head of the Supreme Court in all the other Australian colonies, and in every British colony where there was more than one judge.[4]

Charles Cooper's attempt to formally call himself "Chief Justice" in 1844 had been ignored, and he does not appear to have tried again. Boothby, however, never let go of an issue. He was a pedantic Anglophile who insisted on everything being done as if everyone were still in London. His continual obstruction of the business of the courts drove Charles Cooper to retire early in 1861, and eventually led to Boothby's own removal in 1867. But in the 1850s, Boothby was one of those who pressured successive governments to retitle the judges' offices.

The titles of "Chief Justice" and "Puisne Justice" were finally approved on 19 June 1856 in the first section of Act No. 31 1855-1856:

> That the said Supreme Court, so established as aforesaid, shall continue, and shall be holden by or before one or more Judge or Judges appointed, by the Governor, with the advice and consent of Executive Council, one of whom shall have the title of Chief Justice, the present Judges being Charles Cooper, Esquire, and Benjamin Boothby, Esquire; and that the said Charles Cooper shall be the first Chief Justice (…).

The Act then described the functions of the Supreme Court and its officers, but did not suggest any distinction between the role of the Chief Justice and a puisne justice. After Richard Hanson was appointed Charles Cooper's successor, not him, Benjamin Boothby took up this lack of distinction before a select committee of the House of Assembly in 1861:

> I would remark on the great mistake made by the Government and others, as to the Judges; it would seem as though the other Judges are regarded as inferior in power and functions to the

---

4   Ralph Hague, *Hague's History of the Law in South Australia*, 1837-1867, p. 183.

Chief Justice. Correspondence goes on between the Government and the Chief Justice, and I know nothing at all about the matter, until it has been decided ... In this Colony the Chief Justice can do nothing which the other Judges cannot do. The duties are precisely the same. It is merely a title given to the headship of the Supreme Court, and the Chief Justice is simply primus inter pares.[5]

How correct was Justice Boothby? If the duties of all the judges are indeed the same, then how can the Chief Justice be, as Boothby described him, a "first amongst equals"? Yet the very term does suggest a distinction.

In fact, the "first among equals" term encapsulates the essence of the office of Chief Justice. As we already mentioned, as a judge she or he will be on equal terms with the other judges. But in relation to the outside world, as titular head the Chief Justice will be the first point of contact in regard to fundamental matters concerning the courts.

In South Australia there is no formal, constitutional separation of powers. Nevertheless, there is a constitutional judicial independence, and in practice, this has produced an unofficial separation of powers between the judiciary, and the legislature and executive.[6] By extension, the Chief Justice is head of this judicial arm of government. Other heads, such as the Premier and the Governor, consult the Chief Justice about matters concerning their internal relationships. For the courts, the Chief Justice is the spokesperson for the other judges and magistrates. Since Len King's term of office (1978-1995), he has also become a spokesperson to the media, with the aim of increasing public understanding of the courts and justice.

The Chief Justice also had a traditional role as a substitute Governor. On the official table of precedence, the Chief Justice is seventh – after the Governor-General, the Governor, the officer administering the government, the Lieutenant-Governor, Governors of other states, and the Premier. But if both the Governor and the Lieutenant-Governor are absent, then the Chief Justice acts as the "officer administering

5   Hague, as above, p. 184.
6   Bradley M Selway, *The Constitution of South Australia*, p. 120.

the government".[7] From 1891 until 1967 the Chief Justice was in fact always the lieutenant-governor, but John Bray declined to accept the lieutenant-governorship because he believed that the judicial and executive arms of government were best kept apart. The Chief Justice swears in new Governors, newly elected members of parliament and new puisne justices.

The Chief Justice to some degree controls the membership of the senior bar. All applications for Queen's Counsel must be made each year to the Chief Justice, and although they consult with the other judges and the South Australian Bar Association before any recommendations to the Attorney-General, only those applicants the Chief Justice agrees with ultimately will be recommended. But the Chief Justice is not – as is the Chief Justice of the United States – the titular head of the bar. That role for centuries in England, and more recently in Australia, is reserved for the Attorney-General.

From 1883 until 1983 the Chief Justice was also almost always the Chancellor of the University of Adelaide. The first Chancellor of the University was Chief Justice Richard Hanson, from 1874 until he died suddenly in 1876. His replacement as Chancellor was Bishop Short, head of the Church of England in South Australia. Bishop Short resigned in 1883 and went to England and died the same year:

> A successor was not immediately appointed and the idea was raised in the press that the Church of England was waiting for Dr Short's successor as Bishop, so as to make the office of Chancellor an attachment in perpetuity to the Bishop's throne.[8]

But Hanson's successor to the Chief Justiceship, Samuel Way, was voted Chancellor. Except for two separate periods of six years each, the Chief Justice would also be the University of Adelaide's Chancellor for the next hundred years.

The role of the Chief Justice has changed somewhat from the first days of the King's Bench in fourteenth-century England when his role was primarily to preside at treason trials and ensure that those ac-

---

7   Same, p. 95.
8   W G K Duncan and Roger Ashley Leonard, *The University of Adelaide 1874-1974*, p.9.

cused were found guilty and executed.[9] But over the mere hundred year period that we study in this book, the office has changed little in its essential duties. It has no doubt faded in public prominence from the days when Samuel Way was Chief Justice. But South Australia was smaller then – 160,000 people lived in the capital and 200,000 in the rural areas. And Way dominated in many other areas during the founding of institutions like – to name only some – the University of Adelaide, the Art Gallery, the Museum, the Children's Hospital, and the Methodist Church. He also filled in as Governor when that role was more prominent.

From Federation until Len King's retirement in 1995, the State of South Australia changed dramatically. It added a million people to its population. The two world wars and the Depression stripped away the old class structure. Technology and industry replaced the old rural economy. Mass-produced cars and airlines gave ordinary people unprecedented mobility. Electricity, public housing, multicultural immigration, radio and television broadened lifestyles and perspectives beyond the imagination of the Victorian age. A moral and cultural revolution in the 1960s challenged and revised generations of barely questioned values.

How well did each Chief Justice adapt the courts to these changes? Should he have changed them at all? Surely the basic principles of justice do not change? One of the hardest roles of a Chief Justice is to reconcile contemporary expectations with unchanging principles. When Gerard Brennan was being sworn in as Chief Justice of the High Court in 1995 he stressed that a court of law is not a "parliament of policy":

> Judicial method is not concerned with the ephemeral opinions of the community. The law is most needed when it stands against popular attitudes sometimes engendered by those in power and when it protects the unpopular against the clamour of the multitude.(...)
>
> Judicial method starts with an understanding of the existing rules; it seeks to perceive the principle that underlies them and, at an even deeper level, the values that underlie the principle.[10]

---

9   Anthony Mockler, *Lions Under the Throne*, p. ix.
10   http://www.hcourt.gov.au/brennanj/brennanj_swearing.htm

Even a long-serving judge can make a mistake in the approach to "judicial method". The whole of the South Australian criminal justice system was shown to be out of touch in 1959 by the Rupert Max Stuart trial and the Royal Commission that followed. Although Stuart was still found guilty of murder, several aspects of the case, from the circumstances of the initial arrest and confession to the trial, appeals and Royal Commission, revealed serious systemic flaws. Chief Justice Sir Mellis Napier was not the only person guilty of error but most certainly the most important. The Stuart case radically diminished his influence over his judicial colleagues, and the Supreme Court's reputation between then and his retirement in 1967 was at its lowest ebb.

The five Chief Justices come from surprisingly different backgrounds. Each one filled the office differently; emphasis on one or other aspect of the office varied according to individual personality. For that reason people sometimes speak of the "Murray court" or of the "Bray court". All except for John Bray remained for over twenty years - Samuel Way was Chief Justice for almost forty. The lengthy periods of office, in contrast with the much shorter terms of the other heads of government, gave stability to South Australian justice. The lengthy terms also gave each Chief Justice the opportunity to mould the office according to their own interpretation, and distinguish South Australia from other jurisdictions. South Australia had just seven Chief Justices in 156 years (if we count Charles Cooper from his arrival in 1839). Over that period England had fifteen (from Denman to Taylor); New South Wales, fourteen (from Dowling to Gleeson); Queensland, sixteen (from Cockle in 1861 to Macrossan); and Victoria, ten (from a'Beckett to Phillips).

Because of the importance of personal interpretation of the role, the book is divided accordingly into chapters on each successive Chief Justice. This biographical structure acts as a foundation for a more socio-historical exploration of the way each Chief Justice dealt with not only changing community expectations of justice but broader changes in society overall. This is a somewhat unconventional methodology, risking criticism from both biographers and historians, but one I felt was born of the topic and hopefully yields the best results.

CHAPTER 2

Sir Samuel Way (1876-1916)

THE LEAD INTO FEDERATION

When the province of South Australia became the State of South Australia on the first day of January 1901, Sir Samuel Way was its "most distinguished citizen" according to J J Pascoe's *History of Adelaide and Vicinity*, published that same year. But Way was not in the State for that famous New Year's Day. He was part of the South Australian delegation for the proclamation of the Commonwealth in Sydney with Premier Frederick Holder and ex-Premier and constitutional draftsman Charles Kingston, who would subsequently be a minister in the first federal government.[1]

Way held an impressive list of offices and honours: Chief Justice since 1876, Chancellor of the University of Adelaide since 1883, Lieutenant-Governor since 1890, Australasian representative on the Judicial Committee of the Privy Council since 1897 and a Baronet since 1899. He was also Grand Master of the United Grand Lodge of South Aus-tralian Freemasons, President of the Public Library, Museum and Art Gallery, President of the Adelaide Children's Hospital and on the board of several other organisations.

---

1   Alex C Castles and Michael C Harris. *Lawmakers and Wayward Whigs*, pp. 223-224.

Samuel Way was involved in founding an impressive array of South Australia's core institutions. Not long after being appointed Chief Justice he convinced the government of the need for the Adelaide Children's Hospital, and in June 1878 he laid its foundation stone as Acting Governor. Through his leadership of the Acclimatisation Society, he helped establish Adelaide's zoological gardens on the bank of the Torrens in the early 1880s. He also helped establish North Terrace's reputation as the cultural heart of South Australia. Since 1872 he had been involved in the plans to set up the University of Adelaide, which started teaching in 1876, and he was Vice-Chancellor when it opened its first building – called since 1961 the Mitchell – in 1882. He presided over the building of the Art Gallery next door which opened in 1890, of the Museum next door to the Art Gallery, which opened in 1895 – and of the University's Elder Hall in 1900.

Adelaide during Samuel Way's lifetime was a completely different city from the over-extended metropolis it would later become. At the end of its first year in 1837 its population had reached 2,220. The first colonists lived in tents, and huts of mud or reed, along streets that were mere tracks scratched through the gums between Colonel Light's survey pegs. By 1901 its population had grown to 162,094, and 39,000 of those inhabitants lived in the city centre and North Adelaide.[2] In between there had been a too-often-forgotten sacrifice: the end of thousands of years of the Kaurna people's culture. Even Pascoe in 1901 already recognised the loss:

> Soon the opportunity of close observation will be gone, for the Exterminator has immolated nearly all. Contrary to the general opinion, their customs and habits offer supremely interesting matters for study. (…) Few peoples have secured less scientific attention and the omission is almost a slur on the British student.[3]

In King William Street, the towers of the Town Hall and the General Post Office were the tallest constructions in sight. Elsewhere, since commercial buildings and hotels rarely exceeded three storeys, the

---

2   J J Pascoe (ed.), *History of Adelaide and Vicinity* , p.617.
3   As above, pp. 12-13.

city skyline was noticeably spiked by church steeples and factory chimneys billowing smoke. In the centre of the busy city streets, horses struggled to pull trams laden with workers and shoppers. Grand carriages and humble carts filed by on either side.[4] The first motor car was yet to interrupt the clamour of hooves. The city speed limit was 12 miles per hour (18 km/h). But the drivers of the trams would risk a fine for exceeding 10 miles per hour, or for carrying prostitutes. Beyond the parklands in all directions, the suburbs were scattered unevenly from the sea to the foothills, separated by tracts of scrub so that they resembled a collection of English villages. The metropolitan population at this stage was still less than that of the country – then around 200,000 – and it would be twenty years before metropolitan Adelaide would outnumber rural South Australia.

Sir Samuel Way in 1901 (SCLSA)

The city had infiltrated international literature through the visits of two of the world's most famous writers of the time: Anthony Trollope and Mark Twain. Trollope (1815-1882) arrived in Adelaide as the guest of Thomas Elder in April 1872 during his grand tour of Australia. He wrote eighty pages on South Australia in *Australia and New Zealand*, published in 1873, introducing Adelaide as a "pleasant, prosperous town".[5] The celebrated author praised the Botanic Gardens, the parklands and the buildings, in particular the size of the Town Hall and the Post Office, given the metropolitan population then of only 60,000.

Twenty years later, Mark Twain (1835-1910) arrived by train in the hills and was taken by open carriage down to the city:

> The road wound around gaps and gorges, and offered all varieties of scenery and prospect – mountains, crags, country homes, gardens, forests – color, color, color everywhere, and the air fine and fresh, the skies blue, and not a shred of cloud to mar the downpour of the brilliant sunshine. And finally the mountain gateway opened, and the immense plain lay spread out below

---

4   Derek Whitelock, *Adelaide 1836-1976: A History of Difference*, p. 134, illustration 45.
5   Anthony Trollope, *Australia and New Zealand*, p. 636.

and stretching away into dim distances on every hand, soft and
delicate and dainty and beautiful. On its near edge reposed the
city.[6]

Twain was also impressed by the wide streets, the fine homes
and the imposing public buildings. He was especially impressed by the
religious diversity of such a relatively small population – it had reached
320,000 – that he published the statistics from a recent census of all the
denominations represented. It is true that two-thirds of the population
were Church of England (89,271), Roman Catholic (47,179) or Methodists of some kind (76,575). There were also several hundred Jews,
Muslims and Confucians. But among the category of "other religions"
were listed 3 Cosmopolitans, 9 Infidels, 2 Maronites and one each of
Memnonists, Shakers, Hussites and Zwinglians.[7]

Beatrice (1858-1943) and Sidney Webb (1859-1947), the English socialists, arrived in Adelaide in November 1898. Sidney Webb
found Adelaide "a charmingly attractive city" that resembled a "German
Residenzstadt" – the capital of a little principality, with its parks and
gardens, its little court society, its absence of conspicuous industrialism,
and its general air of laying itself out to enjoy a comfortable life."[8] Beatrice Webb found Adelaide "perhaps the pleasantest of all the Australian
colonies":

> The luxuriously laid out city surrounded by beautiful hills, the
> pleasant homely people, the air of general comfort, refinement
> and ease give to Adelaide far more amenity than is possible
> to restlessly pretentious Melbourne, crude chaotic Sydney, or
> shadily genteel Brisbane.[9]

The key personalities in the province's original colonisation had
all died by 1901, but many of those in influential positions had known
them. Way, for example, remembered Henry Jickling (1800-1873) who
had filled in as the sole judge of the Supreme Court from when Sir John
Jeffcott drowned in December 1837 until Sir Charles Cooper's arrival
in March 1839. Jickling had been Master of the Supreme Court when

---

6   Mark Twain, *Following the Equator*, p. 181.
7   As above, p. 182.
8   A G Austin, *The Webbs' Australian Diary 1898*, p. 93.
9   As above, p. 96.

Way was admitted in March 1861. Charles Kingston (1850-1908), who had been Premier from 1893 to 1899, was the son of George Strickland Kingston, Colonel William Light's Deputy Surveyor. Both George Kingston and William Light were part of the group waiting on the Glenelg shore on 28 December 1836 to greet the arrival of HMS Buffalo at 2pm and witness the proclamation of South Australia as a province of the British Empire.[10]

Early South Australia was governed– to borrow R M Hague's term – by a "reign of squabble". Governor Hindmarsh's quarrels with Charles Mann, his Advocate-General, had begun even before the Buffalo had left England. The enforced closeness of the five-month journey on board the Buffalo founded his hatred for Resident Commissioner James Hurtle Fisher and his scorn for his own secretary George Stevenson. Robert Gouger and Osmond Gilles – Colonial Secretary and Colonial Treasurer respectively – were arrested in August 1837 for fighting in public outside a gin shop in Franklin Street. Even the only person capable of mediating the warring factions – first Supreme Court judge Sir John Jeffcott – had arrived in the colony having only narrowly missed being convicted of murder after killing an opponent in a duel, and the very idea of colonising South Australia had come to Edward Gibbon Wakefield while he was in Newgate prison serving time for abducting a schoolgirl.[11]

Almost sixty years later the colony's leaders had changed but there was no less a reign of squabble. Premier Charles Kingston – who had done his legal training with Samuel Way – was on a good-behaviour bond when he was elected in June 1893. Two years later – and he would be Premier for four more – he was in a fight on the corner of Grote Street and Victoria Square with Henry Sparks, the manager of the South Australian Company. The statue erected in Kingston's honour in Victoria Square in 1916 gazes defiantly over the very spot where this scuffle took place.[12]

Kingston was also responsible for illegally detaining a political opponent and one of the two leaders of the bar. Paris Nesbit QC was a gifted lawyer, but suffered occasional psychotic episodes. In 1896 he ran unsuccessfully for Parliament and inflamed the incumbent Premier

---

10   J J Pascoe, cited earlier, pp. 34-35.
11   R M Hague, *Sir John Jeffcott*, pp. 65-87.
12   Derek Whitelock, cited above, pp. 21-24.

by encouraging electors to "thrust Kingston's great fat unwieldy despotic carcass on to the Opposition benches". Two years later, when Nesbit was spending time in Parkside asylum, Kingston took revenge. He held a special cabinet meeting and sent Dr Cleland, the medical superintendent at Parkside, a memo which ordered that: "Mr Nesbit must not be released on any pretext whatever without Ministerial authority". This directive was entirely illegal and effectively made Nesbit a political prisoner. Four months later Justice Bundey ordered his immediate release.[13]

Samuel Way's former articled clerk left State politics in 1901 to become the first Commonwealth Minister of Trade and Customs. The legal profession at this time numbered around 170 practitioners. Such a small legal profession meant that everyone inevitably knew each other and that the four practising silks led almost all the major cases. At the beginning of the 1890s these were Kingston, Nesbit, John Downer (1843-1915) and Josiah Symon (1846-1934), who was Samuel Way's former partner. Kingston and Downer became more and more involved in their political careers and this left just Symon and Nesbit to dominate the Bar from the mid 1890s. This was not always a happy affair, as Graham Loughlin describes:

> On one occasion, for example, they opposed each other in court shortly after Nesbit had been released from the asylum. During Nesbit's address to the court Symon suggested that the judge should disregard the opinion of a lunatic. Symon, who was the father of one or more retarded children, instantly regretted his remark, for Nesbit scornfully retorted: "I may be a lunatic but at least I have the decency not to populate the countryside with imbeciles!"

Unlike the other arms of government at the beginning of the twentieth century, the judicial one had been at its most stable. Way had been appointed in 1876, James Boucaut (1831-1916) had replaced Justice Edward Gwynne in 1881, and Henry Bundey (1838-1909) had replaced Justice R. B. Andrews in 1884. This meant that for sixteen years the bench had had the same three judges, and that unbroken run would

---

13   Graham Loughlin, "Paris Nesbit, QC" *Journal of the Historical Society of South Australia*, vol. 3, 1977, pp. 55-61, for all on Nesbit on this page.

remain until Bundey retired from ill-health in 1903. Boucaut followed
him two years later. All three of these long-serving judges had been Attorney-General at some time before their appointment – Boucaut from
1865 to 1867, Way from 1875 to 1876, and Bundey from 1878 to
1881. Combined legal and political careers appear more intricately in-
tertwined than a hundred years later.

Samuel Way in his sixty-fifth year could look back with special pride
at his collection of achievements. Unlike Kingston, Downer, or
Baker – the now President of the Legislative Council who Kingston had
challenged to a duel – Way did not have the advantage of a wealthy and
influential father. James Way was an impoverished Bible Christian minister earning just twenty-eight pounds a year when Samuel was born in
Portsmouth, Hampshire, on 11 April 1836. To get an idea of the buying power of that income, James Way two years earlier had bought the
eight volumes of Clarke's Commentary on the Holy Scriptures second
hand for nine pounds, when he was earning then just twelve pounds a
year.[14] John Jeffcott in April 1836 was arguing for five hundred pounds
a year as Judge of the Supreme Court of South Australia instead of the
four hundred offered to him.[15] In England then, the annual salary of
Lord Chief Justice Thomas Denman was eight thousand pounds.[16]

The Bible Christian denomination had formed only in 1815 in
Shebbear, North Devon, as a direct response to the lack of any support
in the region from any of the churches – not just Anglicans but even
the Wesleyan Methodists. James Way was frequently transferred, continually uprooting his growing family. After Portsmouth they lived in
Exeter, the Isle of Wight, Bideford and finally Chatham. By this time
– 1850 – many Bible Christians had gone to South Australia to work
in the Burra Mines, and they needed a minister. James Way was asked
if he would like to fill the position.[17] He hesitated at first, as his wife's
aging father lived in Chatham, but he accepted and took his wife and
his four younger children – Florence, Elizabeth, Edward and Jane. They
left Samuel in Chatham to continue his schooling. By the time he left
England in November 1852, Way had completed a total of five years

14   A J Hannan, *The Life of Chief Justice Way*, pp. 7-8.
15   R M Hague, cited above, pp 55-56.
16   Anthony Mockler, *Lions Under the Throne*, p. 194. Lord Denman's predeces-
      sor, Charles Abbott, had been paid 10,000 pounds a year for the position.
17   A J Hannan, cited above, pp 1-9.

– two at Shebbear College and three in Chatham under the Reverend Joseph Means. This was the only formal education he ever had.

At this point Way apparently had no specific ideas on what ca-

Shebbear College in Devon where Samuel Way completed the first two years of his five years total formal schooling around the 1840s. (SLSA)

reer he would pursue. He had already visited a court but this early experience is likely to have put him off the law. He accompanied a family friend, a butcher called Veale, who had been called to jury duty in Exeter:

> When the jury went into the box I was left alone and the Judge inquired who I was and did me the honour of ordering me out of the Court. I did not know the way out and a small procession was formed, a javelin man, myself, and a policeman, and thus ended my first appearance in a Court of Justice.[18]

In England, Samuel Way could never have been called to the bar and hence become a judge. Neither could he have been articled as a solicitor. The costs for both professions were prohibitive and had the

---

18   Sir Samuel Way, letter to Reverend T Braund, 19 July 1910. SLSA Archival Collection, South Australia, PRG 30. Javelin men were part of the sherriff's retinue whose duty was to carry pikes.

effect of generally restricting the profession to the sons of gentlemen with large incomes.[19]

Neither could have Way entered Oxford or Cambridge, as they did not grant degrees to dissenters, that is, non-Anglicans, until the 1850s. His decision at the age of 16 to follow his family to South Australia was the most important one of his life, as during this early period of the colony he would be exposed to opportunities that would never have been possible had he remained in England.

Way arrived in Adelaide after four months at sea on Sunday, 16 March 1853. The colony was sixteen years old with a total population of 126,830. The city of Adelaide had 18,303 residents, and the fast-expanding areas of Kensington, Norwood, Port Adelaide, Glenelg and Gawler already had municipal councils. There were still no railways (first line 1856), no telegraph lines (1856), nor mains water (1861). Copper had just been discovered in Wallaroo and Moonta. Young Way made the journey from Port Adelaide on a bullock cart drawn by oxen, and being the end of summer, the unpaved road would have been billowing dust.[20]

At some time in the afternoon he arrived at his parents' home in Gouger Street (they moved later that year to Gilbert Street), and surprised them and his three younger sisters and a younger brother – they had not seen Samuel for two and a half years, and with only a very slow international mail service would not have known exactly when he was due to arrive. In the evening, according to a letter written in December 1911, they all went to the Sunday service.[21]

But from Monday Samuel Way had to look for work, as his father was in no different a financial situation than he ever had been. One advantage Samuel Way had was that ship-loads of men had for months been leaving Adelaide and South Australia to go to the gold diggings in Ballarat. There was therefore less competition for available jobs. On the other hand, the local economy was consequently very depressed, and there were not many jobs on offer.

---

19   See Richard L Abel, *The Legal Profession in England and Wales*, p. 39.
20   J J Pascoe, as above, p. 617 and Derek Whitelock, cited above, p. 75.
21   A J Hannan, as above, pp. 17-18.

Way firstly had the idea of following the example of so many of the men – going to the gold diggings – but his father disapproved. Then he wondered if he would be suited to farming. In order to find out, he went out to a farm near Noarlunga owned by an old couple, the Looneys, who were Bible Christians and friends of James Way. The Looneys must have been quite impressed by their friend's eldest son, as they offered him a section of land if he stayed in South Australia. Samuel accepted it, named it "Seaview", and used it all his life as a holiday home.[22]

Without any real prospect of immediate income and no capital to invest, Samuel Way applied for work with the Bank of South Australia, the Post Office, the Public Service and the Burra Copper Mining Company – all without success. Eventually, after four months of rejected applications, he was offered a job as a junior clerk in John Tuthill Bagot's law office in King William Street.

John Bagot's practice was small and he also devoted much of his time to his pastoral and mining interests near Burra. Nevertheless, he later became a member of the Legislative Council, and his two male clerks at the time – Samuel Way and Henry Bundey – would become judges of the Supreme Court. A.J. Hannan believed that it must have been during his employment at Bagot's that Samuel Way became aware of the possibility that he could become a lawyer. But Way did not commence articles with John Bagot. After a year as junior clerk with him, Way joined Alfred Atkinson and R B Andrews in their conveyancing department as a searching clerk. This was a much larger practice located at 69 King William Street. He worked a further 18 months before entering into articles under Alfred Atkinson – at the beginning of 1856.

That Way could have entered into articles is an excellent example of the opportunities offered in South Australia then. Mr Atkinson asked a similar premium to that asked in England, but the difference was that he also paid Way a salary of three pounds a week. Thus – unlike his English counterparts – Way avoided the greater expense of his own maintenance. Apparently, during his two-and-a-half years of working he had saved enough for the premium. Even better, like all lawyers in the State since Charles Mann was admitted by Sir John Jeffcott in May 1837, Way was admitted in 1861 as a "barrister, solicitor, attorney and proctor", thus having the best chance of future success by being able to take on the complete range of legal work.

---

22   A J Hannan, as above, pp. 20-24.

An observer at this time would have been justified in predicting an average legal career for Samuel Way. He himself did not foresee anything remarkable, yet just over eight years after arriving in Adelaide, with little idea of what of he would like to do with his life, Samuel Way was the sole partner of one of the city's largest established legal practices. He had only just turned 25. He writes of the amazing sequence of events that made it possible in a letter to his uncle, 31 July 1861:

> You will have seen in the newspapers which I forwarded that Mr Atkinson died on the 4th of June. I purchased the goodwill of the business, the lease of the offices, the furniture and the book debts of his executrix for 1000 pounds, payable by two instalments of 500 pounds each. The first is paid – the other is due in June next. The purchase was settled on June 24th, but I was too busy to notify it for some weeks, and then I determined to delay issuing circulars until July 31st, because on that day seven years ago I entered this office as a searching clerk. At that time Mr Atkinson was less than 30 years of age and in the zenith of his popularity; his conveyancing clerk was an able lawyer, the mainstay of the business; and there was articled in the office a young man, the son of a wealthy and influential member of the legislature. Soon after, Mr Atkinson went into partnership with one of the ablest barristers in the colony [R B Andrews], who took a relative into the office with a promise of a future share in the firm, and articled his own stepson [Atkinson's]. So that there was no likelihood of my ever becoming the head of the office. However, in the course of a few years, he quarrelled and separated from the partner and the relative I have mentioned – the young man and the conveyancing clerk got involved in intrigues and had to leave the Colony – his stepson didn't like it and left the law – he himself, poor man, went mad and died, and I became his successor.[23]

Way had revealed in an earlier letter that Alfred Atkinson had been certified insane in October 1860. This had meant that Way had been managing the firm even before he had been admitted.

---

23   SLSA Archival Collection, PRG 30, but also quoted in A J Hannan, cited above, pp. 30-31.

The year 1861 was a particularly dramatic one in South Australia's legal history. The profession in Adelaide at this time numbered around 30 practitioners. The reputation of the Supreme Court was at its lowest ebb, exclusively because of a judge called Benjamin Boothby. He had been terrorising and bullying his brother judges, barristers, politicians and the Governor since his appointment as Second Judge in 1853. Boothby had been directly appointed from England by the British government and would be the last judge to be so. His attacks expanded from the courtroom to parliament from 1857 when South Australia gained self-government. Boothby did not recognise the new State government as valid and consequently viewed every piece of its legislation as illegal and every office holder as an usurper.[24]

By 1861 his behaviour had become such a threat to effective government that a special ministry was formed whose sole purpose was to carry out the necessary official steps to have him removed from office. Petitions complaining about his behaviour had totalled 7,000 signatures. Although they hoped for a quick amotion – removal from office – it would take six years. The situation was further exacerbated when Richard Davies Hanson was appointed the State's second Chief Justice in November 1861 to replace Charles Cooper, whose frail health could no longer cope with the disputatious Boothby. Boothby was appalled as he had been admitted to an Inn of Court in London, whereas Hanson and Edward Gwynne – already Third Judge– had been mere attorneys in England. Boothby refused to accept their appointments as Supreme Court judges and he told them so frequently. In a petition against Hanson's appointment to the House of Lords, Boothby even refused to recognise the office of Chief Justice, praying "that the instrument by which Mr Hanson claimed to act and preside as Chief Justice should be declared null and void, as being unjust and contrary to law."

That year was also the one when a shepherd named Ryan discovered copper near Moonta. The amoval of Justice Boothby and the court case resulting from the Moonta copper discovery would play key roles in establishing Samuel Way's reputation as a barrister over the next few years. But Way's first two years in practice were devoted more to solicitor's work, at least if one examines his court appearances. Before the South Australian Law Reports began appearing in 1865, the daily

---

24   See Castles and Harris, cited above 126-134, and 143-148, but for greater
      detail R M Hague, *Hague's History*, pp 219-528.

newspapers – *The Advertiser* and *The Register* – provided the sole written record of court proceedings and judgments. In Way's first year he appeared in eight reported cases and in 1862, in seven. He got his big break in 1863 when he was briefed to appear before a Select Committee of the House of Assembly in the Moonta mines case.[25]

The details of Way's involvement in this case appear in A.J. Hannan's biography. The case would drag on through the courts until 1866 and become South Australia's first appeal to the Privy Council. The core problem was that Mr Ryan had been unable to convince anyone at first of the truth of his discovery, and then had ended up forming agreements with two syndicates. One was led by Samuel Mills and the other by Walter Watson Hughes, the owner of the land and Ryan's employer. The Mills syndicate arrived at the Lands Office at 8.30 am and the Hughes syndicate at 10 am. The office opened at 10.15, and because the Chief Clerk knew Hughes's representative personally, he served him first.[26]

Way represented the Mills syndicate which claimed that they should have been given priority at the Lands Office. In the end, the Privy Council ruled against the Mills group, but Way was able to obtain a settlement for his clients of ten thousand pounds from Walter Hughes. This was a certainly a large sum of money – at around a hundred times the median annual wage – but was nothing in comparison to the total value of

Justice Boothby (SCLSA)

the copper produced at Moonta until it ran out in 1923: twenty million pounds.[27] But it made possible the early establishment of the University of Adelaide in 1874, for Walter Hughes and Thomas Elder (1818-1897) – one of the mine's main investors – each contributed twenty thousand pounds, and over the following 23 years Thomas Elder added a further seventy-five thousand pounds including the legacies in his will.

For Way, the Moonta Mines case gave him an indispensable opportunity to demonstrate his ability as a barrister. It was the State's biggest case so far, with Bagot, Boucaut and Way acting for Mills; and Bakewell, Fenn, Strangways and Ingleby acting for Hughes. The case

25   A J Hannan, cited above, p. 41.
26   Hannan, pp. 34; 41-8; 61; 68-69.
27   Derek Whitelock, cited above, p. 102.

had not been made any easier or less drawn out by Justice Boothby's frequent denials in court of the existence either of an Attorney-General or of a Chief Justice in South Australia. The failure to remove Boothby had the effect of making him even more confident in his opinions and therefore more obstructive.

Samuel Way at 34, the age he holidayed in England (SCLSA).

Among other incidents, at the May Criminal Sessions of 1866, Boothby refused to acknowledge the legitimacy of the At-torney-General in the colony and released prisoners waiting in the cells, much to their surprised glee. In June 1867, Governor Sir Dominic Daly (1798-1868) set up an in-quiry and gave Way the job of conducting it. In a document drafted by former Attor-ney-General Boucaut, Justice Boothby was charged on five accounts:

1.　　　Conduct and language contumacious and disrespectful to the Court of Appeals, and obstructive to the said court in the performance of its duties.

2.　　　Perverse refusal to recognise the authority of Parliament, and to administer the laws of the Province.

3.　　　Expressions on the Bench disparaging of and insulting to the Legislature, the Government, and the institutions of the Province, and language and behaviour on the Bench calculated to bring the administration of justice into contempt.

4.　　　Language on the Bench offensive and irritating to the other Judges, and public denial of their authority.

5.　　　Allowing private and personal feeling to interfere with the fair and impartial administration of justice.

On 4 July Way made his final address. Justice Boothby predict-ably considered the entire proceedings illegal and attended on the first day to say only that. On the evening of 29 July 1867 a Gazette Extraor-dinary published the finding of the Governor and Executive Council ordering the amoval of Justice Boothby. A week later, Attorney-General and Crown Solicitor William Wearing replaced Mr Boothby as Second

Judge. His shocked predecessor spent his newly gained spare time preparing a petition to the Privy Council but died in June 1868 before he
had completed his submission.[28]

In 1868 Way took on a partner, James Brook. The arrangement
worked so well that by the following year Way was confident enough
of his firm's reputation to take a year off to go to England. He went
both to take a holiday and revisit his friends and family and to appear in
two Privy Council appeals on behalf of his clients.[29] He was away from
Adelaide from May 1869 until April 1870.

At this point Samuel Way could look with considerable pride
on his life. He had in sixteen years become one of Adelaide's leading junior barristers. From the humblest of social backgrounds, he was
now regularly mixing with leading politicians and business people. He
turned 33 just before he left for Britain. He was dedicated to the Bible
Christian church that he had grown up with and he was a member of
the Freemasons. But to 1869 we can trace the beginnings of the two
great regrets of his life.

The first was widely known, and that was his desire to live in
England. His correspondence from his return to Adelaide in 1870 until
his last letters in 1915 show how he was constantly preoccupied with
the great legal world of London. For example, he writes to a friend in
England after being appointed Queen's Counsel at the age of 35 years in
September 1871, thus placing him at the top level of the bar in South
Australia:

> I often think of the happy holiday I had in 1869-70, and wish it were
> just beginning again. There are no incidents in it I more frequently
> recur to or which I wish more I could live over again than my return
> and first visit to Chatham and the happy Christmas I spent there.
> (…) I have no intention of being transported for life, and if I can't live
> in England I will, if I am spared, visit it as often as I can.[30]

---

28   See Hannan, already cited, pp. 55-75 for more on Way's role in the amoval of
      Justice Boothby.
29   *National Bank of Australasia v Mullen* [1869] SALR 157 and *Randall and
      Others v South Australian Insurance Company* [1869] SALR 151.
30   Hannan, p. 89; and p. 79 for the second quote on the demands of his prac-
      tice.

The month before he had written to a London tailor, ordering a silk gown, waistcoat, knee-breeches, black stockings and a pair of shoes with silver buckles, telling him: "I could get them in Melbourne, but prefer your work to Colonial". Symptom of a fading dream rather than concern for quality was behind these words.

The second great regret of Samuel Way's life would remain a secret in Adelaide during his lifetime: the five children that he fathered with Susannah Gooding. It would take another 120 years until legal historian Alex Castles was examining some Tasmanian shipping records and realised there was a curious pattern to Way's visits. Way usually went to Tasmania annually, but every so often he returned after nine months. Further researchers uncovered the truth.[31] Way's first biographer A J Hannan must have known as he curiously omits Way's holidays in Tasmania in their entirety. It may be true, as John Bray notes, that Way's sister destroyed his personal diaries.[32] But Way records his trips to Tasmania in other diaries available in his SLSA Archival Collection files.

Sir Richard Hanson, Chief Justice 1861-1876 (SCLSA).

This alone contradicts Hannan's introduction to Chapter 5, "A Visit to England", referring to his trip in 1890:

> The substantial justification for the journey to England was that Way badly needed a holiday. He had for years been giving unremitting attention to the demands of his expanding practice (…).

Way worked hard and never wasted a moment, but he took advantage of any break in the Supreme Court program to travel, particularly the summer break of two months. In 1890 he gave a speech to the Tasmanian Masons and confirmed that he had been in the habit of visit-

31   Anne Rand, Margaret Glover, Shirley Eldershaw and Sue Edgar. Investigated further by Andrew Parkinson who then published "The Regret of Samuel Way." (1995) 1 *Aust J Leg Hist* 239-257.

32   J J Bray, "Sir Samuel Way", *Australian Dictionary of Biography*, 1891-1939.

ing Tasmania regularly for 22 years, which dates his first visit to 1868. Parkinson found circumstantial evidence suggesting that Samuel Way and Susannah Gooding met slightly earlier – in the mid-1860s.

The fact that Way's trips to Tasmania were not always during the summer court breaks, and that he did not necessarily go even then, made it easier to trace the connection between him and the births of the five children. On five particular visits to Tasmania, or to Melbourne in the case of the fifth child, there had been an earlier visit precisely nine months before. The researchers located baptisms, and the names of the children revealed the truth: James Samuel Gooding was born on 16 July 1869 – not long after Way had arrived in England. Frank Brook Way Gooding was born on 4 October 1872; Alfred Edward Rowden Gooding on 5 November 1874; Florence Elizabeth Jane Gooding on 9 January 1877; and Edward Rowden Gooding was born on 14 November 1881. Way's middle name and father's name was James; James Brook was his first partner – who notably died in August 1872; Rowden was the surname of his maternal grandfather; and his three sisters were Florence, Elizabeth and Jane.[33]

Way's relationship with Susannah Gooding lasted until her death in 1888. He moved her and the children to Melbourne in 1881. Here they took the surname of White. He set her up in a millinery business and sent the sons to Geelong Grammar. James died in 1895 and Frank in 1902, and the two younger boys, Alfred and Edward, became medical practitioners. Alfred became a well-known philanthropist in Melbourne and gave many thousands of pounds for medical research, libraries and art. He was knighted and it is after him that the Rowden White Library in the Union Building at the University of Melbourne is named. Edward's son James Northcote Rowden White is listed in the Geelong Grammar School Register along with his father and uncles. He was born in 1921 and enlisted in World War II, dying in March 1942 after the first Japanese air-raid on Darwin. James White knew about his distinguished grandfather in South Australia.[34]

Why did Way keep this relationship with Susannah a secret? Was it simply because she was a servant? He would have been aware of the

33   Andrew Parkinson, "The Regret of Samuel Way", *Australian Journal of Legal History*, vol. 1, 1995, pp. 242-247.

34   One of his fellow soldiers was the Hon. F R Fisher QC, South Australia's first federal court judge, and direct descendant of Joseph Fisher (1834-1907), joint owner of *The Register* and politician. .

hardening of attitudes towards the notion of class over the course of the nineteenth century. Susannah Gooding had been a servant. Way would have sympathised more than many would have realised with Chief Justice Sir Richard Hanson, who was ostracised by respectable society in Adelaide for having married his housekeeper, a higher position than a servant. This apparent gaffe was maliciously seized upon in 1863 when Justice Boothby tried to prevent Mrs Hanson from attending a ball at Government House with the aid of, among at least fourteen others, Bishop Short, Joseph Fisher (a joint owner of *The Register*) and John Morphett. Both Fisher and Morphett were members of the Legislative Council. Colonel Light had earlier been ostracised by Adelaide's founding fathers for cohabiting with his mistress, Maria Gandy.[35] The righteous conveniently forgot that in order to secure the Hanoverian succession King William IV himself had been obliged to leave his defacto partner of twenty years and marry Princess Adelaide of Saxe-Coburg and Meinengein, after whom the city of Adelaide is named.

Why Way decided to keep his family a secret from all but perhaps a few intimate friends will itself remain a secret. He records his visits to her in the diaries available, but only briefly.[36] It shows the extent to which he was a pragmatist, as opposed to Colonel Light and Sir Richard Hanson, who were visionary and idealistic. Hanson had even been sacked in England from the legal firm of Bartlett and Beddome for his utopian ideals. But neither of these two had grown up in the extreme poverty that Way had known. It is very likely that in his own career he wanted to put himself as far as possible from having to endure that misery again, and to him that seems to have meant conforming to established practices, rather than challenging them. If it was not the done thing to marry a servant if one aspired to high public office, then he would keep that side of his life to himself. This division of private and public life was no exception in Victorian society. As Parkinson points out, Way's friend in Melbourne, Justice Redmond Barry, also had a mistress and children living near Susannah Gooding and hers in Carlton.[37]

So after Susannah's death in 1888 Way was more a widower than a bachelor when, aged 62, he married Katherine Blue in 1898. His

---

35   Whitelock, cited above, p. 6. Maria Gandy was a grandmother of future
      Justice Herbert Mayo.
36   SLSA Archival Collection, PRG 30/1.
37   Parkinson, pp. 253-254.

Way bought Montefiore in 1872, now part of the University of Adelaide's Aquinas College (SLSA).

history with his new wife may also have been longer than is publicly known. Being wise after the event about the reality behind the cryptic references in his official diaries to the "W's" or "my dear S" leads too easily perhaps to reading other entries by extension as also meaning more. In 1903 Samuel Way celebrated the jubilee of his arrival in Adelaide. An article in *The Register* cites a speech in which he mentions that he had fallen in love with his wife when she was still a child.[38] In fact, fifteen years before they married, and while she was still married to Dr Blue and living in Strathalbyn, she was a regular guest of Samuel Way at his house in North Adelaide. For example, his entry for Friday, 26 October 1883 notes: "Annual [unreadable] Children's Hospital. Mrs Blue arrived." At the head of each page until the 5 November is written "Mrs Blue's visit continues." She stays again from 12 November until 21 November, and then again from 22 November until 24 November. This was not long after Susannah and the family had moved to Melbourne.[39]

In the light of Way's private life, the discipline and energy which he applied to his professional life is even more impressive. On his appointment as Queen's Counsel in 1871 he and Randolph Stow constituted Adelaide's senior bar. Two years later, Stow entered politics and

38   SLSA Archival Collection, PRG 30/36.
39   SLSA Archival Collection, PRG 30/1, diary for 1883.

won representation of the electorate of Light in a by-election in 1873. Then in February 1875 he was appointed to the Supreme Court to replace Justice Wearing, who had drowned off the Queensland coast after the first circuit session in the Northern Territory. Way entered politics in June that year as one of the two representatives for Sturt. James Boucaut formed a government, and Samuel Way became his Attorney-General. This would prove the key event in his eventual appointment as Chief Justice.

In the early 1870s, Samuel Way was also becoming involved in another activity in which he would dominate during his life: the University of Adelaide. This was to be Australia's third university after Sydney's, established in 1850, and Melbourne's, established in 1853. The initial idea in Adelaide was not the establishment of a university but a training college for Baptist, Congregational and Presbyterian ministers. Classes began in 1872 and proved successful enough to justify immediate expansion. The college leaders approached Walter Watson Hughes, who had made a fortune from the Moonta mines for a donation. His offer of twenty thousand pounds was so significant that the college leaders realised that they could establish a university.

A meeting was held in September 1872, and the organisation and appointment process began. After a lot of debate in Parliament about the site and the avoidance of denominational and sectarian tendencies, the University Act was finally passed in November 1874. It provided for a council of twenty members, no more than four of whom should be ministers of religion. The Chief Justice, Sir Richard Hanson, was elected Chancellor, and Bishop Short Vice-Chancellor. This was an surprising combination, since Bishop Short was part of the group in 1863 that boycotted Sir Richard Hanson's wife from Government House. Samuel Way was one of the founding members of the Council. The Government assisted by donating five acres of land on North Terrace.[40]

Sir Richard Hanson died suddenly on 10 March 1876 and Samuel Way's life changed very quickly as a result. As Attorney-General, he had the responsibility of recommending a successor as Chief Justice, and under English law could recommend himself. This he did, but backed by Premier Boucaut and the rest of the cabinet. He was 39 years old

---

40   W G K Duncan and Roger Ashley Leonard, *The University of Adelaide Centenary 1874-1974*, pp. 4-9.

and had been a practising lawyer for barely the 15 years required by law. His entire career spanned almost exactly Sir Richard Hanson's time as Chief Justice.

In his relatively short career at the bar, Way had nevertheless saved forty thousand pounds – or the equivalent of four hundred times the annual wage of a tradesman in 1876.[41] He had bought his house, Montefiore, in North Adelaide four years earlier and a large Merino sheep property near Mintaro in the north. He had his southern country property, "Seaview", the gift of the Looneys. His average annual earnings in his last years at the bar had reached six thousand pounds a year. Although the Chief Justice's salary at that time

The Supreme Court in the 1890s when the judges arrived by carriage (SCLSA).

was much less at two thousand pounds a year, it was still comfortably more than his needs.

Such a rapid move to the Chief Justiceship was certain to provoke frowns on the brows of some of his legal and judicial colleagues. His partnership with Joshua Symon is a distant ancestor of contemporary firms such as Finlaysons, Piper Alderman, and Murray and Cudmore. Symon held a bitter grievance against Way for the abrupt manner in which he left the firm. Symon was on his way to England at the time, and had made it as far as Colombo. He had to turn back as a result, as only the two managing clerks were left to operate the practice and they did not have the right of audience in the Supreme Court. One of the clerks was Charles Kingston, who would become a lifetime critic of Way.

The two other judges on the bench were Randolph Stow, Way's former co-leader of the bar, and Edward Gwynne, who had been Second

---

41   Hannan, cited above, p. 97. For annual wages in 1876 see William Harcus (ed.), *South Australia: its history, resources and productions*, pp. 272-275.

Judge fifteen years earlier when Way had been admitted. Neither of the two spoke to Way after his appointment except in an official capacity. Stow died in 1878, but until Gwynne retired in 1882, Way must have found the corridors of the Supreme Court building occasionally uncomfortable.

Bishop Short replaced Hanson as Chancellor of the University of Adelaide and Way was elected Vice-Chancellor. His first day as Chief Justice was 27 March 1876, and the opening meeting of the University was held on 25 April in the Town Hall. The first classes had already begun in March that year, with a total of sixty students, including thirty-three women. Adelaide was therefore the first university in Australia – and no doubt among the first in the world – to enrol women. Melbourne did not admit women until 1879, and Sydney until 1881. The first University building was opened in 1882 –in 1961 named the Mitchell building.[42]

Way in full robing with breeches and buckled shoes (SCLSA).

Thus began Way's golden period. Over the next twenty-three years, he would join or preside over the boards of the Children's Hospital, the Public Library, Museum and Art Gallery, and the Geographical Society. He filled in as Acting Governor and was permanently appointed Lieutenant-Governor in 1891. His double crowning glory was to be the first Australian judge to be appointed to the Judicial Committee of the Privy Council in 1897 and the first South Australian to be awarded an hereditary baronetcy.

Judges and barristers in South Australia had been wearing wigs since Justice Crawford arrived as Second Judge in 1850. Before that, Justice Cooper as sole Judge did not permit them due to the hot summers. A year after his appointment, in 1877, Way indulged his passion for English legal tradition by introducing the scarlet robe trimmed with ermine for criminal trials. Alex Castles and Michael Harris in their

---

42   Duncan and Leonard, cited above, pp. 14-15. Sir William Mitchell was the Hughes Professor of English Language and Literature and Mental and Moral Philosophy from 1894-1922, Vice Chancellor from 1916-1942 and Chancellor from 1942-1947.

1986 *Lawmakers and Wayward Whigs* were suspicious of the new Chief Justice's motives:

> Today, when the use of wigs and gowns in higher court proceedings in South Australia and elsewhere continues to be supported, it is sometimes claimed that this is necessary to uphold the dignity and the standing of these tribunals. It is unlikely, however, that Way had this argument in the forefront of his mind when he introduced his new robes to the public. Rather, he showed for the remainder of his life that seeking honours and titles, and the accoutrements which went with these, was one of the abiding passions of his life. At the inaugural function for the University of Adelaide, for example, after he had been elected to be Vice-Chancellor, he insisted in appearing in his black judicial gown and wig. Even his normally adulatory biographer, A.J. Hannan, remarked of this attire that there might have been some who disapproved "for that was not the uniform of the vice-chancellor".[43]

Way no doubt annoyed those who believed he should have had a university education. But his ambitiousness was well-known. The weekly *Critic* and the daily *The Register* would often satirise it. In the edition of 10 June 1899 after his baronetcy was confirmed, "Outis" in *Critic* published "Biography of a Baronet":

> Scion of a simple manse
> Pert and snazzy legal lance;
> Busy with his briefs while others slept.
> > Politician, picked of Sturt;
> > An Attorney-G --, alert;
> On the Chief Judicial Bench he leapt.
> > Substitutionary gem
> > Of vice-royalty, pro dem;
> Privy C --, the Press and people's pet;
> > Might have been a pretty knight,
> > Wouldn't – offer was a slight;
> Nought would do but this – a baronet.[44]

---

43   Castles and Harris, cited above, p. 74.
44   SLSA Archival Collection, PRG 30/45, Box 1. *Critic*, 10 June 1899.

The poem was accompanied by drawing of a ladder, with each rung labelled:

Baronet
PC 1896
Lieut-G 1891
CJ 1876
AG 1875
MP 1875
QC 1871
Bar 1861
SA 1853
Born 1836

The rise of Samuel Way (SLSA).

These quotes come from clippings his secretary collected on his behalf and bound into books. They leave out the honorary doctorates he was awarded from Oxford in 1891, Adelaide in 1892, Queen's (Canada) in 1895 and Cambridge in 1897. The University of Melbourne also awarded him a fifth honorary doctorate in 1901. Meanwhile, he became Chancellor of the University of Adelaide in 1883 after the death of Bishop Short. In short, a man of extraordinary distinction who may have inspired envy or jealousy.

There was a notable change in the way *The Register* reported his accession to Chief Justice and his appointment as Vice-Chancellor. The article about him becoming Chief Justice recognised him as the "natural leader of the bar", his "sheer hard work and thorough devotion", a "thoroughly shrewd lawyer", and concluded: "In a word, he has many of the qualities that go to make an excellent judge.[45] A month later, the

---

45   Hannan, cited above, pp. 96 and 105.

paper questions the wisdom of his selection as Vice-Chancellor: "We think it would not have been difficult to find among the members of the Council more than one eminently qualified by their University standing to fill the position." It was referring to the fact that Samuel Way had no university education while several of his fellow university council members did. It certainly would be interesting to know exactly how he was chosen as Vice-Chancellor and subsequently Chancellor when Bishop Short died in 1883. Was he an intriguer or did he show an obvious ability to lead the University's development?

In the court, Way brought a maturity and dignity that it needed after the damage done to its reputation during Boothby's pedantic decade. The period of exceptional stability from the 1880s to the early 1900s with the same three judges

The Supreme Court was one of the tallest buildings in Victoria Square in 1883 (SCLSA).

– Way, Boucaut and Bundey – gave South Australia a solid judicial arm of government, particularly during the tempestuous Kingston years of the 1890s. Way dominated the Court, and in the single instance when he was in the minority of a Full Court judgment, the Privy Council upheld his.[46]

Way also chaired a number of Royal Commissions, the most notable being the inquiry in 1883 into welfare services. Although the impetus for this had been concerns by Catholics that some of their orphaned children had been placed in Protestant homes and converted, Way quickly discovered two real sources of concern. The first was a leaking ship used as a boys' reformatory. Way was appalled by the "pallid and dull appearance of the boys" when he visited. Their diet was primarily "cold and indigestible pudding" and they were kept on board for periods of up to seven months at a time. He also was shocked at the "Lying-in Home" on North Terrace. Unmarried mothers were imprisoned for six months and forced to wash clothes six days a week.

---

46   Bray, cited above, p. 418.

The stench from the City Morgue next door in summer was, in Way's opinion, a possible danger to their health. His report was damning and obliged the government and parliament to take immediate action against the Destitute Persons Board.[47]

We get an insight into Way's personality in his peak years from writer Beatrice Webb who met him during her 1898 visit to South Australia:

> Chief Justice Way is a character. A grizzled, bearded little man, insignificant in features, voluble and diffusive in speech, with more authority than dignity in his manner; he neither pleases nor impresses the casual visitor. At first he seems a fussy little Methodist deacon; presently you discover that he is both good and wise. With intimacy one learns to appreciate his wide experience of men and things, his large-minded cultivation and above all his continuous application in advancing what he believes to be right. We found him peculiarly interesting to talk to; he had known every colonial of note for the last thirty years; he had served as Acting Governor many times, had been practising barrister, minister of the Crown and lastly Chief Justice.[48]

Webb's description of Way is particularly interesting for its comparison of the first impression he gave and later insight into his character. Hannan notes aspects of his court behaviour, perhaps when he was a bit older:

> The Chief Justice's appearance in court was always dignified and impressive, especially in the scarlet robes he wore in the Criminal Court, but he had a tendency as the case proceeded to poke at his wig with the large, cork-handled pen in his right hand until he had pushed it to one side. He would also sometimes push his spectacles up on to his forehead, and then call upon his tipstaff to find them for him.[49]

---

47   Hannan, pp. 119-121, and Castles and Harris, pp. 194-195.
48   A G Austin, pp. 97-98.
49   Hannan, p. 99.

Way also amused counsel and members of the public with his insistence on taking his own notes, even after shorthand writers and typists were introduced. Way viewed them as "dangerous resources of the indolent". He spoke each word as he wrote it, but caused smiles when he frequently misheard what had been actually said. But Way in turn liked to make fun of counsel if the opportunity presented itself, which would usually provoke polite laughter. Paris Nesbit once countered such a humorous attack: "I suppose we must all laugh now, your Honour" – without Way being the slightest offended.

Change was in the air already in the closing years of the nineteenth century, even as Way achieved his highest appointment, the baronetcy. For almost twenty-four years his carriage was a familiar sight in King William Street four times a day. His coachman William Henry George not only drove the Chief Justice in to the courts from his grand home in North Adelaide, but also returned in the middle of the day with his lunch, and waited for the tray, often with one of Way's dogs on the front seat with him. But in September 1899, William George died, and, in a way, for his employer the nineteenth century died with him.

The end of that century was also the end of the independent Province of South Australia. Way, as we mentioned at the start of this chapter, was considered the State's most distinguished citizen. His entry in Pascoe's *History of Adelaide and Vicinity* is by far the book's lengthiest, outdoing the ones for great founders and developers such as George Fife Angas (1789-1879), Sir Thomas Elder (1818-1897), Sir Henry Ayers (1821-1897) and Sir Samuel Davenport (1818-1906). It is little surprise then that, having succeeded within the mechanisms and structures of the Province, Way viewed federation with more than a little suspicion.

His most immediate concern was the loss of appeals to the Privy Council. His appointment to the Privy Council had renewed his longtime wish to live in London, and now, with a general movement to replace it with a new federal High Court, Way's ambitions were threatened. Early in 1900 he wrote a memorandum attacking in particular section 74 of the draft constitution which struck out Privy Council appeals, and sent out copies to all those concerned in Australia and England. His memorandum arrived in England at the same time as the colonial delegates arrived to witness the Imperial Parliament pass the bill to constitute the Commonwealth of Australia and accept the draft constitution. Charles Kingston was there to represent Australia and, having been the key to Way's appointment to the Privy Council three years earlier, was furious. Way had not warned him about sending the memorandum, and since the arrangement had been that the draft constitution would pass unchanged, Way's memorandum almost stopped the bill being passed.[50] The Constitution was hastily altered to allow for the continuance of appeals to the Privy Council and the Bill finally passed and received Queen Victoria's assent on 5 July 1900.[51]

The most symbolic event that signalled the passing of the colonies and the passage to a new century was the death of Queen Victoria, who only lived twenty-two days into the year 1901. She had been Queen of the British Empire since June 1837, only six months shorter than South Australia's history. Nearer to home, Way's brother Edward, who had become an eminent surgeon, died at fifty-five years old after

A garden party at Victoria Park around 1900. Katherine Way is second from left (holding the umbrella) and Samuel is third from left (SLSA).

collapsing suddenly in the operating room in September.

---

50   Castles and Harris, pp. 237-239.
51   For a detailed examination of Way's argument, see Hannan, cited above, pp. 184-193.

Way no doubt realised by now that he would never live in England, and anyway was too well-established in South Australia to leave. He was anxious nevertheless not to lose his vast number of friends and colleagues in the mother country, so he sent two hundred of them a case of apples each from Adelaide Hills orchards, for fear of them forgetting him before he had the opportunity to return. He did not know that his visit in 1897 when he sat on the Privy Council had been his last, and that the High Court of Australia to which he was so opposed would be the reason.

He had been watching the Court's establishment with great interest, and knew from his connections that the choice for its first Chief Justice came down to Edmund Barton or Samuel Griffith. Way knew that he would not be considered because of his memorandum against the High Court being the final court of appeal. He felt entirely vindicated when the first three judges of the High Court were from the eastern States: Chief Justice Griffith from Queensland, and both Edmund Barton and Richard O'Connor from New South Wales. In a letter in April 1903 he wrote:

> Everybody sees now what a mistake it was to limit the right of appeal. What chance would South Australia have in any litigation to prevent the waters of the Murray being diverted with a majority of NSW and Victorian judges on the Bench? I see that Jenkins and Gordon are having a hard time at the meeting of Premiers in upholding our rights as to the Murray.[52]

A hundred years later the use of the River Murray remains a point of dispute between South Australia and its more populous eastern neighbours. But what would change Samuel Way's life for ever - and many Supreme Court judges across the country - was that the High Court began reversing decisions from State courts.

Until the High Court came into existence the judges gave their judgments ex tempore in all but the most complex cases at the end of argument by counsel. This was at least part of the reason why Samuel Way had been able to dedicate himself to so many other ex-judicial duties – Chancellor, President of the boards for the State Library, Art Gallery, Museum, Adelaide Children's Hospital, and so on.

---

52   SLSA Archival Collection, PRG 30/5, letterbook, 1903.

Way had rarely known the experience of being overturned on appeal. In a letter to Sir Robert White-Thompson in 1905, he writes:

> There have been less than half a dozen cases in twenty-nine years in which my judgment has not been the judgment of the Court, and the Privy Council has only overruled me once, and on that occasion I had great difficulty in persuading my colleagues to reverse my decision as a judge in the first instance.[53]

Even in the single instance when the Privy Council reversed the decision of the Full Court, they returned to Way's original decision at trial. With such an unblemished record, he became very anxious when he noticed the new High Court reversing many State Full Court decisions. In the same year, having watched the High Court in operation for two years, he expressed his fears to New South Wales Chief Justice Sir Frederick Darley:

> It certainly appears as if the High Court approaches the judgments of the State Courts with a presumption that they are wrong. It seems to me in the last degree improbable that the State Courts should be wrong in so many cases, and I observe that the Appellate Jurisdiction is attended with the same results in Victoria as in New South Wales. I dare say that it will be our turn next.[54]

Two other factors also combined to add to his work load. Firstly, the number of judges remained at three while the State's population increased sixty per cent from 1876 until 1901, correspondingly increasing the case load. Secondly, businesses had grown bigger, and commercial litigation became ever more complex.

Retirement was not an option if the workload became too much, as appointments were for life, and a judge could not retire with a pension unless he was ill. At the turn of the century as Samuel Way approached his seventies, he was healthy: he swam, lifted weights and every Sunday went on a country walk. He was 167 centimetres tall, 70 kilograms and very fit. He therefore had to continue working, or lose his primary

---

53   SLSA Archival Collection, PRG 30/5, letterbook 1905.
54   SLSA Archival Collection, PRG 30/5, letterbook 1905.

income. After 1903, until the end of his life, he would work almost every day.

His wife Katherine began to take on a more public role and showed an interest in the increasing status of women. South Australia was the second place after New Zealand to give women the vote in 1893, and the University the first in Australia to enrol female students. The dominance of men in this period is clear in Pascoe's *History of Adelaide and Vicinity*: all of the 225 biographies (which make up over half of the book) are of men. In June 1904, *Every Journal* published Lady Way's address to the National Council of Women, in which she looks forward to the year 2000:

> The women one foresees in Anno Domini 2000 will be as different from the present as she is from the past.
> In the year 2000 her household duties will no longer claim her attention, for they will have disappeared. Food will be taken in tabloid forms. (…) Clinging skirts and frills will have changed into short skirts, and mayhap divided ones; strong square-toed boots will replace the dainty shoes of today, and long, luxurious tresses will be close-cropped.
> What is to become of the children of the year 2000? I can only suppose that man will have degenerated (the word is quite admissible in the face of women's fast-growing contempt for the feminine) into femininity and will stay at home to fondle babies, while the breadwinner goes forth into the market place.[55]

This speech is not only revealing for its speculation about our present from a century ago, but also for its insight into an important aspect of Samuel Way's married life. It is obvious that Katherine Way would have been an intellectual companion. For Way to marry her at all, he must have been relatively open to new ideas, even if he thought himself a little conservative.[56] We see a perfect example of this cross between conservatism and liberalism in his own attitude towards the women's movement in a letter to a "Mrs L" many years later (1913):

---

55   SLSA Archival Collection, PRG 30/45, Box 2, 1904-1909.
56   See for example, the letter to Reverend Horwill, 18 June 1906: "As you know, I cannot be called an advanced radical (…)." PRG 30/5, Box 3.

"I disapprove strongly of the actions of the suffragettes though I am in favour of their cause."[57]

Way lost his long-time colleagues on the bench in this period. Bundey retired in December 1903 and Boucaut in 1905. Bundey was replaced by John Hannah Gordon (1850-1923), who as Attorney-General, like Way earlier, recommended himself for the vacancy on the bench. Way was horrified. In one of several letters in 1904 in which he refers to Gordon's appointment, large sections have been physically cut out of the copies available in his SLSA Archival Collection papers, for example:

> Gordon, the A.G., a brilliant advocate, but nothing of a lawyer. [cut out] strong point rhetoric not logic.

In another letter the same year, Way makes a biting comment:

> Gordon the Attorney-General was appointed in Bundey's place. He is a brilliant man and knows a good deal more about everything else than he does about the law, of which, honest, he is not entirely ignorant.[58]

In the following year – in March 1904 – Way is further scandalised by his new colleague. To his close friend Pennefather, he writes:

> We sat yesterday in Full Court for the first time since the Vacation and Gordon disagreed with us in our first case. On a literal construction of the contract he was right, but he looked at the letter and not at the spirit of it. As I sat listening to his chirruping on it seemed to me exactly like Andrews, but I am bound to add that Andrews never dared to disagree with me![59]

But Way changed his opinion very quickly of Gordon and wrote in 1905 that "[he] is turning out an excellent judge, and I find him a

57   SLSA Archival Collection, PRG 30/5, Box 6.
58   SLSA Archival Collection, PRG 30/5, Box 3 (both quotes on Gordon).
59   As above. Frederick William Pennefather (1852-1921) was Professor of Law at the University of Adelaide 1888-1896, although he was absent during two years. See Castles and others, *Law On North Terrace*, pp. 13-15.

most agreeable colleague". Similarly when Robert Homburg was appointed in early 1905, Way was at first highly prejudiced, but soon realised his early impressions were wrong. It is very likely that his feelings were more the result of fear of change after such a long period without it, than from the actual personal qualities of either of the new judges.

In May 1904, Way took on the most expensive and complex civil trial since the Moonta Mines case forty years before: *Weingarten Bros. v G. & R. Wills & Co.*[60] The "Corset Case", as it was called, became the *cause célèbre* of the time. An innocent wholesale drapery in Adelaide had been importing corsets from Great Britain for over nine years, and reselling them. The corsets had the trademark registered in Great Britain "W.B." after the American firm, Warner Brothers, who licensed the English manufacturer.

An American firm arrived in Adelaide in 1902 – the plaintiff Weingarten Brothers – with the plan to market their own "W.B" corsets, registered in America. Their corsets were more expensive, and they sued Wills for attempting to pass off their cheaper corsets from Britain as theirs. This was not the case at all, but the trial lasted for fifty-three days over 1904 and cost more than twenty thousand pounds. Weingarten engaged J. H. Symon KC, Paris Nesbit KC and E E Cleland to advance their cause, while Wills defended themselves with John Downer KC, George Murray and J. Henderson. In this case Way decided to rely on shorthand reporters after day twelve to record proceedings. He was pleasantly surprised at how useful it was to be free to "watch the demeanour of the witnesses".[61] The reporters took down 10,000 questions and answers; Way had already noted down 4000.

E E Cleland (1869-1943), who would come to dominate the bar and join the Murray court thirty years later, employed two girls to go on a shopping spree around Adelaide, buying corsets everywhere they went, in an effort to see how Wills's retail clients were marketing them. But Way was not impressed by the plaintiffs' argument. It nevertheless took him eighteen months to deliver his judgment, in favour of Wills. which takes up a full quarter of the 1906 SASR volume. Citing Lord Macnaghten in *Payton v Snelling*,[62] he found the defendants "perfectly honest traders". His correspondence shows that he was furious at the "waste of

---

60   [1906] SALR 34.
61   SLSA Archival Collection, PRG 30/45, Box 2, 1904-1909.
62   [1901] AC at 309.

time" that the plaintiffs were causing, calling it "a dam across the stream of litigation". He was impressed, though, by the apparent lucrativeness of the corset industry in that it provoked such rivalry that traders would spend so much money in acquiring or guarding their markets.

Way sometimes found the act of sitting in court during a trial itself a trial. *The Advertiser* on 23 June 1904 published an article headlined "A Drowsy Judge". Way is addressing George Murray:

> "The atmosphere of the court is as stuffy in summer as it is intensely cold in winter. I listened intently to your sensational argument yesterday, Mr Murray," said His Honor smilingly. "In fact nothing but so able an argument could have kept me awake."
>
> Mr Murray smiled audibly, and the Chief Justice asked him to explain his hilarity. The learned counsel said he was trying to reconcile the two statements that while His Honor was sleepy he was yet fully alive to his argument. The judge remarked that it was not Mr Murray's argument that made him drowsy, but rather the foul air, which was caused by the continuous burning of the gas in court for heating purposes. "The only choice for us in this court is between suffocation and freezing," added His Honor.

Murray had been Way's associate from 1889 to 1891, and proved one of the most gifted lawyers in the State. Life had changed since then. Now Way's current associate, Dr Frederick Richards (1869-1957) worked with Way five nights a week until the departure of the eleven o'clock tram, and every weekend.

The increasing complexity of the cases compounded the need to write the judgments, and at one stage, Way wondered if his labours were "those of Sisyphus". His exasperation at being forced to work day and night and weekends led him to accuse the legal profession of conspiring to get all the heavy civil cases before him. But occasionally he still delivered ex tempore judgments, despite the worry of a High Court Appeal:

> I delivered a judgment yesterday in a great case between the Government and the Tramways Corporation involving two or three hundred thousand pounds. My judgment took an

hour and five minutes to read and it is necessarily imperfectly reported. If I undertook the labour of writing them all it would be impossible for me to overtake my work.[63]

In 1906 Samuel Way received a letter from Prime Minister Alfred Deakin offering him an appointment on the High Court bench, which was being increased to five judges. Way's official response was published in *The Advertiser* and is a highly polished example of his masterful diplomatic skills. His final sentence was:

> I must therefore ask you and your colleagues to permit me gratefully to decline the invitation with which you have honoured me.[64]

The tone in the official letter back to the Prime Minister contrasts sharply with that in a private letter to Sir Cyprian Bridge:

> You will see by the newspapers I have sent you that the Federal Government offered me one of the two new judgeships. As you may imagine, after having been at the head of a court for over thirty years, I am not inclined to take 5th place in any tribunal, and to join a peripatetic court would deprive me of all home life. Besides, I would rather be first in a small court.[65]

Way was even stronger in a letter to another correspondent cited by Hannan, where he declared that he did not intend to "tramp about the Continent as a subordinate member of the itinerant tribunal".

Samuel Way was not alone among the South Australian legal profession in his low opinion of the High Court. Paris Nesbit appeared before it in a matter concerning trusts law:

> Chief Justice Griffith asked Nesbit for the legal authority for what

---

63   Letter to Rev. Tacon, 8 August 1905. SLSA Archival Collection, PRG 30/5, Box 3, .
64   Cited in Hannan, p. 216.
65   SLSA Archival Collection, PRG 30/5, Box 2, 1906 volume.

Victoria Square around 1910, looking south from the GPO towards the Supreme Court. (SCLSA)

the judge considered to be a "startling proposition". Nesbit replied by asserting that he had considered it "unnecessary to require authority for anything so obvious". He turned to his instructing solicitor and asked him to get a book on the subject from a nearby library. As the solicitor was leaving, Nesbit spoke out sufficiently loudly so that everyone in the court could hear him, much to the amusement of some onlookers, that "any elementary book will do".[66]

Probably the annual visits of the High Court represented for Way and other South Australians, as much as anything else, a symbol of the continuing intrusion of the Commonwealth Government into what they had known as an autonomous Province.

Way's opinion of federation never improved, and he actively did what he could to retain the State's independence. In 1907 his opinion was that most people were disappointed with federation and he declared himself "an upholder of State rights". That year he was dismayed at the Commonwealth annexing of the Northern Territory:

> At the present moment I am bemoaning the coming severance of the Northern Territory from the Central State, that will reduce South Australia to the status of a third class colony.[67]

In 1913 he declared in a letter to Sir John Forrest that "the Federal Government is worse than a foreign occupation". Way, like all land holders, resented the new federal land tax, and the fact that it raised a quarter of a million pounds more than anticipated pleased him even less.

---

66   Castles and Harris, cited above, p. 331.
67   SLSA Archival Collection, PRG 30/5, Box 3.

But his anxiety about the High Court reversing his decisions was to prove largely unfounded. By 1912 he admitted to his friend Pennefather that the court had been kinder to South Australia than to Victoria and New South Wales – an interesting comment given that the bulk of the judges (and litigants) then, and since, have been from those States:

> Four of my decisions were appealed against – two were upheld, the third will be and the fourth ought to be so. They had the grace to pronounce one of my decisions a very able one![68]

Alex Castles and Michael Harris point out that the High Court had one beneficial effect on Way's approach to his judgments. We saw earlier that he criticised Justice Gordon for being too literal in his interpretation of the law; Way was more concerned with its spirit. This involved a certain degree of value judgment, and as a result, left him open to being overturned on appeal:

> It was a defect he set out to try to remedy, once the High Court had taken his measure, by undertaking much more detailed research than previously in preparing his judgments.[69]

Castles and Harris also speculate on whether an appointment to the High Court of a South Australian would have placated the antagonism towards the court. It could only improve South Australians' participation in federal government, but the High Court remains, at least until 2006, notable for the absence of either a South Australian or a Tasmanian appointment. There have been offers: Way in 1906; Gordon in 1912 when the court was expanded again; a third offer much later to Justice George Ligertwood – Way's associate in 1912. There have no doubt been others but Way may have unintentionally founded a tradition of South Australians not accepting appointments to the High Court.

One of the other major cases that Way tried in this first decade of the twentieth century was a customs fraud. It became instantly a scandal as one of the accused, Charles Tucker, had been Lord Mayor of Adelaide from 1895 to 1898, and a member of the House of Assembly.

68   SLSA Archival Collection, PRG 30/5, Box 11.
69   Castles and Harris, pp. 332-333.

Pascoe's *Adelaide and Vicinity* dedicates four pages of praise to his biography:

> Mr Charles Tucker, ex-Mayor of Adelaide, has, by his own industry and perseverance, won his way to the front. His capacity for high and onerous positions has been proved and verified by the ability with which he has discharged the manifold functions of the offices he has held.[70]

In reality, Mr Tucker during the years 1896 to 1906 was fraudulently augmenting his personal income by 2000 pounds a year – the Chief Justice's salary – with the help of his brother Wallace and his nephew F W Forwood. Charles Tucker was customs agent for department store John Martin's:

> It appeared that Charles Tucker had, during the eleven years covered by the frauds, delegated to Forwood without the knowledge of Martin's almost all of the duties that he had agreed to perform personally for Martin's when he accepted the position of Customs Agent for the firm. Tucker's bank account, in which Martin's lodged the money required to pay the duty, was drawn upon from time to time by Forwood, who used for this purpose whole books of cheques signed in advance by Tucker, which Forwood filled in after signature for any amount he pleased. It was Forwood too, who prepared the false invoices that were produced to the Customs officials and the false Customs receipts that were given to Martin's.[71]

The three men shared thirty-four thousannd pounds between them over that lucrative period. The trial took around 30 days and Way's address to the jury took six hours: "In the midday adjournment, I flung myself on the sofa in my chambers and had nearly half an hour's sleep." After the jury returned with a guilty verdict, Way gave two years each to Tucker, his brother Wallace, and Forwood, in Yatala Labour Prison. The only part of the case that appears in the law reports is the

---

70   Pascoe, p. 367.
71   Hannan, p. 219.

re-argument of the admissibility of certain evidence: *R v Tucker and Another*.[72]

By then Way had not had a weekend off in four years. Neither was life on the circuit any easier. One of his early administrative reforms as Chief Justice was to establish the circuit courts in Gladstone and Port Augusta in 1881. There had been one at Mount Gambier, in the south, since 1856. He wrote to his friend Mrs Bourne in November 1911, telling her about a recent experience in Mount Gambier:

A signed photograph of Way in 1914 held in the Supreme Court of South Australia (SCLSA).

> I sat on the bench for 17 ½ hours, with a break for 1 ½ hours for lunch, when I entertained a party of local magnates, and an hour for dinner. The case was one of intricate circumstantial evidence, but the jury were not long in coming to a decision. The court rose at three a.m. and I got to bed at four, and was out again at half past five and had a railway journey of twelve hours and a quarter, and all this without much sense of fatigue.[73]

Way's health at 75 years old remained as it had always been, which meant he still could not retire. This was fortunate, as Gordon's was failing, and Way and Homburg had to make up for his increasing forced absences. The pace of work remained intense. In 1910 Way had to miss a night's sleep entirely to keep up with a complex divorce case that lasted three weeks. He waded through the pile of oral and documentary evidence through Friday, Saturday and Sunday in preparation for his charge to the jury on Monday:

> When Sunday night came I found I was not nearly through my

---

72   [1907] SALR 30
73   SLSA Archival Collection, PRG 30/5, Box 4.

work, and I sat at it right through the night, not rising from my chair until 9 o'clock on Monday morning. I almost went to sleep in my bath, but I was on the bench at half past ten, and got through my charge, which took three hours, without fatigue. When I got home I had a hot bath and went to bed and slept from 7 o'clock until 9 the following morning.[74]

Way seemed indefatigable, equal to the men he admired such as his near neighbour George Sara at Willunga who was 99 years old and still chopping his own fire wood, and Douglas Mawson (1882-1958), who led his own Antarctic expedition in 1911, still in his twenties.[75] It is curious given his immense working hours that, although the State government told him in 1912 he "only had to say the word" to have a fourth judge, and although he felt there should be six, he did not take up the offer. The workload was all the more given that Gordon was often away ill. Yet it was Gordon who lived on to stay on the bench until his death in 1923 and Homburg who would die in office in 1912. Nevertheless, Alexander Buchanan began filling in as acting judge that year until being permanently appointed in 1916.

The University of Adelaide at this time had grown to serve a student population of one thousand with an annual budget of twenty-six thousand pounds. It remained a small cluster of buildings around North Terrace – the Mitchell, the now demolished Prince of Wales Building and the Elder Conservatorium of Music – and a few smaller buildings behind them. There was still an oval used for the Royal Adelaide Show on the lower end of Frome Road. The largest building in the vicinity was the grand domed Jubilee Exhibition Building, built in 1887 and demolished in the early 1960s to make way for the new Law School building, Napier building and underground car park. Students and academics both wore gowns for lectures, which were solemn readings in dark rooms that chilled bones in winter and baked their overdressed occupants in summer.

Way had only managed recently to achieve a degree of respect among the students. From the mid-1890s, degree-conferral ceremonies had become a huge joke often at his expense. During one early cer-

---

SLSA Archival Collection, PRG 30/5, Box 5; letter to Bailey.
75   Douglas Mawson was born in Yorkshire and was Professor of Geology at the University of Adelaide from 1920 until 1952.

emony held in the library upstairs in the Mitchell building, alarm clocks concealed among the books interrupted the proceedings for an hour. After 1900, when the ceremonies were held in Elder Hall, the Chancellor would wait patiently while some students sang:

> We're Varsity students all!
> Sir Sammy is our father.
> We throng the Elder Hall
> And love the ladies, rather!

The disruptions increased until 1905 when, with the exception of those receiving degrees, students were banned from conferral ceremonies. That year several hundred of them marched through the streets in a procession that worried their elders about entrusting the future of the State to such "hooligans".[76] In 1906 a group of students blew tin whistles during Samuel Way's speech for the unveiling of Sir Thomas Elder's statue on the lawn in front of the Conservatorium. This attracted a meeting afterwards with Vice-Chancellor Dr William Barlow and the State Governor, Sir George Le Hunte, who obtained a public apology, and that seemed to have been the end of that era's general student pranks.

The only times Samuel Way had been ill were when he caught influenza in 1892 and enteric (typhoid) fever in 1899. In May 1913 his record run of good health came to an end when he first contracted flu, and then suffered a heart attack in July. He was forced to stay away from the Court for six full months, and he rented a house on the seaside in Grange for his convalescence. He probably could have finally taken his retirement now, but instead he was determined continued to write his judgments and plan for the day he could return.

In April 1914, just a few months after being back, he noticed a lump on his left upper arm. When the test results came back, the news was the worst: it was a sarcoma – a malignant tumour. His doctor was opposed to an operation due to Way's cardiac problems and predicted that he would at best make it to the end of that year. With that knowl-

---

76   Duncan and Leonard, p. 61.

edge the Chief Justice continued working, unaware that just a month later he was to receive an even deeper shock.

On Thursday 14 May 1914 Way was eating breakfast when his wife Kitty came down the stairs for her bath. Way was forbidden to go upstairs because of his heart, so he was now sleeping in a downstairs room. Kitty suddenly felt giddy, and he had to help her to his bed to lie down. Then she had a bilious attack, but soon recovered. Way chatted to her for a while, and then went to court. Kitty had appeared in perfect health until then and he had no reason to believe that there was cause for concern –particularly as she was eighteen years younger than he.

Katherine Way got worse and a doctor was called to Montefiore at half past two. When he discovered that she was suffering from uraemia, caused by kidney dysfunction, Way was sent for urgently. He arrived before five but his wife was now unconscious. He was with her barely more than an hour when she died at one minute to six. *The Advertiser* described her in its leading article the following day as "a fitting life's partner for perhaps the most notable figure in South Australia".[77] Way had now seen the two great loves of his life die before him, but unlike the death of Susannah, this time he did not have to hide his grief.

He found relief, as can be imagined, in work, working on a long-standing judgment from *Wallaroo and Moonta Mining Company v Commissioner of Taxes*.[78] The case had hung about the various courts since 1905 and had been sent back to the Supreme Court from the Adelaide Local Court. Way delivered his judgment on 18 June.

His other preoccupation was the growing cancerous tumour on his arm. Dr Marten, his regular doctor, did not believe that he would survive any form of operation. Way consulted other doctors and received opposing opinions. He also consulted two particular Melbourne doctors, Dr Alfred Rowden White and Dr Edward Rowden White. His two sons, aged 42 and 33, were now established general practitioners.[79]

Way was determined not to be beaten; neither by the death of his wife, nor by cancer. At the beginning of July he took the train to Sydney to consult Australia's most eminent surgeon:

---

77   Hannan, p. 239.
78   [1914] SALR at 207.
79   SLSA Archival Collection, PRG 30/5, Box 6, 1914.

Sir Alexander McCormick, when he had examined me, said, "The sooner you are operated on the better." I said, "When?" He said, "Tomorrow morning." "At what time?" "Half past seven," and I said, "I shall be there."[80]

Way woke half an hour later with his left arm gone. He spent a month in Sydney recovering, and a crowd was waiting for him at Adelaide station when he returned on 5 August. He returned to court in October.

The neuritis caused by the split nerves was very painful. In court and at his desk he had to use a lead weight to hold the law reports open. Defective circulation in his legs caused great expanses of sores. At night he took a cachet of Trional, which allowed him uninterrupted sleep. But he had come to the point of his life where he could see the end looming ever closer, and his legendary will started to dwindle. Then the death of his long-time friend, John Thorne, seemed to affect him as deeply as the loss of Kitty. Thorne's grandfather had been one of the co-founders of the Bible Christian Church at Lake Farm in Shebbear, North Devon. His father James became one of the first ministers, and had been a friend of Way's own father. John Thorne himself had married Samuel Way and Katherine Blue in April 1898, and in his old age came to live with the Ways in Montefiore, together with his sister Margaret. Thus John Thorne was not just the second person in Samuel Way's household to die, but was also a link to Way's own religious beliefs and to his family.

That year as well, the world that Samuel Way had known was threatened: the Great War began. During the next year Way would see the return of his nephew Neil Campbell with a bullet from Gallipoli lodged next to his heart and the death of his stepson Bill Blue, and wonder if another nephew, Jim Way, would survive.

In December 1914 he drove out to Kadlunga for the first time in nine years, to see drought starving his two-and-a-half thousand Merino sheep to death. He spent Christmas and New Year at Seaview, but the visit brought back too many sad memories:

My dear father died there and my wife and I spent our honeymoon and nearly all our holidays during the sixteen years

80   Hannan, p. 241.

of our happily married life. I found myself frequently exclaiming, "Oh for the touch of a vanished land, and the sound of a voice that is still".[81]

He wished he could see England once more. It was now nearly twenty years since he had last been there. He wanted to "see the places and people who are dear" to him and take his place again on the bench of the Judicial Committee of the Privy Council.

In 1915 Sir Langdon Bonython organised a fund to commission a statue of Way and sufficient donations of a hundred pounds each came in within a few days.[82] Sculptor Alfred Drury, who had also done the statues of Thomas Elder in front of the Mitchell building and of Charles Kingston in Victoria Square, began meeting Way regularly in his chambers to prepare the model. But although the model was completed, the war prevented the brass being cast in England, and further delays prevented it from being unveiled until 1924.

In October 1915 Way went on circuit to Mount Gambier, but came back with a cold and rheumatism. A month later he was dogged by a persistent cough, and before long it became apparent that the cancer had invaded his lungs. By mid-December, he knew his days were coming to their close. His last day in court was Saturday 18 December. He told Doctor Brown that he would meet his fate with fortitude, and that he did not want the public to know. He could not bear the idea of his illness being the topic of general conversation. On 4 January 1916 he wrote to Fred Beach:

> I am very ill unable to stand. Very confidential [double underlined]. The Doctors have given me my sentence of death. The sarcoma has recurred, of which there is always danger in cases of this kind. (...) We do not know where the enemy is burrowing.[83]

81   SLSA Archival Collection, PRG 30/5, letterbook 1915/16.
82   These were from Robert Barr Smith, Sir Edwin Smith, Sir Charles Goode, George Brookman, Peter Waite, A.M.Simpson, Richard Smith, Henry Rymill, G.A. Jury, T.R.Scarfe, James Gartrell, John Lewis, Charles H. Angas, Arthur Waterhouse, George Murray and Sir Langdon Bonython.
83   SLSA Archival Collection, PRG 30/5, letterbook 1915/16.

Four days later, near midnight on Saturday 8 January 1916, Samuel James Way died.

His death had an impact on the State in a way that has never been known since. He was very much the beneficiary of the period he lived in, and astute enough to recognise its opportunities. With the natural increase in the size of South Australia, no individual is likely to be able to hold so many key positions and exert singly so much influence. No Chief Justice is likely to have the time to dedicate to so many other activities as Way did. Way lived long enough to see that change himself. *The Register* on 10 January 1916 noted also that he had filled in as Governor on sixty occasions, for a total of six years, 279 days. This was longer than any permanent Governor in the entire British Empire had served. He was given a State funeral like Crawford, Hanson and Stow.

The auction of his household goods by Theodore Bruce took place in May at Montefiore. There were more than nine hundred items, including an ancient crossbow and ceremonial axe that had hung in the hallway, and two identical 91-piece gold-embossed Minton china dinner services. There were more than one thousand pot plants from his greenhouses. From his cellar there were hundreds of bottles of port, sherry, special Lafitte, whisky, ale, and several dozen bottles of vintage wine.

With an estate worth fifty-five thousand pounds, Way was not in the league of the great capitalists of his day such as Thomas Elder, who left over six hundred thousand. But Way would have still been a multi-millionaire in today's terms. He was also one of the many South Australian men of the colonial period – George Fife Angas, Elder, Robert Barr Smith, Samuel Davenport and Peter Waite – who built their fortunes and influence from scratch. Way left almost half of his estate to religious, educational and charitable purposes. He left fifteen thousand books to the University Library. The copy of J J Pascoe's *History of Adelaide and Vicinity* used for this chapter was once in his library at Montefiore: it bears his signature in copperplate on the frontispiece.

Way was a model colonial leader, but was he a great judge? Many years later, his future successor John Bray seemed to believe so, according to his entry on Way in the *Australian Dictionary of Biography*:

His pragmatic cast of mind inhibited intensive historical research or jurisprudential analysis. At times he strained the law to produce the result which he thought justice and common sense demanded (see *De Pledge v Australian United Steam Navigation Co.*, 1904). But he was conscientious, intelligent and industrious, and his verdicts gave general satisfaction. His judgment in the celebrated corset case (*Weingarten v. Wills & Co.*, 1906) which took nearly four hours to read, demonstrated his ability to marshal and assess a complex array of facts.[84]

Way was never a jurist with the academic depth of Bray, but he was a great judge. If he was a little inclined to mould the law to fit justice, then he was the perfect opposite of Benjamin Boothby, who could see nothing but the law, and English law at that. His ability to bring justice to the law, rather than the opposite, shows how intimately Samuel Way could connect and empathise with his litigants; understanding their problems and doing his best to relieve them, if he could not solve them.

With all his other achievements - as Chancellor of the University of Adelaide, Lieutenant-Governor, sheep-breeder, Chairman of the boards of so many key organisations - Way was a towering giant in the cultural development of South Australia. His influence at a fundamental level in so many varied areas is surely unique.

---

84   John Bray's entry on Way in the *Australian Dictionary of Biography, 1891-1939*, p. 419.

CHAPTER 3

Sir George Murray (1916-1942)

BETWEEN THE WORLD WARS

George Murray would continue the traditions that Way established in the office of Chief Justice, yet he was a very different man.

He was the first native-born South Australian to have been appointed King's Counsel and to be appointed a judge on the State's Supreme Court. He was also the first judge appointed in over forty years – since Wearing in 1867 – who was not a former politician; who, in other words, could not be accused of using a political career as a stepping stone to judicial appointment.[1] None of the seven former politicians appointed since Wearing had proved anything but excellent judges, but

---

1   Prior to Wearing, Edward Gwynne (Second Judge, 1859-1881) had been Attorney-General in 1859, and the State's second Chief Justice, Sir Richard Hanson, had been the State's last Advocate-General before that office was renamed Attorney-General in 1857. Hanson was also Premier for a brief time in 1860. Subsequently, all seven judges appointed between Wearing and Murray had been Attorneys-General, though not generally at the time of appointment: Randolph Stow (Third Judge, 1875-1878); Samuel Way (Chief Justice, 1876-1916); James Boucaut (Third/Second Judge, 1878-1905); Richard Andrews (Third/Second Judge, 1881-1884); William Bundey (Third Judge 1884-1903); John Gordon (Third/Second Judge, 1903-1923) and Robert Homburg (Third Judge, 1905-1912).

after almost half a century of appointing only politicians, there was at least one sigh of relief when Murray was appointed. *The Register* commented that the Vaughan government had avoided the unfortunate example set by its predecessors. Samuel Way was also very relieved, but for a different reason. He had been hoping Murray would join him on the bench as early as 1905 when James Boucaut retired. Later, in 1911, Murray refused an offer to be an Acting Judge. (This was taken up by Alexander Buchanan, who was permanently appointed when Way died in 1916.) Only one person is recorded as having been disappointed at Murray's appointment, and that was Sir John Downer KC (1843-1915), one of the leaders of the bar and another ex-Attorney-General. But he was twenty years older than Murray and may well have worried some in

Sir George Murray at the age of 69 in 1932. (Advertiser)

power by the tumbler of neat whisky he needed frequently refilled during his attendances at the bar table.[2]

Justice Robert Homburg died on 23 March 1912. Samuel Way called George Murray into his chambers a week later. Murray must have already been approached by the government and indicated his reluctance to accept an appointment to the Supreme Court, and the Chief Justice must have hoped to change his mind. He did not succeed and wrote to Murray the next day:

My dear Murray,
In the discussion we had yesterday morning I doubt if we raised

2　　Sir John Downer KC is a grandfather of Alexander Downer, Minister of Foreign Affairs in the Howard government. His disappointment was noted by Samuel Way in a letter to John Gordon dated 16 April 1912 (SLSA Archival Collection, PRG 30/5). His habit of keeping the whisky tumbler at the bar table is reported by W A Norman in *Random Reminiscences*.

it quite high enough. Although we spoke of self-sacrifice we did not dwell on patriotism.

Every citizen owes a debt to his country which he ought to try and discharge when the need arises. Surely there is a call to you of duty at the present crisis. The prestige and efficiency of the Bench are imperilled, and there is no one else who could maintain both as effectively as you could.

Let me add to patriotic claims your duty to yourself. In my interview with Professor Maitland at Cambridge in 1891, he said he confidently expected you to win distinction. And now the opportunity has come for which you have unconsciously been preparing for thirty years and more. Moreover, it has come in the most opportune way. You are at an ideal age for entering upon judicial work, you have the public confidence, the possession of ample means, and the temperament which would enable you to become a great Judge. The change, so distasteful to you in your daily habits, is as the dust in the balance when weighed against these public and personal considerations.

You know well the pleasure it would give me to have you as a colleague. I have no right, and do not desire, to ask you to take this into account. But there is a hope in which I indulge on public grounds. It is that when, at no distant date, my place is filled by another, South Australia may have a Supreme Court Bench as strong as it was before I came up, when we had such judges as Hanson, Gwynne and Stow. On your decision hangs the possibility of this ambition of mine being realized.

Believe me, my dear Murray,
Your old and faithful friend,
S.J. Way.[3]

Way succeeded in convincing Murray. He accepted the next day. A little vainly, Way confided about Murray to his friend Horwill in April 1912 that "…the great inducement to him to come up was to take his seat by my side."[4]

---

3   Way papers, Mortlock Archival Collection. PRG 30/5, 1912 volume.
4   As above, to Horwill. Similar sentiments are quoted in A.J. Hannan, pp. 233-235.

Murray took his seat on the Supreme Court bench on Monday 7 May 1912. The previous Friday, Samuel Way gave a dinner at the Adelaide Club to celebrate. The High Court was in town, so among the guests were not only the Governor, Sir Day Hort Bosanquet, but also Chief Justice Samuel Griffith and Justices Edmund Barton and Isaac Isaacs. "No pleasanter dinner has ever been held in the Adelaide Club", Way enthused in a letter written the week after.

The letters that Samuel Way wrote over the next year to his various correspondents refer to Murray with such expressions as "He is one of the most brilliant graduates our University has sent forth…", "Murray is a great comfort to me…", "Murray is an ideal colleague in every way". Way had been aware of George Murray's outstanding ability for almost thirty years. Murray had taken his Arts degree in 1883, the first year of Way's Chancellorship of the University of Adelaide. His high grades won him the prestigious South Australian Scholarship to study at Cambridge for four years. Way must have also been struck by the twenty-year-old student who towered over him by thirty centimetres.

In February 1889, after Murray's return from England, Way appointed him his Associate. Two months later Murray was in hospital with a sporting injury. The Chief Justice had to make a special trip for his admission. Murray recalled the incident at a dinner in 1938:

> I have told the story before of how I signed the roll and took the oaths as a practitioner when I was lying in bed at a private hospital in Wakefield Street, and I would not refer to it again were it not that my dear old friend the late Mr Justice Piper liked to twit me with doubts as to the validity of my admission. It does not matter now, but I never shared his doubts. What happened was that an order nisi for my admission was made with all due propriety in Court, and the Chief Justice and the Master (then Mr Scott) were authorised to obtain my signature to the roll and administer the oaths to me at the Hospital. Possibly such a thing had never been done before, but if not, it created a precedent, which as far as I know, has never been upset. Six months later, I may say, the rule was made absolute, and I was then present.[5]

---

5   Speech made at the South Australian Hotel 29 April 1938.

This was in April 1889. Murray spent several months unable to walk and could not play sport again. The details of his injury are unclear, as a New Zealand correspondent thought he had "a broken knee cap" and a Londoner heard he had fallen "down a lift and broke your toe".[6]

Attorney-General Charles Kingston queried Way's appointing Murray over the heads of the two existing Associates, to which Way responded:

> I don't think you should be "troubled" on "the question of Murray's appointment over the head of the second associate".
> (...) There is no rule that the associates ought to be promoted in succession. For example, Mr Murray's predecessor was appointed over Mr Castle and Mr Taylor who were neither of them qualified for the first place.
>
> Before appointing Mr Murray I looked around the service. Mr Castle was the only member of it fitted for the office. I offered it to him but he declined.
>
> I consider it fortunate that I was able to secure Mr Murray. He is quite distinguished as an accomplished lawyer in England as well as here. He is a member of the English Bar, a BA of Adelaide, where he took the South Australian scholarship and he is an LLB of Cambridge where he was bracketed first in the Law Tripos [examinations]. He was also Gold Medallist at the Inns of Court. His appointment is no disparagement to Mr Taylor and I know he does not "feel aggrieved" at it.[7]

But if there had been this slight query over Murray then, there was certainly not by the time he was appointed to the Supreme Court. By then he had been one of the leading civil and commercial lawyers in the State for more than a decade.

After Way died in January 1916, the Labor Attorney-General and Premier Crawford Vaughan offered the Chief Justiceship first to Justice Gordon as the senior surviving judge. Gordon declined, ever concerned about his health, as he had been four years earlier when he

---

6   SLSA Archival Collection, SLSA Archival Collection, PRG 259/54, Box 2
     (1880-1900).
7   As above, PRG 259/52.

declined to join the High Court. *The Register* reported that George Murray was then approached and accepted:

> His appointment is one which will be accepted by the profession and the general public with great satisfaction and pride.
>
> Sir Samuel Way said to George Murray once after a case: "I congratulate you Mr Murray on the skill with which you presented your arguments, you know I am looking forward to the day when you will be occupying my seat on the bench."
>
> Mr Murray smiled, no comment.[8]

The salary of Chief Justice remained the same as forty years before in 1876 when Samuel Way had been appointed: two thousand pounds a year. According to the Australian Bureau of Statistics Consumer Price Index, prices in 1911 had returned to 1850 levels. But by 1916, prices had risen by a third.[9]

The main news topic since September 1914, which filled several pages of each issue of the daily papers, was the Great War in Europe and Asia Minor. In particular, the Gallipoli campaign ended in January 1916 after nine fruitless months of fighting the Turks. More than half a million men died in that battle, including 33,000 Australians. The war would claim a total

Moore's Department Store in 1911 looking north-west from the Supreme Court on Gouger Street. (courtesy Jeffcott Chambers)

---

8   *The Register*, 20 January 1916.
9   See *abs.gov.au/Ausstats*. The index for both 1850 and 1911 is 53 and 71 for 1916. (The index for 2002 is 2462, which translates the annual salary of the Chief Justice in 1911 to $185,811, but in 1916 down to $138,704.) The salary of the puisne judges was 1,700 pounds a year. The pension was 1,300 pounds a year, but only payable if a judge had to retire for reasons of illness, not of age.

of six thousand South Australian lives, and leave scarcely a family without a loss. Day after day, the papers greeted readers with yet another list of soldiers killed or reported missing. One patriotic backlash in South Australia during the course of 1916 was to change the 67 names of "enemy origin" such as Hahndorf and Klemzig. Curiously, the city of Adelaide itself survived, named after the Princess of Saxe-Coburg and Meinengein, King William IV's consort.

South Australia in the past few years had undergone some important political changes. The Labor Party win in 1910 provoked the other parties to unite and form the Liberal Union. This was the beginning of the modern parliamentary party system in the State, and since then these parties have dominated the political scene.[10]

In 1933, looking south, Moore's department store has been rebuilt on the corner to model the Galeries Lafayette in Paris. Since 1983 the building has housed the District Court as the Sir Samuel Way building. (Jeffcott Chambers)

Previously, governments were formed by coalitions of several small parties and independent members. Labor lost office to the new Liberal Union in 1912, but won it back in 1915, aided by a severe drought and economic depression. George Murray was briefly a member of the Liberal Union – resigning as soon as he became a judge.

Election day in 1915 also saw a referendum on the issue of closing-times for hotels. The members of the Woman's Christian Temperance Union had fought for many years to reduce the number of hours which men could spend in hotel bars getting inebriated. They began opening coffee palaces in the nineteenth century as a non-alcoholic alternative to the hotel, the real forerunners to Adelaide's modern café society. Voters were given a choice of six closing times – each hour from 6pm to 11pm. Only a few thousand opted for the in-between times of

---

10   Dean Jaensch. *The Flinders History of South Australia: Political History*. See pp. 212 and 226-242.

7, 8, 9 and 10pm. Of the remaining two times, 96,140 voted for 6pm closing, and 60,160 for 11pm.[11]

This simple win had a huge impact. South Australia gained its reputation overnight as the "Wowser State". It would be 1967 before hotels could again open until late evening, despite several attempts during the following decades to relax the early closing times. The period of early closing – 1915-1967 – is the same period, except for a year, as the Murray and Napier Courts, which Alex Castles and Michael Harris have called "an age of judicial conservatism", "preserved and cosseted" by Murray and maintained and continued by his successor, Napier.[12] It was a period of enforced social order that may have offered a bedrock of stability during two world wars and the Depression, but grew increasingly less relevant as the State expanded and its population grew more diverse.

Murray's conservatism showed itself quite early in the letters he wrote back from Cambridge. Being of the second generation of a family of immensely wealthy Scottish colonial pastoralists, he was, not surprisingly, wary of changes to the economic and political system by which his family had built its wealth. In a letter to his mother written from London in November 1887, he described the processions of unemployed that had been taking place every day for the past month. He mentioned a member of Parliament who got up to speak on behalf of the protesters at Trafalgar Square and was arrested. George Murray was not sympathetic:

> He received his well-merited reward of some months imprisonment for his temerity in attempting to defy the order of the police.[13]

Murray was an academically gifted twenty-four year old student when he wrote this, but obviously not curious about the reasons that would motivate a politician to risk arrest and imprisonment. Later on,

---

11   Jaensch, p. 230.
12   Castles and Harris, p. 348.
13   SLSA Archival Collection, PRG 259/56. Letter to Mrs. M T Murray, dated 14 November 1887.

he would worry about South Australia having three "labouring men" in the Upper House: "The prospect is anything but pleasant."[14]

His view was no doubt representative of the new generation of South Australians whose fathers had been pioneers and fortune-builders, but who themselves never knew the initial hardships. Being brought up during the latter part of the Victorian era, on incomes increasingly distanced from direct trading, mining or property speculation, these daughters and sons now had more respectable "old money" and they became more class-conscious. The most obvious sign of this tightening of attitudes was when the Adelaide Club blackballed Edward Holden's nomination in 1914, because he was classified as a trader. So were members such as R J H Wills, John Darling II, Charles Hayward and Lavington Bonython, but now a new direction took hold.[15] Ironically, Holden's name will outlive any of the rest, since it was given by General Motors to the first Australian mass-produced car.

George John Robert Murray's background and education were therefore considerably different from those of his predecessor, Way. By the time he was born on 27 September 1863, his father, Alexander Borthwick Murray, was forty-seven and one of the wealthiest pastoralists and most successful merino sheep breeders in the State. The year before, Alexander had been elected as a Member of the House of Assembly for Gumaracha. In January 1863, no doubt because of his prominence, his house guest was the explorer John McDouall Stuart (1815-1866) who had just returned from his epic journey as the first European to cross Australia through the centre from Adelaide to Darwin.

Alexander Murray was one of the great pioneers of South Australia. His biography is included in J J Pascoe's *History of Adelaide and Vicinity*. He was born in Langshall Burn, Dumfriesshire, Scotland in 1816 and as a young man learned about sheep breeding and husbandry. By the mid-1830s he was in the highlands of Inverness, acclimatising sheep to the harsher mountain climate.

Around this time, a distant relative, Admiral Sir Pulteney Malcolm, recommended Captain John Hindmarsh to his close friend Lord

---

14   Letter to George Tinline, January 1892, SLSA Archival Collection, PRG 21/1.
15   Dirk van Dissel, "The Adelaide Gentry, 1850-1920", in Eric Richards (ed.), *The Flinders Social History*, p. 359.

Glenelg to be Governor of the yet to be settled colony of South Australia. Once a Governor had been appointed, interest in the new colony grew and the Admiral encouraged his brother Sir James Malcolm to get in quickly and take up some land. Sir James took a city allotment in what became Gouger Street and a country allotment of 134 acres of what became Murray Park, now part of the Magill campus of the University of South Australia.

Governor Hindmarsh has since gone down in history as the most incompetent Governor in the history of the State, and he was quickly recalled to England in 1838 before he could do further damage. Nevertheless, he was in South Australia long enough to have a say in the naming of the city streets and in gratitude to the admiral he named Pulteney Street after him. Sir James bought up a number of properties and although he sent both his sons out to manage them, he still needed someone who knew about sheep. He asked twenty-three-year-old Alexander Murray if he would take on the sheep management on his distant colonial properties.

When Alexander Murray arrived in Adelaide in 1839 with his brother Pulteney - named after the admiral - the sheep on Sir James's Barossa property had scab, but before his twelve-month contract was complete, the best of them took a prize at the State's first agricultural show, held at Noarlunga.[16] Brothers John and William immigrated the year after Alexander and though William later went into manufacturing, the three brothers began acquiring land and buying merino sheep. Alexander Murray married Charlotte Scott in 1842, just after he bought Murray Park from James Malcolm, and Pulteney Murray married Charlotte's sister Mary in 1846. Both Scott women died after a decade of marriage. Before Charlotte died in 1853 she had eight children, though only one would survive Alexander, and sister Mary had nine children before she died around 1856. Pulteney married again and fathered thirteen more children before he died in 1879.[17]

It was Alexander's second wife, Margaret Tinline (1823-1907), who would be George's mother. George was the second of their three children. Margaret was the sister of the Murray brothers' partner from

---

16   J J Pascoe (ed.). *History of Adelaide and Vicinity*. Adelaide: Hussey & Gillingham, 1901, pp. 492-494.

17   A family tree is available in Murray's papers PRG 259, in the series list. Due to copyright restrictions I could not publish it.

the 1850s, George Tinline (1815-1895). In December 1851, when Tinline was acting manager of the Bank of South Australia, he had saved the State single-handedly from bankruptcy.[18] The gold rush in Victoria had caused a currency crisis. George Tinline argued that Adelaide should outbid Melbourne for Victorian gold and use it to back a paper currency. As a result, the Bullion Act of 1852 backed the currency with gold ingots at the rate of 71 shillings an ounce, confidence was restored, and the economy boomed.

In gratitude to George Tinline, 200 leading Adelaide citizens held a public dinner and presented him with two thousand guineas (one thousand one hundred pounds). The Bank of South Australia gave him a further one thousand pounds. Despite George Tinline's significant contribution to the continuing development of the infant colony, Pascoe's history mentions him as no more than Alexander Murray's partner. Even though George Tinline returned to England in 1863 (he died there in 1895), he should not have been so soon forgotten for his resuscitation of the South Australian economy.

Three children out of eight from Alexander Murray's first marriage survived into his second. George would outlive all of his siblings – both half and full. He was seventeen when his first half-brother died and twenty-two when half-brother John died. His half-sister Esther died in 1930. His full brother Pulteney Malcolm Borthwick died in 1900 at forty. George's older full sister Margaret (1858-1936), or Maggie as she was known within the family, would live her entire life with him at Murray Park. Charlotte (1867-1920), known as Lottie, married Frank Downer (1864-1938), the nephew of John Downer QC and uncle to the Howard government's foreign minister, Alexander Downer.

George Murray's early education was at the Adelaide Educational Institution run by John L Young. In 1874, Alexander Murray sent all four children from his second marriage with their mother to Edinburgh. The older three went to Edinburgh High School - Maggie was 16, (Pulteney) Malcolm was 14 and George was about to turn 11. Lottie, who was 7, went to a primary school. The four children arrived in London in June and were met by their uncle, the former Bank of South Australia manager, George Tinline. Later, young George wrote:

---

18   *Australian Dictionary of Biography*, 1851-1890, pp.. 278-279. George
      Tinline's entry is by Christine Hirst.

We spent some very enjoyable days at Uncle George's, and saw most of the wonders of the world. We then came to Edinburgh by train and at the railway station we met Mr and Mrs Balfour and all went to the Royal, the best hotel there.
(...) The boys are very ignorant of Australia – the master asked Malcolm if Adelaide was in England.[19]

This letter was written to his "Papa" on 10 June 1874, when George Murray was still 10 years old, and he signed it "G J R Murray". Maggie wrote later that "George has been at the top of his class several times". She added:

One of the masters asked George if he was at a good school in Australia. George said: "I was at a better one than this." "What did you come here for then?" "Not to come to school, I came to see what was to be seen."

Lottie at seven was openly candid with her father and gives us a rare glimpse into family life:

I have been fighting with George as usual and nearly knocked his eye out when I threw him against the piano. I did not get a thrashing for it for a wonder.

The family returned to Adelaide after the end of the Scottish school year in mid-1875 and George returned to Mr Young's school. His report for September 1876 (Mr Young may have operated according to the English calendar) reveals:

Writing (pretty well)
English composition (exercises not done)
Grammar (very satisfactory)
History (pretty well)
Geometry (very satisfactory)
Arithmetic (very satisfactory)

19   SLSA Archival Collection, as above, PRG 259/70.

French (very satisfactory)
Drawing (very fair)
Conduct (talkative)

From 1877 until 1880 George attended St Peter's College and was top of his class at the end of each year. He won four College scholarships while at St Peter's: Prankerd for French and German in 1877; Westminster for Classics in 1878; and in 1879 the Farrell Open for Classics and Mathematics and the Wyatt for Physics. As a result, he won a three-year government scholarship to attend the university.

When he began studies at the University of Adelaide in 1881, the University was still using rented rooms in the city. Its first building, now known as the Mitchell building, had been under construction since 1879 and did not open until 1882. George Murray was therefore in the first group of students to use the University of Adelaide's foundation building. But the single University building rapidly proved inadequate. It had to house 153 students and four professors - and within a year, the law school as well as the arts faculty.

George Murray around 1883. (SLSA)

North Terrace must have seemed very open in 1882. There were still none of the great buildings that house the museum, libraries and art gallery, and vacant land east of the university to Frome Road. In 1937, hen Murray laid the foundation of the University building named after him, he recalled:

The nearest neighbours were the police barracks, the Adelaide Hospital and the powder magazine.[20]

20   *The Advertiser*, 21 May 1937, p. 30.

Fortunately, the police barracks and the powder magazine remain, tangible links to Adelaide's early period of settlement.

Murray's exceptional academic achievements during his studies for the Bachelor of Arts degree were rewarded with the South Australian scholarship to attend Cambridge University. He left Adelaide in July 1884 for England. He arrived in September via Paris where there had been a cholera outbreak. He would live in Trinity College, Cambridge for the next three years. Although he had won the South Australian Scholarship of two hundred pounds a year, his father had to add an additional four hundred pounds a year to meet his total costs of six hundred pounds a year. These costs were way out of reach of average income earners: in Adelaide around that time, for example, a first-class cabinetmaker earned 150 pounds a year; a butcher, 125 pounds; a jeweller, up to 200 pounds a year.[21]

At first, George did not find his "fellows" at Cambridge very friendly:

> They are cold, reserved and one may almost say, suspicious. You require to be introduced three or four times before you know an English or Scottish fellow sufficiently well even to nod to him.[22]

But at least one fellow South Australian was already at nearby Trinity Hall:

> Tom Barr Smith called on me and I subsequently took lunch with him. He is very nice and not a bit affected. At Trinity Hall he is one of the most popular men but not the most learned. He was plucked in his final examination for the ordinary degree.[23]

---

21   William Harcus (ed.), *South Australia: Its history, resources, and productions*, pp. 274-275.
22   SLSA Archival Collection, PRG 259/56, Letter to (Pulteney) Malcolm, 22 December 1884.
23   As above, Letter to Maggie, 19 November 1884.

Tom Elder Barr Smith (1863-1941) later joined George Murray as one of the University of Adelaide's biggest benefactors.[24]   After a few months, however, Murray was regularly spending Saturday nights with a group of British friends.   One was Austen Chamberlain (1863-1937), son of Joseph Chamberlain (1836-1914) and brother of future British Prime Minister Neville Chamberlain (1869-1940).   Half a century later, in September 1939, Neville Chamberlain's solemn voice announced to the British public that they were now at war with Germany.   Murray considered Austen Chamberlain "the leading light of the company" and thought him quite clever:

> He is very like his father, and each of them wears an eyeglass so that the resemblance is all the more striking.[25]

Murray missed home and often wished he could return.   On 30 July 1885, he wrote a poem to mark the fact that it was a year since he had left Adelaide, and for the loss of his half-brother John, who had died at thirty-five just over a month before.   He concludes:

> Oft in my dreams I've seen thee, brother mine,
> > Thine eyes of woe,
> Now closed in peace for which they used to pine.
> > A year ago.
> A year ago! How fleet the foot of time!
> And yet now slow.
> But hope and love can make those words sublime,
> A year ago.

Murray nevertheless lived a full life at Cambridge, balancing his study with plenty of recreation.   He rowed and was an accomplished cricketer.   According to his colleague on the bench, Justice Angas Parsons, Murray once filled in for Trinity Hall when they were short and

---

24   Tom Elder Barr Smith gave almost 35,000 pounds in 1927-1928 to build the Barr Smith Library Building, complementing the 20,000 pounds given previously by his father Robert to buy books.

25   SLSA Archival Collection, PRG 259/56. Letter to Mother, 12 February 1885. Also the poem.

made a hundred runs for them before he was out to a ball "which killed a swallow in its flight".[26]

He took up dancing lessons with the ambition of learning how to waltz. He once wrote to Maggie in 1887: "It would be fatal, wouldn't it, if waltzing were to go out of fashion?" The legendary Johann Strauss II was alive at this time in Vienna, and he had made the waltz the most popular dance at balls, especially since writing "The Blue Danube" in 1867. Murray's interest in dancing remained eight years later, back in Adelaide. He was part of a group of Adelaide Club members who successfully lobbied the club committee to allow women to enter the club building for a ball in 1895.[27]

Only very occasionally in George Murray's letters from Cambridge are there references to romantic topics. In 1886, he reported to Maggie that he had received a letter from Estelle Hyland, whose family owned the neighbouring Penfolds Winery at Magill, that she would be in London from 7 to 19 November that year. Estelle wanted to see if he had changed, and especially to see if he had grown a moustache. Murray also reported to his older sister that he had replied to Estelle, gallantly telling her that he would also like to satisfy himself as to:

> whether Miss Estelle herself has altered for the worse, for that she could possibly alter for the better is quite out of the question and that she should alter at all is in no respect to be desired.[28]

A few months later, early in 1887, he answered a query from Maggie about another girl:

> You want to know why I correspond with Emmy Edwards. Well, she is a very great little flirt and has fallen in love with me.[29]

Murray also informed his older sister that Emmy's mother had an income of 10,000 pounds a year. An undated and unsigned limerick among his papers refers to his romantic frustrations:

---

26   [1942] SASR V.
27   E J R Morgan. *The Adelaide Club, 1863-1963*, pp. 91-92.
28   SLSA Archival Collection, PRG 259/73. 4 November 1886.
29   SLSA Archival Collection, PRG 259/56. 23 February 1887.

There was a young man called Murray
Who to the ladies was a fearful worry.
    He came to the plains,
    With several swains,
But left in a terrible hurry.[30]

By chance, one night Murray met the Prime Minister of Britain. Newnham College, Cambridge, had been founded in 1871 to cater for the educational needs of women who were not eligible for admission to universities in Britain. In 1887 the Head of Newnham was the daughter of twice Prime Minister, William Gladstone (1809-1898). Through this connection, the 78 year-old leader came to dinner as a guest of the Master of Trinity College. Murray was present:

> I can now say that I have [had] the honour of dining with William Gladstone. To me it was a most curious sensation seeing the old fellow in the flesh. He has been nothing to me hitherto than a photograph or a cartoon, but there was actually the original himself with his big nose (and it is simply immense), his stick-up collar, and the white flower in his button hole.[31]

Murray did not, unsurprisingly, get to meet Queen Victoria, then approaching her seventieth birthday, but he did see her on a trip to London, along with the Kings and Queens of Denmark, Greece and Belgium. She was opening the Imperial Institute:

> The Queen is beginning to look somewhat old. Her hair is getting white but her complexion is scarlet. Perhaps the heatwave was the cause of this, but it is said her natural colour varies from red to purple.[32]

Being brighter than many other students in Cambridge, Murray could earn extra money by giving tutorials to fellow students who

---

30   As above, SLSA Archival Collection, PRG 259/61.
31   SLSA Archival Collection, PRG 259/73. Letter to Mother, 9 February 1887.
32   As above, Letter to Mother, 30 July 1887.

were struggling; he charged them eight pounds a year each. His own academic record at Cambridge was predictably at the top level, but he himself believed that his talents were more of "bronze than of gold" and wondered if he "should have made better use of his opportunities".[33] It is hard to imagine what else he might have thought he should have done. At the beginning of 1887 – three months from the final exams – he confessed to Maggie:

> People have got the idea into their heads here at Cambridge that it will be a fight between me and one Smith of Trinity Hall for head of the Law Tripos test. For my own part I do not think I shall even be second.[34]

As it turned out, Murray was bracketed equal first with three others in the Law Tripos. A total of 77 students had taken the exams, of whom 39 obtained Honours and 18 failed.[35]

With such results, Murray won an Inns of Court Scholarship which helped him spend a year in London reading with a barrister named Wartzburg. He was a student at the Inner Temple, and he was called to the bar there on 25 April 1888. He would often go to the Courts to see a trial in progress. The Lord Chief Justice was Lord Coleridge, great-nephew of the poet. He was known for falling asleep. Some of the judges still powdered their wigs: notably Baron Huddleston of the old Exchequer Division and Justice Sir Henry Hawkins of Queen's Bench. Murray had the opportunity of listening to what the *Encyclopaedia Britannica* called "the most remarkable State trial of the nineteenth century", *Parnell v Walter*.[36]

Murray returned to Australia in late 1888. With such a record of academic achievement and membership of the English bar, Samuel Way made him his protégé almost from the moment he got

---

33   SLSA Archival Collection, Letter to Maggie, 4 November 1886.
34   Letter to Maggie, 23 February 1887.
35   PRG 259/56. Letter to Father, 10 June 1887.
36   1902 edition, Vol. 31, p. 488. Charles Stewart Parnell, leader of the Irish nationalist party, sensationally sued *The Times* for publishing what proved to be forged letters implicating Parnell in the assassination of Irish Chief Secretary, Lord Cavendish, in 1882.

back. Murray's two-years associateship with Way firmly established the path of his legal career. From what Murray wrote in a letter to his uncle, George Tinline, Way may have already begun thinking of him as a potential successor:

> The Chief Justice has been very kind to me, and has spoken good words for me to the leading lawyers in Adelaide. I have made the acquaintance of all our own prominent men and many from the other colonies. He has always asked me to meet any distinguished visitors who might be passing through Adelaide even when he invited no one else. I have met at his home no fewer than six colonial Governors.[37]

At the end of his time with Way in 1890, Murray set up practice in partnership with his old school friend, William Magarey, father of the Magarey Medal, out of Eagle Chambers near the intersection of Pirie and King William Streets.

Also that year, at 28 years old, Murray was elected to the Council of the University of Adelaide. Except for building up the only known complete collection of South Australian postage stamps, the University would be the only other activity he would dedicate himself to outside the law. In his speech at a dinner held in the South Australian Hotel to mark the fiftieth anniversary of his call to the bar, Murray confessed to guests that he always put work before pleasure and that his work with the University of Adelaide was the only diversion he had "any inclination for".

This self-styled diversion was fortunate for the University's nascent Law School, as its first officially designated Professor of Law wanted to take two terms off to travel with Samuel Way. Professor William Pennefather had been appointed in 1888 in circumstances that were publicly questioned in *The Advertiser* and satirised in *The Lantern*. Both papers accused Chancellor Way of nepotism, by appointing Pennefather over a far better qualified candidate, William Cullen. Cullen later justified the papers' support: he became the seventh Chief Justice of New South Wales in 1910, and was Chancellor of the University of Sydney, 1914-1934.

37　SLSA Archival Collection. Papers of George Tinline, PRG 21/1.

Murray agreed to fill in for Pennefather while he was absent, and he taught six subjects. Murray joked in that 1938 speech that it helped fill in the time while waiting for clients to turn up. Murray was not impressed by his students' capacity for work, however, and wrote to Samuel Way in England that "the students as a body are inexpressibly callous and lazy". From what V A Edgeloe wrote, Murray's contribution to the Law School was crucial: "he not only taught but also examined, and was three times appointed Dean."[38] It is probable that Murray provided a lead to the many legal practitioners who taught at the university over the following sixty or seventy years. Apart from his absence in 1890, Pennefather also took the first term off in 1893 for illness, and again in 1896, when he resigned finally and was replaced by John Salmond, a scholar who retains his reputation over a century later.[39]

Despite his heavy lecturing load, Murray was able to develop his practice with W A Magarey, and his name first appears in the South Australian State Reports in 1892 in *R v Koster*. This was a perjury case and one of the few criminal trials in which Murray was involved. He represented the Crown and Paris Nesbit was for Mr Koster, and Acting Chief Justice James Boucaut quashed the count.[40] Murray would build his reputation in equity, and the majority of his cases that were reported were over disputed estates.

One of the larger cases in which Murray was involved in his early career was as junior to Josiah Symon QC in a complex Crown lease case, *R (On the relation of John Bowman) v The Land Board for the South Eastern District*. Murray and Symon represented Mr Bowman, and Paris Nesbit QC – he took silk just two weeks before the case began in late September 1893 – appeared with James Stuart, the Crown Solicitor.[41] This case alone occupies two-thirds of the volume for the years 1893-1895 – over 100 pages. Murray and Symon won the case for their client, a grazier. He had leased around 13,000 acres of Crown land near Lake Albert for his sheep to graze on under the regulations of

---

38   V A Edgeloe. "Sir George Murray (1863-1942): His Public Community
      Career". *Journal of the Historical Society of South Australia*. No. 19, 1991, (pp.
      172-182), pp. 176-177.
39   See Alex Castles, Andrew Ligertwood & Peter Kelly (eds.) *Law on North Ter-
      race*, pp.13-15.
40   [1892] SALR 1.
41   James Martin Stuart (1834-1908) was appointed silk in 1900. He had been
      admitted at 41 years old and was Crown Solicitor 1889-1905.

the *Crown Lands Consolidation Act* 1877. Prior to that date the Crown had the power to resume leaseholds for any reason with six months notice, but after 1877, it could only resume the land for "the purposes of public utility".

Mr Bowman was the victim of two bureaucratic bungles. The first was that his leasehold had incorrectly been executed on an old form, predating the 1877 restrictions on the Crown taking back the land. The second was that the Commissioner of Crown Lands intended taking back 4,500 acres, not for the benefit of the community in general, but to subdivide and resell to private individuals.

In the judgment Way repeatedly referred to Murray's arguments in preference to those of other counsel, including Murray's senior, Josiah Symon QC.[42] But while Samuel Way often praised George Murray in his judgments, this did not necessarily mean that he always agreed with him. Murray represented the Crown in an appeal against a judgment of Way in which the Chief Justice now sat in review in banco with Boucaut and Bundey. (This situation was normal and unavoidable before 1919 when a fourth judge was appointed.) The case was *In re Simms* (1899), a dispute over death duty payable, which was 7 per cent.[43]

William Simms, a successful brewer, had died at the end of 1898, leaving 315,000 pounds, which would have the same purchasing power in 2006 as $40 million.[44] The Registrar of Probate found that Mr Simms had two years earlier promised two hundred thousand pounds to his five children, by way of a covenant asserting that the money was a debt payable to them with three months notice. The family claimed that his estate was therefore only worth 115,000 pounds.

Way agreed with them and the Crown appealed. The appeal was one of the very rare instances when the longest serving Chief Justice found himself in dissent with his two brother judges. Way could find no reason to change his mind when the case came back, with Murray for the Crown, and Symon QC (with P F Bonnin) for the children. Way called Murray's argument "subtle but candid", yet eventually had to disagree: "I find myself unable to accept the conclusions which have

---

42   *R (On the relation of John Bowman) v The Land Board for the South Eastern District* [1893-1895] SALR 1 at 34.

43   [1899] SALR 1.

44   See CPI rates at abs.gov.au.

been drawn from the evidence laid before us in this bald manner."[45] But as he was in the minority, the family were liable for duty on the whole 315,000 pounds. Justices Boucaut and Bundey believed that William Simms had set up the debt only to evade the death duties, and discussed at length the difference between "evade " and "avoid". The Simms family looked set to pay over twenty-two thousand pounds in duty.

Naturally, with such a large sum to lose – for example, Sir Langdon Bonython bought Carclew house, over the road from Samuel Way, in North Adelaide ten years later for 3,500 pounds – they took their case to the Privy Council, where it was heard in February 1900. The Privy Council reversed the order of the Full Court upholding not only Way's dissenting judgment, but his original one as well. They found that there was no evidence of any deliberate intent to evade duties, the Crown's argument was based only on inferences.[46] Way's win was Murray's loss, and the Crown was only able to claim death duties on the net 115,000 pounds William Simms had kept to himself.

George Murray's regular appearances over the years before the Chief Justice attracted an anonymous poet. It is worth reproducing in full because Way and Murray feature so strongly. Neither dated nor attributed, it mentions he is the "great KC" so it must have been written after Murray was appointed silk in 1906:

> The Chief Justice, in delivering his judgment said:
>
> For forty years I've been familiar
> With the practice of the Court –
> And with the advocates before it
> Broad, long, thin, fast and short.
> But unhesitatingly I say,
> I, the great Chief Justice Way –
> Thro' all the life I've lent
> My ear to argument –
> I have never heard so deuced
> An able, clear and lucid
> Legal argument.
>
> With unseemly hurray

---

45   *Simms* [1899] SALR, at 52 and 53.
46   *Simms v Registrar of Probate* [1900] AC 323 at 330.

Proceeded Mr Murray
There was nothing to diminish
From start to very finish
The pathos that he felt upon
The arguments that he dwelt upon
Throughout his royal road
And its very mighty praise
When the Lord Chief Justice strays
And stops his judgment fairly
in the middle
To make a kind allusion
To the Piper in conclusion
And to say that he succeeded in
but playing second fiddle.

Then Hey! for the Bench!
And Ho! for the Bar!
And ha! for the recognition
Of a pardonable ambition
To become a shining light
Not an ordinary light
That only shines at night
But a sort of second Symon
(Not that simple child the Pieman
But the great, great, great KC!)

We can picture in the scurry
Of a busy world – our Murray
Sitting calmly taking fees
With his chin upon his knees
Sending junior briefs to Symon and to Nesbit
His engrossing work to Kingston
Now that Collyer's nearly dead
With copying the briefs that float
round Murray's head.
While Downer, Grundy, Fenn
And the balance of the Bar
Walk to and fro like laden ants
With books for "GJR".

He gives up active practice
And devotes his time and nerve
To preparing all the judgments
That the judges must reserve
For fear of contradiction from
This lordly source of law.[47]

As well as a high income as a successful lawyer, Murray was a legatee in several considerable fortunes left by his wealthy relatives. In 1886 his uncle John Murray died leaving the family 150,000 pounds. George had been hoping for more

The Murray family's homestead on the Wirrabara Estate. (SLSA)

– he was in Cambridge at the time – and wrote to his older half-sister Ettie (Esther, 1847-1930):

> I confess I am disappointed, I thought a quarter of a million would more nearly hit the mark.[48]

Murray's uncle on his mother's side – George Tinline – died in London in 1895 and left sixty thousand pounds to the family. Then his father Alexander died in 1903, leaving 107,000 pounds. This was mostly the value of the 8,000 hectare property at Wirrabara in the state's mid-north. Nearby Murray Town was named after Alexander Murray. He left one of the best merino flocks in South Australia and had been a regular prize winner at the Royal Adelaide Show and elsewhere since that first win at Noarlunga in the early 1840s. In the last decade of the nineteenth century, the Murray flock increasingly found itself sharing

---

47   SLSA Archival Collection, cited above, PRG 259/61.
48   SLSA Archival Collection, PRG 259/56. Letter to Ettie, 18 November 1886.

first and second prizes with another merino breeder: Samuel Way, on his Kadlunga property. For example, in 1899 Way came runner-up to Murray in the Adelaide Show for merino ram, but won first for champion ewe.

Murray's correspondence from the 1890s on reveals that none of the fortunes of which he was a major legatee gave him peace of mind. His Scottish upbringing had firmly branded him with a need to squeeze the best return out of each and every solitary pound, no matter how many of them there were. This was where his correspondence differed from his predecessor's. Way wrote about people and their latest successes and failures to win power or honours. Murray's letters – whether they are to his stock and station agent or to a close relative – ended up being entirely about his property and share transactions. He never seemed to have felt as though he had enough money to feel safe, and was incensed at the idea that others found him or his family rich. He wrote a letter to the editor of *The Register* in September 1904, in response to local criticism of the size of the property:

> The Wirrabara Estate was bought and paid for by my father, and utilised by him in the breeding of high quality merino sheep – not, I believe, without benefit to South Australia. The profits he made from it were invested and lost in attempts to develop outlying pastoral country in various parts of the colony. When he died last year he had little more to leave than this property at Wirrabara.[49]

But the criticism about the Wirrabara property was mild in comparison to what he would experience in New Zealand a few years later. His uncle John Tinline died in Nelson, South Island, in 1905, where he had built up a group of pastoral properties. George Murray had to make two trips to Nelson in 1907 to organise the best management of the estate. Soon after arriving, he received a letter:

---

49   SLSA Archival Collection, PRG 259/7. Letter to the editor of *The Register*, 28/9/1904.

So you are a lawyer are you we might have known. It's only people like you who are lawless, greedy, groping things and too mean to give away a penny when asked for it.[50]

The writer of the letter offered to sell Murray some sacks he had made to help carry John Tinline's gold back to Sydney, and signed off: "R.I.P" in bold black letters.

Further letters accused John Tinline of being mean to his staff for not leaving them any money, and wanted some of his estate "put to good use in Nelson". They became threatening:

So you take no notice don't you and won't do anything with all your dirty money as you have been told to do. (...) We will give you one more chance and then if you do not do something you will suffer for it.

Murray himself was surprised at the lack of provision for any of the key staff; one in particular had worked on the property for thirty years. He wondered if one of them was the author of the letters, but then one day received an apology:

Sir, I write these few lines in deep regret of the letters I have written you lately. I am really and deeply sorry for them and I apologise most humbly for them and the pain they must have caused you.[51]

He had the impression that the author of this letter was female, and probably the author of all the letters he had received. Murray, despite his Caledonian philosophy, kindly made ex gratia payments of 100 pounds each to the staff he believed were deserving, and allowed one of them to purchase one of the properties through a favourably arranged mortgage. The value of John Tinline's estate was around 160,000 pounds. Each major beneficiary of the estate, among them George Murray, received forty thousand pounds. Murray wrote to his

---

50   SLSA Archival Collection, PRG 259/54. Anonymous letter to George Murray, not dated.

51   PRG 259/73/50/1. Quoted in a letter to Maggie, 16 April 1907.

cousin James Madder Tinline – George Tinline's son – that Uncle John had 345 pounds when he arrived in New Zealand in 1845.[52]

The year 1907 was not a happy one for Murray. In between his two trips to Nelson, his mother died. In her memory, he gave one thousand pounds – his first cash donation to the University of Adelaide – to establish the annual Tinline prize. The year before, Murray had been appointed silk, and so was now officially one of the leaders of the South Australian bar. He was one of the leaders in the famous "Corset Case" - *Weingarten Bros. v G. & R. Wills & Co.* – representing Wills with John Downer KC and James Henderson. Josiah Symon KC, Paris Nesbit KC and E E Cleland represented the American Weingartens. He had been born into one of the State's wealthiest families and he succeeded at everything he attempted himself. Yet, from a letter he wrote to the local manager of his late uncle's estate in New Zealand, he was never at ease: "I am accustomed to a life of worry. A few more come naturally to me", he wrote.[53] Although at the time the letter had been written he was having to manage both his father's property at Wirrabara and his uncle's in new Zealand, as well as his busy law practice, it is obvious his state of mind was not just due to these added responsibilities, nor the recent death of his mother. These brief lines suggest that he may never have been quite comfortable with his life.

Murray and his sister Maggie would continue to live the rest of their lives at Murray Park, except for three year-long holidays spent in Britain – in 1909, 1925 and 1935. In 1909 Murray must have appraised his financial situation and felt more confident in his expenditures, and in his ability to take time off from his practice. He and sister Maggie went to England for a year, while the house at Murray Park was enlarged. While there, Murray enrolled for the Master of Laws at Cambridge, and he received his degree in June.

Murray and his sister would also be able to visit their nephew Douglas studying at Cambridge for a degree in agricultural science, and scold him about his extravagant spending. Douglas was the son of Murray's older brother Pulteney, who had died in 1900 at the age of forty when Douglas was just thirteen. In 1902, George took his teenage nephew on a holiday to New Zealand to visit John Tinline.

---

52   SLSA Archival Collection, PRG 259/29. Letter to "Madder", 24 April 1907.
53   PRG 259/29. Letter to a name that could be Conrad, but equally Connal, 20 March 1908.

The assumption of a paternal role towards Douglas was to prove one of George Murray's most acute worries, and it ended in tragedy. Murray was a reserved, shy man who preferred to retire to one of the quiet rooms of his house with a book or his stamps. His needs were frugal and he preferred to accumulate money rather than spend it. His nephew Douglas, on the other hand, was about as opposite as imaginable. Douglas had little interest in knowledge and spent money recklessly. He preferred parties. Douglas's profligacy was not assisted by the fact that he had inherited seventeen thousand pounds from his father which gave him an independent income of five hundred pounds a year – five times the median income.

In January 1909, two weeks before he left for England, George Murray wrote to Douglas:

> I was greatly shocked when I received your cablegram this morning asking me to wire you one hundred pounds. You drew the whole of your two years allowance – four hundred pounds – in August and before five months have elapsed you are asking for another one hundred pounds. (…) You do not seem to realise that you cannot afford to live at the rate you are doing.[54]

In April, this time writing from the Hotel Russell in Russell Square, London, Murray again attempted to restrain his nephew's spending when he asked for fifty pounds – the equivalent now of several thousand dollars.

Douglas seems to have been far from intimidated by his uncle's stern warnings of imminent ruin. A year later, Murray was back in Adelaide and despite the lectures on thrift that he gave his nephew, Douglas again asked for more money:

> This is absolutely shocking and proves to me that you have neither paid the slightest heed to the advice I gave you or else have not been frank with me in disclosing your liabilities when I was in England.[55]

---

54   SLSA Archival Collection, PRG 259/29. Letter to Douglas, 19 January 1909.
55   SLSA Archival Collection, Letter to Douglas, 26 April 1910.

Douglas had just spent three hundred pounds in four months, around four times more than average students, who were already from families in the upper income level. Murray issued an ultimatum, after consulting with Maggie and Douglas's mother:

> I order you to leave England at once and return to Adelaide. It is both a waste of time and a waste of money for you to continue as you are doing.

Somehow, Douglas convinced him that he should stay, and in 1911 he took his degree. He returned to Australia to work on the pastoral property his father had left, Pinnacle Station near Grenfell in New South Wales. His farm management was more disastrous than his student life. He continued to ask George Murray for money for at least the next five years, but this time the amounts were even larger. At the end of 1914, Murray sent Douglas 650 pounds, asking him for the reason he had not sold his wool. Six months later – in July 1915 – Murray sent another 650 pounds, leaving himself "insufficient funds to go with".[56] The total of these two payments – 1300 pounds – was just four hundred pounds short of Murray's annual judicial stipend then.

Murray had repeatedly warned Douglas that he was eating into his capital and would end up with nothing. But the western world was at war now, and Douglas joined the army. On 25 October 1918 at Damascus (then in Palestine and now in Syria), and a few days short of the final victory over the Turks, Douglas Murray was killed in action. He was thirty-one.

The Vaughan government appointed Murray a puisne judge on 2 April 1912. The year 1912 was also the first year in which all judges in His Majesty's dominions received the title "Honourable" from the moment they were appointed instead of awaiting parliamentary approval.[57] He immediately resigned his membership of the recently formed Liberal Union which had been attempting, without success, to persuade him to run for parliament:[58]

---

56   As above, Letter to Douglas, 1 July 1915.
57   *The Advertiser*, Saturday, 27 January 1912.
58   Alex C Castles, Entry for Murray in *ADB* 1940-1980.

I have never aspired to be a politician. The shock I got when two of those I had lectured to at the University stood for Parliament and were elected – I mean Sir Angas Parsons and Sir Frederick Young – was enough for me.[59]

Murray also curtailed his social life at the Adelaide Club where he was known for his "cheery wit" and "resonant voice":

His play at billiards was always worth watching. However, and perhaps over-scrupulously, he severed all his unofficial and many personal ties after he was elevated to the bench (…).[60]

Murray was elected the first Vice-President of the Adelaide Club in 1915, and would have been President, but he resigned the office in January 1916, when he became Chief Justice in succession to Sir Samuel Way. He then appeared daily at the club with his puisne judges, "led in procession at lunchtime to a table in the dining room which was reverently, although not officially, kept for their use." This tradition continued until his last year, although not all the judges participated. Justice Frederick Richards – Samuel Way's associate from 1901 to 1908 – appointed in 1927, was a strict Methodist and preferred to take his lunch in his chambers.

Margaret (Maggie) and George Murray in Melrose, 22 April 1929. (Advertiser)

Of all the Chief Justices of the twentieth century, only Murray found himself appointed almost simultaneously as Chief Justice, Chancellor of the University of Adelaide and Lieutenant-Governor. All three appointments took place within three months. Way was not

59   Speech, 29 April 1938, cited above.
60   E J R Morgan, p. 86.

made Chancellor until seven years after he became Chief Justice, and, although he filled in for the Governor, he had not been officially made Lieutenant-Governor until 1891. Murray was truly the beneficiary of the triple office that Way established, if only as a tradition. Unlike Way, when Murray was offered a KCMG, in 1917, he accepted. Way in 1889 had declined - and eventually got his baronetcy in 1899.

Murray's election as Chancellor began a completely new period at the University of Adelaide. He had been elected Vice-Chancellor in April 1915 when William Barlow died, but relinquished office to William Mitchell in 1916. For the next twenty-five years the two men oversaw a crucial period of growth. Each of them attributed the university's success during their management to the other. In 1937, at the laying of the first stone of the George Murray building, Sir William pointed out that Murray had had a voice in every single addition to the original University building (eventually to be named for Mitchell himself):

> Neither the length of years nor the number of buildings gave any idea of the influence the Chancellor had exercised. The University had been his peculiar care in a way no outsider could understand.[61]

Murray said the following year:

> That place has since grown to amazing proportions but there again I am entitled to no credit. The chief author of its success has been Sir William Mitchell.[62]

In 1916, the University of Adelaide was made up of four buildings on two hectares of land – the original Mitchell Building, the Elder Conservatorium, the Prince of Wales Building and the Anatomy Building. There were 775 students, though only 284 of these were full-time undergraduates, and 12 professors and 36 lecturers. Over the next twenty-five years the University would expand down to the River Torrens and across to the Adelaide Hospital, with sixteen more buildings and major additions, including the two most admired today – the Barr Smith Library and Bonython Hall. By Murray's death in 1942 there

61   *The Advertiser*, 21 May 1937.
62   Speech, 29 April 1938, cited above.

were almost 2500 students, including 1221 full-time undergraduates, taught by 23 professors and 89 lecturers.[63]

In his first year as Chancellor Murray made a very significant decision regarding the location of the University. The Labor Government wished to move the entire University to the site of the new Glenside Mental Hospital so that there would be room to establish colleges. Murray believed that the university benefited from its central position on North Terrace and successfully prevented the move. The university is not entirely without a link to an asylum, however: in 2003 the university took a long-term lease on the failed National Wine Centre: it is built on the same land as the long-forgotten North Terrace Asylum.

Another example of Murray's defence of the university was in 1934. G V Portus joined the university that year as Professor of History and at the request of the Workers' Education Association (WEA) gave a public talk on "What Marx did for Socialism". Portus reminisced:

> A member of the local Parliament who happened to be in the audience wrote to the university complaining that I was a Marxist. He added that I ought to be silenced, and unless something was done about it, he would bring the matter up in Parliament when the University estimates were next under consideration.[64]

Portus had been an Anglican parson in Merriwa, New South Wales, before becoming a lecturer. The Registrar, Frederick William Eardley, demanded an apology and – no doubt concerned about future State grants – warned Portus not to "quarrel with our bread and butter". When the letter was read in a Council meeting, Murray intervened:

> He said the University could not dream of telling its professors what they had to say or not to say on any question. Having been appointed, professors were free to express their opinions and views, and must not be muzzled.

---

63   V A Edgeloe, *The University of Adelaide: The Murray-Mitchell Era*. Unpublished, Appendix 3.
64   G V Portus, *Happy Highways*, pp. 248-249, and for the other quotes.

Portus realised subsequently that this would be Murray's position in all similar attempts to silence academic staff: "He was a genuine liberal in outlook, and the University of Adelaide was very fortunate to have him as its Chancellor."

Murray's Vice-Chancellor, William Mitchell, was an equally dominating force during the period between the two world wars. He had been born in Scotland in 1861 and would live to the age of 101. Duncan and Leonard describe him as "the nearest approach to a philosopher-king the academic world has ever seen".[65] He was appointed Professor at Adelaide at the age of 33 in English Language and Literature and Mental and Moral Philosophy. This broad title led him to remark once that he did not so much occupy a chair as a sofa. Nevertheless, as though teaching english and philosophy was not enough, he also taught subjects in zoology, anatomy, psychology, political economy, logic, and education.

Murray as Lieutenant-Governor ca. 1930s. (SCLSA)

Mitchell established his reputation in the wider community of philosophers in 1907 with *The Structure and Growth of the Mind*. Consequently he found himself invited to give lectures in England and interstate. After the death in 1915 of his wealthy father-in-law, Robert Barr Smith, Mitchell no longer needed a salary and became part-time Vice-Chancellor in 1916, full-time from 1922 until 1948 - all without a salary. Like Murray, his Calvinist upbringing extended to his professional duties. To save money, he never had his own office, always sharing a desk with the Registrar.

Murray's contribution to the University of Adelaide while he was Chancellor was not only on an entirely voluntary basis, but also financial, initially to cover budget shortfalls. In 1920 he donated one thousand pounds – more than the salary of a professor – for general expenses, and twice that again in 1931. The 1930s were a difficult period for the university due to the Depression, which left Adelaide with over 30 per cent unemployment for almost a decade. The great saviour for the State

---

65   Duncan and Leonard, *The University of Adelaide, 1874-1974*, p. 78.

was Sir Langdon Bonython, who provided jobs by giving one hundred thousand pounds for the completion of Parliament House, and more than fifty thousand pounds to build Bonython Hall in the University.

Murray's donations to the university would come to exceed even Bonython's, the Barr Smiths' and Elder's. In 1936, he again gave fifteen thousand pounds for general purposes, and another ten thousand pounds to build the George Murray building for the recreational and study use of male students. This was a twin building to the Lady Symon, built in 1929 for female students. In 1937, his sister Maggie died, and Murray transferred the fifty three thousand pounds he inherited from her to the university. Finally, in his will, he left a further eighty-three thousand pounds for any use the university could find. His gifts totalled around 165,000 pounds – at least $30 million in 2006 purchasing power – making him the single most important benefactor in the history of the University of Adelaide since its foundation.

George Murray with two of his judges: Mellis Napier and Herbert Angas Parsons. (Advertiser)

South Australia's economy during the period between the two World Wars stagnated, and by the end of the 1930s average incomes dropped below those of the 1880s.[66] The harsh climate was proving that an economy based on agriculture could not sustain general long-term growth. The Moonta mines, a significant source of wealth for over fifty years, closed in 1923. The population grew around 30 per cent between the wars, from around 450,000 in 1916,

---

66   *Wakefield Companion to South Australian History*, p. 160.

to 600,000 by 1940. By this time metropolitan Adelaide held sixty per cent of the State's population.[67]

The bench during Murray's period increased in number for the first time since a third judge had been added in 1859 – still under the first Chief Justice of South Australia, Sir Charles Cooper. The State's population two years later, when Richard Hanson took over, was 126,830.[68] It had quadrupled to almost half a million by the time Thomas Poole was appointed Fourth Judge in 1919. A fifth judge was added relatively soon after in 1927. The eventual total of nine judges in the Murray Court (including him) would form the last exclusively Protestant, all-male Supreme Court bench. No Catholics or women were appointed. All the locally educated judges had been to St Peter's and Prince Alfred Colleges. There was a swing towards a majority of Church of England

Murray doffing his hat at an official function. (Advertiser)

or Scotland men: Murray, Buchanan, Angas Parsons, Poole and Piper. During Way's period as Chief Justice, the judges appointed before Murray were from the diverse "dissenting" Protestant religions: Methodist, Presbyterian and Congregational. All except for Gordon and Cleland were members of the Adelaide Club, and all had been appointed Queen's Counsel except Buchanan. Some were Freemasons, but notably George Murray was not; Angas Parsons was the only other non-Mason.

According to a practitioner of the Murray period, Robert Clark, the Chief Justice "ruled his fellow judges and the profession with a touch that was none the less for being light".[69] Murray became a well-known

---

67   *South Australian Year Book.* Vol. 1, 1966. Adelaide: Commonwealth Bureau of Statistics, p. 84.

68   J J Pascoe, p. 617.

69   *Law on North Terrace*, p. 17, for both Clark quotes.

figure in the city, even to people who had nothing to do with the courts, simply because of the impact of seeing a tall man every day at the same time striding between the Supreme Court and the Adelaide Club. Professor Portus described Murray as having the face of a Roman stoic.[70]

Murray's frequent companion around the city from 1920 was brother judge Herbert Angas Parsons (1872-1945). Angas Parsons was a great-great-nephew of pioneer George Fife Angas (1789-1879), hence the additional surname, and he had married Sir Langdon Bonython's daughter Mary in 1900. Bonython (1848-1939) was the sole owner of *The Advertiser* daily newspaper, which bought out *The Register* in 1931, and thus a dominating personality in Adelaide's society and politics.

Robert Clark remembered that because of the size difference between the two judges – Murray a "colossal figure" and Angas Parsons quite short – they were known around the city as 'the long and short of it". Cedric Isaachsen, associate to both judges in the mid-1930s, recalled Murray and Parsons crossing North Terrace opposite the Adelaide Club, when a police officer told them they were breaking the law by jaywalking. Murray replied that he was the Chief Justice. The policeman replied: "Alright then, who's the short chap?"

Jack Elliott in his *Memoirs of a Barrister* recalled that the Chief Justice presided over his admission ceremony in April 1937. Murray advised Elliott and his newly admitted colleagues:

> You are entering the wrong profession if you regard it as a highly remunerative occupation. The law is essentially a profession dedicated to the service of the public. If you work hard and honestly, as I hope you will, the most you can ordinarily expect is an income that will keep you in reasonable comfort. To any of you who think otherwise I say you'd probably be wise to seek your fortune in another sphere.[71]

This warning was especially true at that time because of the Depression. Elliott also commented on George Murray's physical presence: "a tall, imposing figure of great solemnity and little speech."[72] El-

---

70   G V Portus, p. 247.
71   Jack Elliott, p. 15.
72   Jack Elliott, p. 17; and p. 18 for the following quote.

liott only appeared once before George Murray, representing a 19-year old country youth who had broken into a shop and stolen some money. Since it was the fellow's first conviction, Elliott asked for him to be released on a good behaviour bond.

His fellow lawyer and friend Les Wright doubted his chances: "Old Sir George is mid-Victorian. His idea of leniency is a sentence of about ten years, especially if the offence involves breaking and entering." Elliott pleaded so passionately on behalf of his client that he worried he might have sounded like a "cross between a salesman and an evangelist". His efforts were rewarded, despite Les Wright's warning, as Murray allowed the young man the requested bond.

Immediately into his tenure as Chief Justice, Murray became embroiled in a case relating to the war with Germany. This was *R v Snow*, which revolved around Broken Hill ores being sold to a German company. The case would drag on through the entire period of the war and it would require a detailed study to understand the Commonwealth government's persistence in keeping it in the Supreme Court of South Australia and in the High Court. In wartime, issues of defence are a priority. Nevertheless, from the account of the case by W A Norman, one of the defence lawyers, Prime Minister Billy Hughes wanted to go further than merely suspend trading with Germany due to war. According to Norman, the case was really about the federal government's plan to put an end permanently to the supply of Broken Hill ore to German companies.[73]

Francis Snow's large enterprise was involved in transporting ore for a number of mining operations around Australia. When war broke out, he sent letters to his German client Hirsch via their English and American agents, advising them that business would be suspended during the war, but would resume once it was over. Australian intelligence services seized his letters and charged him under the Trading with the Enemy Act.

Snow's letters had been written before the Act came into force and so, at the first trial in early 1915, Justice Gordon directed the jury to acquit, since the Act could not be applied retrospectively. The Crown applied for leave to appeal to the High Court rather than the Full Court.

---

73   W A Norman, *Random Reminiscences of the South Australian Bar and Bench*. Unpublished manuscript, ca.1950, pp. 31-32.

The application was denied in Adelaide, in Melbourne, and again in Sydney. Norman was present at each of these attempts. At the Sydney application, he described how Chief Justice Samuel Griffith denounced the application as absurd and referred to an "elementary text book on Criminal Law".[74] Justices Isaacs and Higgins attempted to allow it but without success.

The Crown charged Snow again, using fresh information that brought him before Murray for the first time, in November 1915. The Crown – represented by Cleland KC, Villeneuve Smith and Powers – argued that the content of the letters was irrelevant in defining "trading with the enemy". Murray agreed with this broad definition and, though Snow was convicted, Murray encouraged an appeal to the Full Court.

He himself headed the appeal court and reversed his original judgment, ruling that "the mere sending of letters on business matters in which the parties are interested without any resulting arrangement or transaction does not constitute trading".[75] His brother judges Gordon and Buchanan agreed. The verdict of guilty was set aside. It would be interesting to know whether Murray recommended the appeal to his Full Court in order ultimately to counteract the pressure coming from the Commonwealth government with a joint judgment rather than one.

The Crown appealed to the High Court again in May 1917. The federal judges sent the case back to Murray as trial judge (in the second trial) to consider further evidence.[76] Murray found that he had misunderstood some crucial wording in a telegram and referred the case again to his own Full Court. By now – August 1918 – Murray and Buchanan, Gordon dissenting, reluctantly found that there should be a retrial.[77] This would be the third separate trial that Mr Snow had to endure. The Commonwealth was again not satisfied and applied to the High Court for special leave to appeal. This was refused.[78] In 1919 – the war had now ended – Snow was again tried and this time the High Court found him guilty of trading with the enemy and fined him two thousand pounds. This third trial is not reported, but the question of

---

74   Norman, p. 35.
75   *R v Snow* [1916] SALR 55 at 85.
76   *R v Snow* (1916-1917) 23 CLR 256.
77   *R v Snow* [1918] SALR 173.
78   *R v Snow* (1918) 25 CLR 377.

costs was.[79] Norman estimated that Francis Snow paid costs of close to ten thousand pounds over three years. He also permanently lost his agency selling ore to Germany, which is what the Federal Government wanted all along.

W A Norman believed that George Murray was one of the "finest judges that ever graced the South Australian bench":

He may not have been quite as astute as Sir Samuel Way, he was not quite as friendly as Sir Herbert Parsons, he did not possess the silver tongue of Sir John Gordon or the practical common sense of Mr Justice Buchanan, but

George Murray and his Associate G G Noble. (Advertiser)

he had something none of them possessed in so high a degree – a strict impartiality and a passion for justice.[80]

E E Cleland had a reputation for being a larrikin and once during the Snow case, managed to cause George Murray to blush. W.A. Norman recalled that the Chief Justice had accused Cleland of endeavouring to mislead the court:

The atmosphere became electrified and Sir George turned very red in the face as he always did when embarrassed. Cleland made some remark which the Chief Justice asked him to withdraw. Ted, as he was generally known then, remarked in his polite but witty style: "In deference to your remarks I withdraw. If your Honour is wrong the High Court will rectify your Honour's mistake as it did in the Blank case last month."[81]

---

79   *R v Snow* (1919) 26 CLR 506.
80   Norman, p. 37.
81   Norman, p. 40.

The "Blank" case was *Hare v Terry*, in which the High Court overturned Murray's decision against Cleland's client Charles Hare.[82] This was an interesting case itself, the direct consequence of the early closing of hotels that resulted from the referendum of 27 March 1915. The Act enforcing the six o'clock closing allowed hotel lessees to surrender their leases before the agreed term as they could not have foreseen the reduction in trading hours.

Mrs Terry leased her hotel to David Callel in June 1914, and because that lease was signed prior to the referendum date, it became subject to the right of surrender. David Callel transferred the lease, with Mrs Terry's complete and signed approval, to Charles Hare in March 1916, after the referendum date. In February 1917, Hare gave two weeks' notice of surrendering the lease. Mrs Terry sued.

Justice Gordon had ruled that since Hare had taken on the hotel lease after the change in hours, he had waived the Licensing Act's special right to surrender it. E E Cleland had argued the contrary: the lease's rights had transferred in their original form to Mr Hare. Cleland appealed to the Full Court and although Alexander Buchanan agreed with his argument, Murray and Gordon did not.[83] Cleland was convinced he was right and the High Court agreed.

The Murray Court in 1920 in Court 2. L-R at rear: Thomas Poole, John Gordon, George Murray, Alexander Buchanan. (SCLSA)

Cleland appears to have been a fearless adversary with little regard for convention. Apart from reminding Sir George Murray of his High Court win, during the Snow case, Cleland also reminded his opponent – Sir Josiah Symon KC – of his recent High Court win against him. This was in *McBride v Sandland* in June 1918.[84] Every time Sir Josiah entered the robing room Cleland would immediately discuss the McBride case with Frank Villeneuve Smith, highlighting a particular point of Symon's argument

82   (1918) 24 CLR 468.
83   *Terry v Hare* [1917] SALR 128.
84   *McBride v Sandland* (1918) 25 CLR 69.

that had been refuted. Symon consequently avoided them as much as possible:

> Some members of the profession considered this rather a display of larrikinism but Cleland argued it was the only way of dealing with Sir Josiah's domineering attitude in Court to other members of the bar.[85]

Sir Josiah Symon was 23 years older than E.E. Cleland, but Cleland was not intimidated. Neither was he intimidated by judges. In 1935, Jack Elliott saw him defy Acting Chief Justice Angas Parsons, who would not allow him to reply to an address by Villeneuve Smith. Cleland turned to the wall and spoke for a full twenty minutes.[86] The following year, Cleland was appointed by Richard Butler's Liberal government to the Supreme Court to replace Justice A W Piper.

According to Robert Clark, Murray "ruled his judges completely" until Cleland's appointment to the bench. That "marred the cosy circle".[87] One revealing distinction between Cleland and the other judges is that he was not a member of the Adelaide Club. He defied Murray's attempt to stop him smoking in public, and continued to meet his old colleagues in the Arcadia Café on King William Street.

During Samuel Way's record term as Chief Justice little had changed in the day-to-day operations of the Supreme Court. But Murray saw a very important change in the mode of trials in 1927. The Juries Act of that year abolished the use of juries in civil cases, and altered their function in most criminal ones. Capital offences still required an unanimous verdict, as before, but not other offences if the jury had been out for four hours. After that, the decision of ten of them would suffice to give a verdict.[88]

The Juries Act of 1927 was the end-product of a series of five reports on law reform produced since 1923. A Royal Commission on Law Reform had been set up after Harry Young initiated debate in the House of Assembly in October 1922, motivated by criticism of the jury system in some notable cases that year. The Royal Commission's first

---

85   Norman, p. 41.
86   Elliott, p. 9.
87   *Law on North Terrace*, p.17.
88   Castles and Harris, p. 345.

report included observations by some of the most prominent legal personalities of the period. All of them – including Crown Solicitor Fred Richards (who would be appointed to the Supreme Court bench in 1927), Assistant Crown Solicitor A J Hannan, Crown Prosecutor E W J Millhouse, President of the Industrial Court W J Brown, F Villeneuve Smith and E E Cleland – favoured the abolition of the jury in civil cases, and generally wished it retained in criminal ones.[89]

The only judge's opinion recorded was Angas Parsons's who had found in of two-and-a-half years on the bench that he had only disagreed twice with a jury verdict in criminal cases, and they were both acquittals. A W Piper, future judge, spoke as President of the the Law Society, whose official stance was to oppose juries in civil cases, but to retain them for criminal ones.

It is not known what George Murray thought about the changes to the jury system. The year after the Juries Act was passed, the court recommended some changes of its own in its annual report to the Attorney-General, but these were more in the order of getting the legal profession in South Australia closer to its English parent:

> 10.   We are of opinion that it would be in the public interest to separate Practitioners of the Supreme Court into the two distinct classes of Barristers or Advocates and Attorneys, Solicitors and Proctors. This was contemplated in the Ordinance still in force to regulate the Profession of the Law in South Australia, No. 6 of 1845.
>
> We propose to invite the Council of the Law Society of South Australia Incorporated to submit us its views on the matter.[90]

The Law Society conducted a plebiscite among its nearly 300 members. Three-quarters of those who responded were against a division of the profession: 209 "No" to 64 "Yes".[91] Although founding judge of the South Australian Supreme Court Sir John Jeffcott intended fusion of the profession in 1837 to be provisional, ninety years later

89   *First Progress Report of the Royal Commission on Law Reform (The Jury System).* Adelaide: 1923, pp. VII-X.
90   (1928) ALJ at 43.
91   Graham Loughlin, *South Australian Queen's Counsel*, p. 33.

the State's fused profession was too well established to welcome change. Over seventy years later, there is still no likelihood of formally dividing the South Australian legal profession, although a voluntary independent bar was founded in 1964.[92]

The most sensational case that George Murray had before him in the thirty years he was on the bench was *R v Edwards*. Looking back, the case had everything of a court-room drama made for theatre. The Chief Justice was the perfect embodiment of justice: reserved, serious, scholarly, rational. The accused was entirely the opposite. Albert Augustine Edwards was a local celebrity, a flamboyant homosexual, who grew up in poverty and claimed Charles Kingston as his real father. He was the owner of several city hotels, the Labor member for Adelaide, an Adelaide City Councillor, president of the West Adelaide Football Club and a tireless campaigner for reform of prisons and amelioration of poverty.[93] Edwards was represented by the most theatrical advocate of the era, Frank Villeneuve Smith KC (who had served his articles with the similarly dramatic Paris Nesbit) and W A Rollison, and the prosecution by Eric Millhouse with Roderick Chamberlain (Crown Prosecutor).

Edwards had been arrested in December 1930 for a sexual offence against his sixteen-year-old employee, John Mundy. The trial lasted eight days in February 1931, and Frank Villeneuve Smith tried energetically to establish that Mundy was not a reliable witness. He had just been released from Magill Reformatory for a sexual offence with a seven-year-old boy. There was also a problem with the statement from a cleaner at the Newmarket Hotel who originally claimed to be an eyewitness. She withdrew her statement.

The press followed the trial and published verbatim excerpts each day. On Tuesday morning,12 February 1931, the jury returned a 10 to 2 verdict of guilty on the charge of sodomy and not guilty on the charge of indecent behaviour. Until this point, the trial had attracted overflowing crowds into the courtroom each day, eager to listen to its salacious details, but the worst was yet to come. Murray sentenced Edwards to five years prison with hard labour and his associate asked the hotelier if

---

92   See John Emerson, *History of the Independent Bar*, 2006.
93   Suzanne Edgar, "The King of the West End". *National Times*, May 2-8, 1982, p. 14.

he had anything to say. His reply was reported at length in *The Adver-tiser*. Edwards first of all announced that he was not guilty but did not blame the jury. He blamed the Chief Justice:

> In your summing up I find that all excuses were made for the Crown witnesses, while my witnesses were discredited. Apparently this was done because they had the courage to give evidence which supported my defence. My enemies have succeeded; they have done so with loaded dice. Some day they will receive the punishment which they so richly deserve. That is all I have to say, your Honour.[94]

At the swearing-in of the Butler government 19 April 1933. Front: S. W. Jeffries (Attorney-General), R.L. Butler (Premier & Treasurer), George Murray (Lieutenant-Governor), G. Ritchie (Chief Secretary), M. McIntosh (Lands). Back: A.L. Read (Under Secretary), H.S. Hudd (Commissioner of Public Works), A.P. Blesing (Agriculture). (Advertiser)

According to rumour, Edwards also accused Murray of intimate relations with his sister, but this was not reported. This must have been the most unpleasant day of George Murray's working life. *The Advertiser* reported that he replied to this incredible challenge to his impartiality with "apparent agitation", which given his normal reserve, is revealing in itself:

> If you have any real ground for complaint at all, the Full Court can provide the remedy. You have attacked my impartiality by saying that I made every excuse for the witnesses for the prosecution and that I cast doubt on the credibility of the

---

94   *The Advertiser*, Wednesday, 13 February 1931, p. 7.

Swearing in George Murray as Lieutenant-Governor 25 February 1939. L-R Tom Playford (Premier), Justice Angas Parsons, Mr McBryde (Supreme Court Master), Sir George Ritchie (Chief Secretary), A L Read (Under Secretary), S W Jeffries (Attorney-General). (Advertiser)

witnesses for the defence. I did my duty as I conceived it right that I should do. Never before have I heard in this court such a speech as the one made by you from the dock. I hope I shall not hear another like it. That is all I have to say.[95]

Murray continued and confirmed the sentence. Edwards appealed twice that year against the sentence to the Full Court without success; both decisions are reported.[96]

Around the time of the Edwards appeals, a transaction took place that would lead to one of the biggest civil cases in Murray's period as Chief Justice. Like the Corset Case almost thirty years earlier, it involved the clothing industry. This simple transaction led to a series of court cases that would see Murray's judgment – overturned in the High Court – restored by the Privy Council. It was also one of the last cases that would see the two great silks Villeneuve Smith and Cleland at opposite ends of the bar table before Cleland's move to the bench.

On 3 June 1931, a medical practitioner called Dr Richard Grant bought four woollen items from John Martin's department store: two

95   Clyde Cameron, 2003.
96   *R v Edwards* [1931] SALR 121 and *R v Edwards (No. 2)* [1931] SALR 376.

singlets and two pairs of long underpants. Australian Knitting Mills manufactured all four. Later that month he wore one set of the garments for the first time and within nine hours noticed some itching on his shins, which developed into rashes. By the middle of July, his condition deteriorated and he consulted a dermatologist.

Dr Grant returned the undergarments he had bought to John Martin's, but the dermatitis spread, covering his body with papules and vesicles that oozed a clear liquid. He was in bed from July until November. He then went to New Zealand to avoid the summer heat, but suffered a severe relapse after his return. He was hospitalised from April until July 1932.[97]

The cause of the irritation was shown to be from an unusual quantity of free sulphites, residual after the processing of the wool. Murray explained the implications in his judgment:

> The significance of free sulphites in the fabric, it may here be mentioned, is that if sodium sulphite is brought into contact with an acid, sulphur dioxide (SO_2) will be formed, and sulphur dioxide will take up oxygen from water and produce sulphurous acid (H_2SO_3), and sulphurous acid will take up more oxygen from water and produce sulphuric acid (H_2SO_4). There being acid and water in sweat, of which at least a pint, mostly in the form of vapour, is given off by a resting person in twenty-four hours, and more, of course, by a person who is not resting, it is believed that the above is what happens when a garment containing sodium sulphite is worn on the human body, the result being irritation of the skin, for sulphur dioxide, sulphurous acid, and sulphuric acid are all known irritants.[98]

The trial dragged from November 1932 until February 1933 over 20 sitting days. Murray awarded Dr Grant 2450 pounds for general and special damages.

John Martin's and Australian Knitting Mills appealed to the High Court in August 1933. Justices Starke, Dixon and McTiernan did

---

97   *Grant v John Martin and Company Limited and Another* [1935] SALR 457 at 459-461.

98   At 467.

not believe that Grant had proved the existence of an excessive amount of the sulphurous irritants, and reversed the South Australian Chief Justice. Justice Evatt dissented.[99] Grant appealed to the Privy Council.

George Murray was in London that July 1935 and wrote back regularly to his Acting Chief Justice, Angas Parsons. Although he was on holiday and tense about the impending hearing of the Grant case, he could not resist a dinner with the judges or a brief visit to the Courts of Appeal. The dinner for His Majesty's judges was held at the Mansion House on 4 June 1935. George Murray hoped to meet there some of the Law Lords, the judges on the Privy Council:

> But there were 219 guests and as I was seated between two ladies and had no opportunity of talking to a man I was disappointed.[100]

Earlier that day, Murray went and spent an hour in the Courts of Appeal to witness the Law Lords in action:

> In the Courts of Appeal the Lords Justices sit quite a long way from each other. They do not interrupt Counsel except to ask a question at considerable intervals. They speak so softly that it is difficult to hear what they say.

In the following letter to Parsons written six weeks later, Murray reported that the Grant hearing had taken nine days:

> I should have liked to hear the argument but was, of course, the one person in London who could not. Isbister, who has been in Scotland, called on Grant's solicitors yesterday to see if he could glean anything. The impression he gathered was that the judges are not unanimous. They appear to be satisfied with my findings of fact but differ on the law, the bone of contention being the judgment of the House of Lords in the Snail case. The only one of them who was a party to that decision was Lord Macmillan, and he is the one, strangely enough, from whom

---

99   *Australian Knitting Mills Limited and Another v Grant.* (1933) 50 CLR 387.
100 Letter to Parsons, 5 June 1935. Howard Zelling Estate; and next quote.

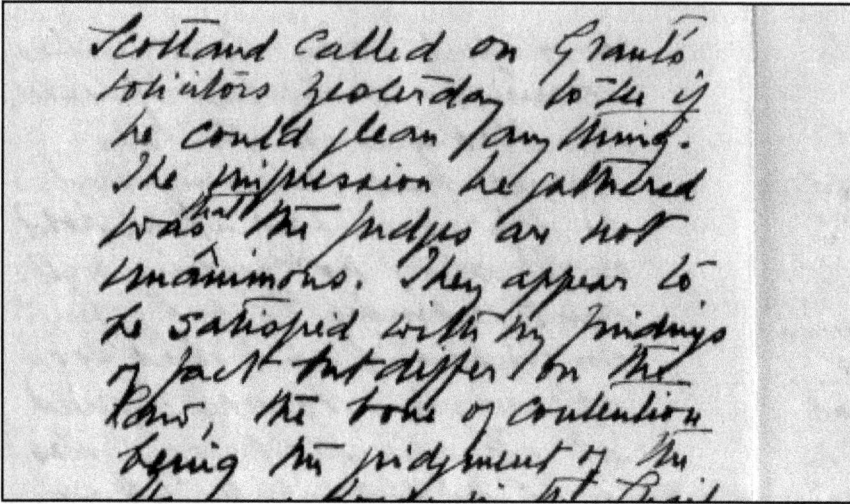

Part of Murray's letter to Parsons, quoted here. (Zelling Estate)

Grant has most to fear. (…) I am not expecting to be upheld, but I am sorry for Grant.[101]

These comments, which at the time were given in the strictest confidence, reveal the self-effacing side of Murray. The decision in the Grant case was still pending at this time, because of the long summer vacation. Judgment was given on the 21 October:[102]

I rang up the Privy Council office at half-past twelve, and was thrilled to hear that the appeal [had] been allowed with costs.[103]

Murray obtained a "print proof" of the judgment from Roney & Co., Grant's solicitors in the case:

It is a most interesting disquisition on both the facts and the law, delivered by Lord Wright, who has twice been appointed Master of the Rolls in succession to Lord Hanworth. The submissions

---

101   Letter to Parsons, 17 July 1935. Howard Zelling Estate. The "Snail Case" is
       Donoghue v Stevenson [1932] AC 562. Donoghue had drunk an entire bottle
       of ginger beer before discovering the remains of a decomposed snail in it.
       Donoghue v Stevenson established modern negligence law.
102   Reported as *Grant v Australian Knitting Mills and Others* [1936] AC 85.
103   Letter to Parsons, 30 October 1935. Howard Zelling Estate; and next quote.

of Mr Wilfrid Green KC, dealt with in the judgment, enable one to understand why there should have appeared to be a want of unanimity amongst the judges when the argument was on. There were some "teasers" to answer, and I cannot help thinking myself lucky that they were disposed of in my favour.

Dr Grant and his counsel, E E Cleland, were vindicated in their attempts to obtain justice in a David and Goliath case.

A week after Murray saw his original judgment in Grant restored by the highest court in the British Empire, he received a telephone call from the Dominion Office: His Majesty would receive him at 11 o'clock that morning, 28 October – "His Majesty" being King George V (1865-1936), grandson of Queen Victoria and grandfather to Queen Elizabeth II. Murray had been Lieutenant-Governor since 1916, but he was never as comfortable with ceremony as his predecessor:

> The ordeal is now over. The King was very kind and told me several things that were not to be made public. His parting words were: "Now, you mustn't let me down." Very human, weren't they?

Later, Murray heard the news from Angas Parsons that their brother judge Arthur Piper, who was seventy years old, had been diagnosed with cancer, and had undergone an operation the day Murray had seen King George. Murray's compassion is again obvious in his reply to Angas Parsons on the 21 November:

> How vain are the pleasures of human life! Here was I amid the glamour of a palace, and there was our dear old friend undergoing the horrors of a hopeless operation. Some day, they say, we shall understand, but shall we?
>
> He will be a great loss to us. So bright, so cheerful, so learned, so ever ready to help. Can he be replaced? I have my doubts.[104]

---

104   Letter to Parsons, 21 November 1935. Howard Zelling's Estate.

Arthur Piper died on 19 February 1936, and he was replaced by E E Cleland, who would never yield to Murray's total dominance of the Court as the other judges had. That year, his sister Maggie with whom he had lived all his life also died.

The thirty hectares of gardens, orchards, streams and vineyards at Murray Park must have seemed a lonely place for the last six years of Murray's life. Except for his times in Britain, it was the only place he had lived, and it had been the centre of the extended Murray and Tinline families. It was during these last years that he began his philanthropic career, increasing his gifts to the University and, in 1938, giving ten thousand pounds to the Law Society of South Australia to establish a library which is now called the Murray Information Resource Centre. That sum then was equal to around $2 million dollars today.

A postcard of Magill Road in Murray's papers. The neo-Georgian building at left still stands. Also surviving further along is the two-storey Tower Hotel. (SLSA)

George Murray died on 18 February 1942 in a private hospital after an appendix operation. He was in his seventy-ninth year. *The Advertiser* reported that Premier Thomas Playford called George Murray "the most distinguished man of his time".[105] In retrospect, his period as Chief Justice was an age of "conservative legal tenets" – in the words of Alex Castles and Michael Harris – but he had also led a court that was beyond reproach during the very unstable political and economic period straddling the two World Wars. In the first World War he did all in his power to defend justice in his court against interference from a nervous Federal Government in the Snow trials. He lived long enough to witness Germany killing again, but died one day before Darwin was bombed by the Japanese.

Murray was left out of the 150 plaques on North Terrace and its companion book, and the *Wakefield Companion to South Australian*

---

105   *The Advertiser*, 19 February 1942.

History confused him with another university benefactor, draper David Murray (not related to George Murray). David Murray gave two thousand pounds to the university in 1908 for general prizes across the faculties but not the travelling scholarships that are funded from the much larger eighty-six thousand pounds that George Murray bequeathed to the university in 1942. His total estate was sworn for probate at two hundred and twenty-five thousand pounds.

It is unlikely though that Sir George Murray would be concerned that he has faded a little from the public memory. Way would no doubt be pleased to find his name on the main courts building on Victoria Square.

St Bernards Road, Magill, from a postcard in Murray's papers. The gateposts at right are at the entrance to Murray Park homestead's driveway. (SLSA)

Murray has his on the building he funded in the University of Adelaide, and in the Law Society's Murray Resource Centre. He has his name on something far more permanent, though, which may well match his cool and aloof personality. Explorer and professor of geology Douglas Mawson named the Murray Monolith in Antarctica after his Chancellor for his continual support during Mawson's frequent absences from the Universtity while on his explorations.[106]

---

106   *The Advertiser*, Saturday, 17 December, 1927.

CHAPTER 4

Sir Mellis Napier (1942-1967)

THE PLAYFORD ERA

The English-style court that Way established and Murray continued found its natural successor in Mellis Napier. But unfortunately for him, over the twenty-five years that he was Chief Justice of South Australia, the State was to change almost beyond recognition. The Supreme Court would grow increasingly out of touch with the South Australian community and finally reach crisis point.

This was the period when Tom Playford was Premier – from 1938 until 1965. It was, and still is, the most sustained period of economic and population growth in the State's history - and of institutional stasis at the highest levels. Tom Playford served as Premier for a record term.[1] Napier's total of forty-three years on the Supreme Court bench places him just behind Edward McTiernan's forty-six year record term of office on the High Court. From 1940 until 1966 South Australia's population consistently increased at a faster rate than the rest of Aus-

---

1   Sir Thomas Playford exceeded the previous record in the Commonwealth of 21 years in office by British Prime Minister Robert Walpole 1721-1742. Stewart Cockburn, *Playford: Benevolent Despot*, p. 291.

tralia.[2] It leapt almost seventy per cent from around 600,000 to just over a million. At the same time the rural population dropped from 40 per cent of the total to around 25 per cent. Metropolitan Adelaide more than doubled in size, from just over 300,000 to 727,916 in 1966.

The sheer increase in numbers tells only part of the story. Complete lifestyles changed as employment in the agricultural sector halved while manufacturing work doubled. Education increased exponentially. Most Australians before World War II left school in their early teens, even future chief justice Len King. By 1964, while the population had risen almost 80 per cent, the number of high school students had risen 466 per cent. University attendance over the same period had increased by 256 per cent. Post-war migration added almost a quarter of a million new residents to the State, having a dramatic impact on the economy and its social fabric. Half of these were from non-English-speaking nations of Europe, in particular Italy and Greece. By the end of Napier's term, 12 per cent of South Australians did not speak English at home.

The State's indigenous population during the Playford-Napier era began to increase for the first time since European settlement. It had fallen from an estimated 15,000 at settlement to a low of 4,229 in 1938. By 1947 it had risen to 5,600, or by a third. By 1966 Aboriginal people numbered just over 8,000, or almost double the numbers when Playford became Premier. While their living conditions improved enough to allow this increase, in 1966 they nevertheless still had an infant mortality rate ten times greater than the non-Aboriginal population. Neither did the Aboriginal people gain citizenship and the right to vote yet: this had to await the national referendum of 1967, the year Napier's term ended.

Playford did whatever it took to ensure that South Australia got its fair share of the developments that were taking place nationwide. His persistence was legendary, as remarked on by former Prime Minister Sir Robert Menzies:

> Playford invariably buttonholed, at Adelaide's airport or railway station, any Prime Minister crossing the continent, no matter how ungodly the hour, for he found that a weary traveller,

2   For precise data refer to Graeme Hugo, "Playford's People: Population change in South Australia", in *Playford's South Australia: Essays on the History of South Australia, 1933-1968*, p. 29.

surprised with some novel demand, was likely to grant at least some concession just to make the troublesome Premier go away.[3]

Menzies, Prime Minister from 1939 to 1941 and from 1949 to 1966, was the Prime Minister most often "buttonholed" during Playford's Premiership. Major industrial developments in South Australia during the Playford years were numerous and remain significant to this day: steel production in Whyalla in 1941, coal mining at Leigh Creek in 1942, the Woomera rocket range in 1948, mass car production at General Motors-Holden in 1948, Adelaide Airport at West Beach in 1955, the satellite town of Elizabeth in 1955, Port Augusta power station in 1960, and shipbuilding in Whyalla in 1962.

Playford worked out early that he needed a clear advantage over the other States in order to attract industry to South Australia. He had a cunning strategy: provide good quality, low-cost rental houses to wage earners. The manufacturers coming into the State could then pay less to their employees, and the State Government itself could keep its own salary costs down.

Although Playford did not originally support the idea for the South Australian Housing Trust, he appreciated its merits by 1940. By then, he had also discovered to his horror the truth about slum housing in Adelaide. In that year, the Building Act Enquiry Committee reported to Parliament that 9,000 people in the Adelaide metropolitan area lived in houses that were unfit for human occupation. This represented 25 per cent of all rented houses:

> Most had no bathrooms, having been built in the 19th century when bathrooms were not considered essential. One or more rooms in each dwelling had no natural light, and the only source of water was an outside tap. Women boiled water in kerosene tins or did their laundry in portable coppers in the backyard. Cooking stoves were sometimes located in open back verandahs, or in sheds, which often did double service as bedrooms. Mean iron and hessian outbuildings were occupied by children, or by

3　　Cited in P A Howell, "Playford, politics and parliament", in *Playford's South Australia*, 1996, p. 49.

single male old-age pensioners who paid up to five shillings a
week for the privilege.[4]

Many had dirt floors and most were damp, dark and infested
with rats. Yet slum rentals made money. The average rental for a five-
roomed house in 1940 was around a pound a week. Even some sub-
standard dwellings were being rented for that. The landlords did not
maintain them. One of these individuals owned 162 slum houses.

Playford needed to be able to market a low-cost workforce that
was happy. From December 1940, the South Australian government
introduced rent controls and the Housing Trust began to build homes
that could be rented out at 12 shillings 6 pence a week. Sub-standard
homes had caps placed on their rentals. If owners wanted more, they
had to raise the standard. Apart from building homes around the entire metropolitan area, the Housing Trust also built a whole new town
– Elizabeth – which clinched the deal with General Motors to build a
second Holden plant. By 1965 when Playford finally lost office, the
Housing Trust – which was the first such government housing body in
Australia – had built 56,000 houses and fixed the rents on 63,000 more
privately owned ones.

It was the Holden motor car that changed the lives of Australians.
Graeme Hugo makes the point in his chapter on population change in
Playford's South Australia that "one of the most profound changes which
occurred during the Playford era was in the personal mobility of South
Australians".[5] The combined effect of an ever-increasing industrial
workforce never better paid, and a locally-made car priced so that they
could buy it, meant that ordinary Australians across the country gained
an independence and freedom they had never known. They joined the
world-wide phenomenon that began in America when Henry Ford's
company mass-produced the first T-model in 1908, and continues to
this day. In 1933 there was one car registered for each thirteen South
Australians; by 1968 there was one car for just over three.

Mobility, industrialisation, more widely-spread affluence, television, increasing education: this was the changing post-war South Australia of Sir Mellis Napier's period as Chief Justice. Such rapid changes

---

4   Cockburn, *Playford : Benevolent Despot*, p. 177. He is reporting what Play-
     ford told Professor Hugh Stretton in 1980.
5   Hugo, in *Playford's South Australia*, as above, p. 41.

in lifestyles – and with the United States replacing England as the dominant overseas culture after the end of the war in 1945 – would inevitably also provoke changes in ways of thinking. Would the brilliant lawyer who became the State's longest serving judge keep up with these changes?

On circuit in the 1930s: (L-R) Neil McEwin (Associate), Mr Justice Napier and Sheriff Stan Blackman. (SCLSA)

Napier's early life in some ways mirrors Samuel Way's. Like his predecessor, he was born in Britain, stayed to complete his secondary education while his family emigrated to Adelaide, and then joined them a year or two later. Like Way, he studied law in Adelaide, also having fallen into it by chance rather than ambition. Even more, he was articled to Charles Kingston, who in turn had been articled to Samuel Way.

There the similarities end. Thomas John Mellis Napier was a Scot, born in Dunbar, East Lothian on 24 October 1882. His father, Alexander Disney Leith Napier was not an impoverished minister of a dissenting church, but a gynaecologist. In 1885, when Mellis was in his fourth year, the family moved to London where his father took up a position with the Chelsea Hospital for Women. Mellis was sent to the City of London School and completed his matriculation in September 1897, aged just fifteen. But for a particularly inflammatory Premier on the other side of the globe, it is probable the Napier family would have remained in London.

From 1894 until 1899 – all but one year of Charles Kingston's Premiership – an ongoing dispute raged between his government, the Adelaide Hospital board and hospital staff. By January 1898, 92 people had either resigned or been dismissed, including at one time the entire board. The total included: "17 Honorary Medical staff, 2 Medical Superintendents, a senior Resident Physician, 6 Junior Medical Officers, 20 members of the Board of Management, 2 Superintendents of Nurses, 2 Superintendents of Night Nurses, 11 Charge Nurses, 3 Probationers,

5 Wardsmaids, a Needlewoman, 2 Assistant Dispensers, a Messenger and 19 medical students."[6]

The dispute had begun in October 1894 with what appeared to be the innocent promotion of a charge nurse to Superintendent of night nurses. The problem with this promotion was that the new Superintendent was the sister of John Gordon, the Chief Secretary (and future judge), and that there were fourteen other charge nurses senior to Miss Gordon.[7] Kingston regarded seniority as important and queried the appointment.

Kingston's intervention was the catalyst for a sequence of events that revealed a deep rift between the management of the hospital and the staff. The Premier called a Royal Commission and in April 1895 its recommendations included appointing two women to the Hospital Board. This created bitter resistance and in March 1896 Kingston appointed a whole new board except for two former members.

The seventeen members of the honorary medical staff refused to be managed by such an inexperienced board and resigned en masse. This created the urgent situation that led to the appointment of Mellis Napier's father. There were no specialists or surgeons available. The honorary staff also were responsible for teaching the University of Adelaide's medical students. Medicine courses at all levels were cancelled. The entire Australian medical profession boycotted all attempts of the Kingston government to replace the honorary staff. As a result they advertised two positions in Britain, although the *British Medical Journal* refused to carry the advertisements. Somehow – the details are lacking – Dr Leith Napier agreed to go to

Mellis Napier around 1894. (Courtesy Napier family)

---

6   Margaret Glass, *Charles Cameron Kingston: Federation Father*, p. 129.
7   Margaret Glass, cited above. What follows is based on pp.107-130, and also on pp. 189-205 in J Estcourt Hughes, *A History of the Royal Adelaide Hospital.*

Adelaide as Resident Surgeon and Dr Ramsay Smith, another Scot who was practising in Wales, accepted the position of Resident Physician.

Dr Napier and his wife Jessie (née Mellis) had five sons and one daughter – Frederick (born 1878), Archibald (1879), Jessie (1881), Mellis (1882), Disney (1885) and Norman (1888). All but Archibald stayed behind in London. Dr Napier and his second son arrived in Adelaide on Tuesday, 21 July 1896 on the Orient mail steamer *Ophir*. According to J Escourt Hughes, Dr Napier decided to leave London in the interests of his wife's health:

> Needless to say, these men were not made welcome by the medical profession in South Australia and, in fact, were ostracised. The British Medical Association expelled them from its ranks. [8]

Dr Ramsay Smith was also on board. Within six weeks the two new doctors were dragged into the ongoing dispute. At the end of September all four junior resident medical officers resigned in a joint letter, published in *The Register*:

> Dr Leith Napier and Dr Ramsay Smith are incompetent to carry out their duties as Senior Surgeon and Senior Physician respectively (...) [and] we are unable to properly fulfil our duty to the Board, whose servants we are, or to the patients in the Hospital, whom we are powerless to protect against the frequently recurring acts of ignorance and incapacity in the treatment of their diseases of which we are almost daily witnesses. [9]

The hospital board interviewed the four young doctors, and dismissed their accusations as unfounded. But then, the honorary consulting surgeon and pathologist, Archibald Watson, also the University of Adelaide's Professor of Anatomy, accused Dr Napier of malpractice, and published a series of letters between the two men. Watson had only recently been appointed to the hospital position, and the board found his accusations as unfounded as those of the four Resident doctors. Professor Watson was forced to resign.

---

8   J Escourt Hughes, p. 201.
9   Glass, cited above, p. 124. Originally published in *The Register*, 30 September 1896.

These allegations against the two British doctors seem to have been made with no other motive than to discredit them and to have them dismissed. But remembering that Kingston had chosen almost all of the members of the current hospital board, it is possible that they felt obliged to be loyal to his wishes, which of course would have been to ensure that Drs Napier and Smith remained. Specific allegations against these two men ended, but the general drama of resignations, inquiries and sackings continued.

When Mellis arrived in Adelaide with his mother, three brothers and sister two years later at the ocean steamers' wharf near Port Adelaide, he was greeted by "lovely weather and bright sunshine".[10] This must have seemed such a contrast to life in Adelaide subsequently. Apart from discovering that everyone of any influence snubbed his father, there was no escape for the family from the ongoing dispute: the Resident Surgeon lived on site at the hospital.

In an interview decades later for the ABC, Napier said that he had no ideas about what he would do for a career. It was assumed that, since his father and uncle were both doctors, he would study medicine. But this was not possible because of the impact of the hospital dispute. Medical courses did not resume until 1900. Napier had little interest in studying medicine or law. But one of his father's few friends at this time, the Premier, Charles Kingston, offered Mellis articles at his law firm. Mellis accepted and began his service on 17 December 1898. In 1899 he joined the ten or so law students at the University of Adelaide.

During his four years as a student he did not stand out in any way academically. When he was awarded his Bachelor of Laws degree in 1902, he was still only twenty. The awards ceremony in Elder Hall was one in which the Chancellor, Sir Samuel Way, was the target of student pranks. The medical students had set up a skeleton to drop from the ceiling right above the Chancellor at the daïs. At that moment, he was conferring a Doctor of Laws on Sir John Forrest. Mellis Napier was next in line. Way – distracted by the dangling skeleton – accidentally named Napier's Bachelor of Laws degree a Doctorate as well, which was quickly corrected.[11]

---

10   Interview for ABC Radio "First Assignment", 1963. SLSA Archival
      Collection, Oral History Collection, OH126/2.
11   Interview with Justice George Walters, November 1968. SLSA Archival
      Collection Oral History Collection OH126/1.

During Napier's student years, his father Leith was appointed Senior Surgeon and Gynaecologist at the hospital. As well as other government appointments, he was commissioned in the medical staff corps of the South Australian military forces as Surgeon Major. Leith was at the peak of his career in Adelaide. He also had a healthy private practice and his own private hospital. In four years, he had quadrupled his income. Kingston had left State politics (he would resurface in greater glory as the Commonwealth of Australia's first Minister of Customs). The antagonistic element that had breathed life into the dispute at Adelaide Hospital was gone.

On the fateful day of 16 January 1900, Leith Napier was on duty with the military camp which was leaving its base at the old Exhibition grounds adjoining the hospital on Frome Road - now part of both the University of Adelaide and the University of South Australia. The camp was on the move to Marino in order to avoid a threatened outbreak of bubonic plague at the hospital. At Marino, Dr Napier's horse stumbled and threw him. He landed on his head, fracturing his skull and sustaining brain damage.

He lapsed in and out of consciousness for six months. In his 1968 interview with George Walters, Mellis Napier spoke of the incredible burden the accident placed on his family. His father could not recover fully and had to forego the private practice he had built up, and his newly established private hospital. The government continued to pay him his full salaries over the almost two years of recovery that followed. But in December 1901, Leith Napier had no choice but to resign his government positions. He would never be able to do any more surgery. He could do nothing more than try to establish a general practice. The Napier family moved out of the residence at the hospital and into a house at 28 Angas Street, Adelaide.

On 12 April 1904 Leith Napier petitioned the Government of South Australia for 6500 pounds compensation. His solicitors were Kingston and McLachlan, where Mellis, after having been admitted on the day of his twenty-first birthday, was now a qualified lawyer. One of his first cases would be on the instructions of his own father. The trial came before Chief Justice Way without a jury over eight days in December 1904. A J McLachlan represented Leith Napier in court, and Sir

John Downer KC, Paris Nesbit KC and a "Mr Nicholls" represented the government.[12]

Leith Napier had already received 525 pounds from the State but he was now claiming compensation for injuries under the Defences Act 1895. This was for "men killed or injured on actual service". When Sir Samuel Way gave his judgment in February 1905, he remarked on Mr McLachlan's "brilliant and exhaustive argument for the plaintiff". He was very sympathetic to Dr Napier, but found that the South Australian legislation limited military service strictly to service in war, invasion and civil rebellions. He also commented on the fact that, had this same incident happened in England, it would have been regarded as "in the performance of military duty". Leith Napier was not eligible for war service compensation.

Around the time of his father's case, the firm in which Napier was working was undergoing changes. Kingston's intense work schedule as a Commonwealth minister and law partner was taking its toll on his health. In July 1903 he resigned, ostensibly because the Federal Cabinet wanted to alter a clause in a Bill he had publicly committed himself to. Yet he had been earmarked to take over as Prime Minister when Edmund Barton stepped down. The real reason was that his health was deteriorating rapidly. He returned briefly to State politics and Alfred Deakin took over from Barton instead.

In October 1905, the Kingston and McLachlan partnership was dissolved. Kingston took his own office in Eagle Chambers near the corner of King William and Pirie Streets. The firm became McLachlan and Vandenbergh briefly, until W J Vandenbergh's death in 1906 created an opening for Napier. It became McLachlan and Napier, with offices located in the Exchange Building, Pirie Street. The two would have worked together for another eleven years. In 1917, Napier joined a firm that would produce over the next half century or so seven Queen's Counsel and, from these, five judges.[13] Originally Glynn Parsons McEwin and Napier, as it evolved the partnership included George Ligertwood and the three Millhouse silks: Eric, Vivian and – until he joined the nascent independent bar – Robin.

---

12   *Napier v Sholl* [1904] SALR 73. Much of the preceding information has been drawn from the reported material.

13   For more details, see Graham Loughlin's Honours thesis, *South Australian Queen's Counsel*, p. A137.

The early years of Mellis Napier's career must have been difficult. At home there were the repercussions of his father's accident, and at work the dramatically varying fortunes of his famous employer. Sir Mellis told George Walters that in those early years he was "working very quietly for quite a while".[14] One has the impression that Mellis kept to himself and offered no opinions.

His first reported case was a boundary dispute in 1906 between the owners of Hindley Street's two major leisure venues, the Grand Coffee Palace and the Cyclorama. The dispute that surfaced between the owners of these neighbouring venues bordered on the absurd – a word used both in argument and in Sir Samuel Way's judgment. Michael Billiet was the owner of the Grand Coffee Palace. In January 1906 Mr Billiet decided to add a second storey to the front part of his thriving café. His architect discovered that the Cyclorama building next door – which had a second-storey tower and wide parapet – protruded seventy-five centimetres over Mr Billiet's existing roof. Further surveys revealed that, worse still, the entire length of the Cyclorama boundary wall protruded eighteen centimetres on average into Mr Billiet's property.[15]

Michael Billiet was unable to build his second storey as long as this outrage continued. His lawyers contacted the owner of the Cyclorama building, the Commercial Bank of Australasia, and demanded that they remove the intruding parts. They would not, and in fact could not, as it would have rendered the Cyclorama building unsafe.

The blame for this situation dated back to a man called William McLean, who had owned the entire town acre and built both the buildings on it: the Grand Coffee Palace in 1887 and the Cyclorama in 1890. McLean was now dead, but his architect for the Cyclorama building, George Soward, was able to explain the history. McLean had never told him that although he owned Town Acre 74, it was held in two separate titles. Mr Soward had made much use of the existing western wall of the Coffee Palace, unaware that it was a boundary. The case was further complicated by the death of Michael Billiet in 1906 and the substitution of his daughters as plaintiffs.

---

14   Interview with Justice George Walters.
15   *Billiet v The Commercial Bank of Australasia Ltd* [1906] SALR 193 at 197. See also pp. 200 and 201.

As a young lawyer in the 1900s, Mellis Napier used to pass time in court drawing the judges, members of the jury, court staff and litigants. Above is an un-named barrister; "an attentive juryman"; and "the foreman in Claude Burrow's case who got him 5 years". Below left: "Move on now! or Oil arrest yer for ..."; 'yes, your 'onour I am the oldest inhabitant at Happy Valley. I was born in the year one when the devil was an infant."; "Henderson"; and "Alfred Savage, sheep stealing, 18 months hard." Below right are Justices Bundey and Boucaut, Mr Bonnin and a barrister. (Courtesy Napier family)

McLachlan and Vandenbergh – as it still was – briefed Herbert Angas Parsons, and Mellis Napier helped prepare for trial. They were going to argue that the protrusions represented a continuing trespass, and that the Commercial Bank was hence trespassing afresh with each new day. Their reason for focussing on the bank was to avoid going back to Mr McLean, because of course, since he owned both properties, he could not trespass on them. Their weak point was that they could cite no authority – no previous case in which this contention had been allowed. The common law since the days of Lord Coke, as Samuel Way pointed out, generally sought out the original wrongdoer or his successors in a case of continuing trespass.

Way collapsed the Napier-Parsons argument by pointing out that "for a continuing trespass, there must be an original trespass." This of course produced the dilemma that Parsons and Napier had been anxious to circumvent: that there was none. Way ruled that since there was no original trespass then there was no continuing trespass. The Grand Coffee Palace was therefore unable to get any grander.

George Murray KC had represented the Commercial Bank. Napier was up against his future predecessor again in 1908, this time alone, and Murray is not recorded as having a junior. Napier was 26, Murray 46. Napier represented a farmer at Riverton called McLachlan – possibly a relative of his partner. The District Council of Waterloo – represented by Murray – had ordered the farmer to destroy noxious weeds in his paddock. He had checked on his obligations and decided not to, and was subsequently convicted of an offence under the Thistle and Bur [sic] Act 1887 by local Justices of the Peace.

There was an apparent inconsistency between the Thistle Act and statutes governing the responsibilities of district and municipal Councils. The Act – which included any plant declared a noxious weed – compelled a landowner to clear not just his own property, but also half of the road adjacent to it. On the other hand, a district council under its governing act, had to keep its roads clear of noxious weeds and could not compel a landowner to clear weeds from his property while the council had not cleared the adjacent road.[16]

Mr McLachlan seems to have decided that it would be pointless to clear his property if the road was still infested and to have believed he

---

16   *McLachlan v Parken*. [1909] SALR 36 at 40.

was justified in so doing. He appealed against his conviction to the Full
Court, which was composed only of the Chief Justice. Way, a farmer
himself, was impressed by "Mr Napier in his able argument", but found
against his client. Way concluded that under the Thistle and Bur Act,
the farmer was obliged to clear his property, despite the apparent contradiction with the District Councils Act.

Napier seems to have built a reputation quickly in his career at
the South Australian bar. In his 1968 interview with Justice Walters, Sir
Mellis remembers that after " the noxious weeds case" he twice appeared
with George Murray KC:

> But the first case I really remember – well, the first case I
> remember taking, this important case – was a taxation appeal
> on the question of income tax, and that, curiously enough, Sir
> George Murray and Nesbit, I think, were in the next case waiting
> for the same point. When it came to the point, they more or
> less adopted the argument that I presented to the court, which
> pleased me very much.[17]

Both cases – *McLachlan v Commissioner of Taxes and Rymill
(Public Officer for Canowie Pastoral Company Limited) v Commissioner
of Taxes* – were heard in November 1911 before the Full Court. Since
they were both also challenging the meaning of the word "profit" in
relation to the sale of rural land holdings, they are reported together in
the 1912 volume.[18] Napier and McLachlan represented brother graziers
A J and H P McLachlan. George Murray KC and A W Piper KC represented Rymill, assisted by W A Magarey. Paris Nesbit KC represented
the Commissioner of Taxes in both cases, assisted by T S Poole.

Napier argued that the "whole question turns on the meaning
of 'profit' in section 6 of the Act of 1908". He insisted that the Tax Act
did not confuse the term "income" with "capital", and that his clients'
land sale was not a source of income, but a conversion of capital from
land to money. Nesbit argued that the sales had yielded a profit, and
that any profit was income. The two judges, Way and Buchanan, agreed
with Napier's distinction. They did not believe either appellant was in

17   Interview with Justice George Walters, cited above, p. 4, transcript.
18   *McLachlan v Commissioner of Taxes; Rymill v Commissioner of Taxes* [1912]
      SALR 138. See also 143 and 146.

the business of selling land with the deliberate intention of making a profit. They derived their income from sheep. No tax was therefore payable. This must have been a huge relief to the McLachlans, who had sold almost 35,000 acres for 204,000 pounds, and had been assessed on the total sum. Following the success of his argument in these taxation appeals, Napier apparently attracted the attention of Sir Samuel Way. According to Napier, Way told one of Napier's friends that he expected that one day Mellis Napier would occupy his seat.

Away from court, Napier was part of the group that brought about the incorporation of the South Australian Law Society. He was a member of the Law Society's Council from 1912, but according to his retirement address in 1967, the Society was then "moribund".[19] It is not clear what he meant by that as the minute books for the period show that although only four or five Council members attended each meeting, they were held twice a month without fail. Napier drafted the Act of Parliament which converted the "South Australian Law Society" as it had been known since 1879, into the "Law Society of South Australia, Incorporated", as from 23 December 1915.[20] The new body was now the official regulator of the legal profession in the State. Most of the Act concentrates on complaints about practitioners.

Napier may have learned a few tips on drafting from his former principal, Kingston, who had built a reputation as an excellent draftsman during his time in the South Australian Parliament. Kingston's policy was to use simple and clear language. At the federal level, he drafted the first Commonwealth Customs Act when he was Minister of Customs. Having taken the baton, Napier drafted the Justices Act in 1921 (No. 1479) and then later, when he was a judge, the Evidence Act in 1929 (No. 1911). Many years later, he was proud when his Evidence Act was cited in *Cross on Evidence* in 1963.[21]

Napier's career at the bar appears, from the earliest days, to have been exclusively in the civil jurisdiction. He established a reputation particularly in industrial matters, often representing the State govern-

19   *Memorandum* [1968] SASR VII at XI.
20   *Acts of Parliament of South Australia, 1915*, "Law Society Act". No. 1220.
21   From an interview with Tony Bishop, former judge's associate to Napier.

ment before industrial tribunals.[22] He was appointed a King's Counsel on 8 September 1921. The month after his appointment, he represented the government with E E Cleland KC and A J McLachlan in an important case with wide ramifications on the way it handled wheatgrowers. The case, *Welden v Smith (Nominal Defendant)*,[23] was appealed first in the High Court, and finally in the Privy Council.

The *Welden* case was a class action. It began with a petition on 29 April 1921 from Elijah Welden to the South Australian Governor on behalf of all the wheatgrowers who delivered their wheat harvest in the 1916-1917 year. Mr Welden alleged that:

> The said Government in the years 1916, 1917 and 1918 by its agents and servants kept large quantities of the wheat delivered to it, as stated in paragraph 1 hereof, negligently and without reasonable or proper care or protection, and carelessly and negligently omitted to keep or protect large quantities of the said wheat.
>
> By reason of the negligence and carelessness of the said Government, its servants and agents, large quantities of the said wheat were damaged by mice and by exposure to the weather, and by reason thereof the said Government has not marketed or sold and cannot market or sell a large portion of the said wheat delivered to it, and has marketed and sold large quantities of the said wheat delivered to it at prices far below the prices which would or could and should have been received therefore if the same had not been damaged (...).[24]

Under the Wheat Harvest Acts of 1915 and 1916, growers received an initial partial payment on delivery of two shillings sixpence per bushel. They received a certificate for each separate delivery and payment, and the government undertook to pay the balance according to the price it received in the market less its normal costs. Thus the growers had a stake in the final price obtained; if the wheat became unsaleable, they would lose money. This is why Mr Welden finally took

---

22   Alex Castles, "Sir Mellis Napier", *Adelaide Law Review*, Vol. 3, No. 1, June 1967, pp. 1-7; p. 2.

23   *Bloch and Others v Smith (Nominal Defendant); Welden v Smith (Nominal Defendant)* [1922] SALR 95.

24   *Welden v Smith* [1924] AC 484 at 490.

action, claiming compensation for the amount that the growers reasonably expected to receive.

The South Australian government appointed a nominal defendant – George John Smith – and Napier, Cleland and McLachlan as his Counsel. The defence argument rested on two major points: 1) that the petition itself was not recognised by the Act under which it was lodged – No 6 of 1853 for persons having claims against the SA government; and 2) that the matter of the petition disclosed no cause of action. Piper KC and W A Norman appeared for Mr Welden before the Full Court in October 1921 – made up of Sir George Murray and Thomas Poole. They both agreed that the petition did not conform to the 1853 Act but found nevertheless that it was good as it "prayed for relief on behalf of the petitioner himself".

The South Australian government appealed to the High Court. The appeal was heard in Melbourne in May 1922 and the judgments read in Adelaide in August. On the first point of the defence, the majority of the High Court judges not only agreed with Murray's and Poole's reasoning, but also did not wish to add anything.[25] But they disagreed on the second point and allowed the appeal. This had the effect that although Welden's petition had been accepted as valid, its complaint was not.

Welden therefore appealed to the Privy Council, who, like the High Court, had no further comments on Murray's and Poole's reasons for accepting the petition in any case – the first point. Welden had already won on that account. On the second point, which he had earlier won in the South Australian Supreme Court, then lost in the High Court, the Privy Council reversed the High Court decision. Welden won his case and the South Australian government had to make compensation payments to the wheatgrowers for not keeping their wheat in better condition so that it could have fetched a higher price.

Two days before Christmas 1923, Justice John Gordon died. Napier was appointed to replace him and the headline of *The Advertiser* on Thursday 14 February 1924 read: "A Popular Appointment":

---

25   *Welden v Smith* 30 (1921-1922) CLR 585 at 597.

Probably no appointment which the government could have made to fill the vacancy on the Supreme Court bench, caused by the death of Sir John Gordon, would have given greater satisfaction to the legal profession (…) His career at the bar has stamped him as an advocate of high ideals, jealous for the best traditions of an honourable profession, a man of great erudition (not only as a lawyer, but as a student of life, literature and history), a keen logician and a sound lawyer. Master of a pleasing and unassuming style in address, alert to see the weak points in the argument or the facts of his opponent's case, always courteous, whether in court or in ordinary professional or social spheres, he has long been regarded as a leader of men as well as a leader at the bar.[26]

The *Advertiser*'s photo of Mellis Napier in 1924 when appointed Judge. (Advertiser)

The new judge was just 41. In Napier's first year he sat on a wide range of cases, including a refused car insurance claim and a charge of indecent language. The latter case, *Norley v Malthouse*, is particularly interesting for revealing the new judge's sensitivity to general community standards.

Miss Norley had appealed to the Supreme Court after a Special Magistrate dismissed her complaint against Mr Malthouse for using indecent language in public. They were on a roadway, and within the hearing range of several other people, he called her "a bloody bitch".[27] Her lawyer, Magnus Badger junior, argued that according to the dictionary, the term was plainly indecent. The Special Magistrate defined "indecent" as being the same as "lewd or obscene" and excluded Mr Malthouse's epithet.

Napier disagreed with such a restriction in meaning. He believed that "indecent" covered much wider territory than "obscene", and that the words used by Mr Malthouse in such a public manner could be

---

26   *The Advertiser*, 14 February 1924, p 6.
27   *Norley v Malthouse* [1924] SASR 268.

classified as indecent. But at the same time he qualified the application of the relevant legislation, for it needed to be tempered with community standards:

> The section is not intended for the special protection of people who are easily shocked. It should be used to protect the public in their use of the public ways against "nuisance" in the form of any substantial breach of decorum. As with other forms of nuisance, the standard ought not to be estimated according to any "elegant or dainty modes or habits" of thought, but according to "plain and sober and simple notions" among the community in question.

This is an example of the common-sense approach for which Napier would become known in his judgments. His concern with the Special Magistrate's decision was that it was not tempered by community standards at that time. He believed that this was the real point at stake, and he allowed the appeal and sent the case back to the magistrate for a re-trial in accordance with this approach.

During that first year on the bench, Napier also had the opportunity to assert his independence. Justice Poole referred an indecent assault conviction to the Full Court, as prosecution had begun after a statutory limit of six months. The appeal is reported as *R v Pople*.[28] Pople had been arraigned on a charge of carnal knowledge of a girl under 16, who – as was the custom then – is named in full in the case details. The relevant legislation from 1885 and 1917 placed a statutory limit of six months on any charge of carnal knowledge, but not on indecent assault. It also stated that if a charge of carnal knowledge could not be proved but one of indecent assault could, then this lesser charge could be substituted.

In the trial before Justice Poole, because of the statutory limit on the carnal knowledge charge, Pople had been convicted of indecent assault instead. Chief Justice Murray disagreed with this. He stated in his judgment that since the statutory limit had been exceeded, the prisoner had not been lawfully arraigned. He should not have been in the dock in the first place.

---

28   *R v Pople* [1924] SALR 448.

His brother judges, Angas Parsons and Napier, disagreed with Murray. They argued that carnal knowledge is just a more serious form of indecent assault, and if the prisoner had been originally arraigned for that, he would have been convicted all else being the same. Pople stayed in prison.

Over the next decade most of the reported cases that came before Napier and the other judges followed similar patterns. There were the perennial sexual offences. The severe liquor licensing legislation of 1915 produced a steady flow of offences resulting from liquor being sold after 6pm or on weekends after 12pm Saturday. More and more cases were coming before the courts from car crashes, reflecting the continuing increase in car ownership. There was also a steady stream of divorce settlements.

Dorothy Kay around 1904. (Napier Family)

At home in Unley Park, Napier's family life was much happier than those appearing before him in the court. He was devoted to his wife Dorothy (known as Flossie) and their three sons. He had married Dorothy on his 26th birthday, 24 October 1908 at St Andrew's Church in Walkerville. An early letter to her shows that they must have met each other four years earlier:

> (9 February 1904)
> Dear Miss Kay,
> My sister tells me that you have been so kind as to invite me to a picnic on Saturday next but that she was sufficiently foolish not to assure you that no engagement could possibly stand in the way of my attendance.[29]

In a letter of 5 September that same year, Miss Kay had become "Dearest little girl". The first child – Robert – was born in 1910,

---

29   Napier's private papers at the time of the writing of this book are held by his family.

followed by John in 1913 and Keith in 1915. Around this period –
between 1905 and 1912 – Napier was also actively involved with his
younger brother Disney in competition rowing on the Torrens and Port
Rivers.

Some letters survive from the early 1930s on, from all the family to John, then working on a farm near Cape Jervis. Mellis wrote at
least every Saturday morning, Dorothy twice a week, the two brothers
more sporadically. Eldest son Robert (Bob), studying for a law degree
at the University of Adelaide from January 1932, was articled to Patricia
Hackett, who would become one of Adelaide's legendary theatre personalities. Hackett was just two years Bob's senior and a friend of Dorothy Napier through their shared interest in amateur theatre. She was
born in Perth in 1908. Her mother's family were the Drake-Brockmans,
well-known Western Australian pastoralists.[30] She began her law degree
at the University of Adelaide in 1927 but was expelled the same year for
sitting her sister's Latin exam. She went to London to continue her law
studies, was admitted as a barrister in 1930, and returned to Adelaide
to set up practice.

Despite Patricia Hackett's busy, bohemian lifestyle, Sir Mellis
reported to John that she was impressed by the pace of life at the Napi-
ers:

> Robert went to the SPSC ball last night as an Inquisitor. It was
> a busy evening as Mum had been out all afternoon buying for
> repertory theatre costumes, returned around five to get dinner,
> make Robber's [Robert] fancy dress, see Pat about costumes,
> and get ready for some friends to bridge – all between 5 and 8
> pm. Pat thinks that it must be quite an exciting home to live in
> – that things sort of happen.[31]

Hackett then was acting in the productions put on by the Adelaide Repertory Theatre. In 1934 she opened her own Torch Theatre
in Gawler Place. She shook the foundation stones of Adelaide with her
opening play - Oscar Wilde's *Salomé* - which featured Patricia playing

---

30   See Jo Peoples, "Miss Patricia Hackett", *Journal of the Historical Society of
      South Australia*, No. 25, 1997, for more information. Also Judith Drake-
      Brockman, *Wongi Wongi*, Victoria Park (WA): Hesperian Press, 2001.
31   Letter from Mellis Napier to John Napier, 17 September 1932.

Salomé, complete with the nude finale to the Dance of the Seven Veils. Her second production in June 1934 was of two eighteenth-century

Sir Mellis Napier and Lady Napier in the 1940s. (Napier family)

plays, Henry Fielding's *The Virgin Unmasked* and George Preedy's *Homage to the Unknown*. Her articled clerk was to discover that he had *ex officio* duties. *The Advertiser* reported:

> Robert Napier took the part of Thomas, the footman, at a few hours notice, as H C Goodfellow, who was cast for the role, was unable to play.[32]

The article also drew attention to the fact that the dressing was "in the capable hands of Mrs Mellis Napier". Among the audience were Dorothy and Mellis Napier, Ursula Barr Smith and Frank Villeneuve Smith.

Bob Napier's letters to John reveal a lively personality. One envelope was addressed to "Rear Admiral J A M Napier" and in another

---

32   *The Advertiser*, 20 June 1934.

he addressed his brother as "Mein Geliebtester Bruder". Bob kept John up-to-date with new expressions – "HELL and 40 (This is the fashionable expletive – as used in the best circles)", dances, films and trips in the family car, "Minnie". His liveliness distracted him from other things. His father's letters reveal an ongoing concern about Bob's lack of dedication to his law studies. In one letter he told John conspiratorially that Patricia Hackett secretly planned to make Bob study in the office under her supervision. In November 1932 Sir Mellis wrote:

> Robber [Robert] sat for the other exams. We await the results in somewhat breathless anxiety. It seems to me that he will have to let the degree course go. Even if he gets there it is time and past time that he was getting a move on and qualifying. I think History is a blue duck. His International I don't know. Property he hopes for.[33]

But a fortnight later when the results were in, Napier had to revise his opinion:

> Goober's [Robert] startling success has almost paralysed the processes of thought. It has so surprised G. himself that he now proposes to do some work for next year.[34]

Third son Keith was seventeen in 1932 and still at school – St Peter's College – repeating his final year. His priority in life was sport and he played cricket, tennis and football. His letters to John are detailed analyses of his own matches, and also of those he watched. On 29 January 1931 Keith went to the Test match between South Africa and Australia at Adelaide Oval. Don Bradman almost made 300 runs: "Whatever Cameron did he couldn't stop Bradman hitting fours." Napier refers to his youngest son affectionately as "H.P", which refers to the fact that he had been elected House Prefect, but also is the abbreviation of a family nickname, "His Perfectionism". Keith is revealed, in both his letters and his father's, as boundlessly energetic, bursting with enthusiasm and a keen ambition to experience as much as he could in life.

---

33   Letter from Mellis Napier to John Napier, 12 November 1932.
34   Letter from Keith Napier to John Napier, 28 November 1932.

Sir Mellis's letters to John over this period are mainly dedicated to recounting the latest adventures of each of the members of the family, the pet dog Haggis and the collection of rabbits, ducks and domestic fowls. He regularly discusses his gardening activities. Central to family life are two cars, Minnie and Lizzie, which seemed to break down on every country journey into the Adelaide Hills or down to the Fleurieu Peninsula to see John. Robert is the main driver, but during this period Dorothy and Keith also learn to drive.

Napier also occasionally revealed the emotional trauma of a criminal trial:

> I don't like the final results of criminal trials. It takes someone tougher than I am to pass sentence without feeling discomfortable at times.[35]

He found murder trials even more traumatic:

> No one likes a capital charge, although this was less anxious than a more doubtful case must have been, and it is exhausting from many points of view. It is a strain at any time and in some of these cases there is a sort of emotional shock that is very upsetting. I am glad that it is over. From the personal point of view I naturally hope that it will not be necessary to sign the warrant that has to be issued if the sentence is executed.[36]

But he also revealed a great sense of the comic aspects of life. In August 1932 the family were jointly repainting the interior of their house at 1 George Street, Unley Park:

> The green paint is particularly effective – specially on one's nose or ear. We had a visit last night by the Bishop of Bathurst and his chaplain, and Mum entertained them under difficulties, that is to say with a plentiful application of green paint in the interstices of the left hind ear. She had mislaid the turpentine and the geography was inimical to the use of Oh So Clean so

---

35   Letter from Mellis Napier to John Napier, 3 October 1932.
36   Letter from Mellis Napier to John Napier, 12 June 1933.

finally she accepted my suggestion and dressed her hair to meet the emergencies of the situation.[37]

On 15 November 1935, Napier was appointed by Labor Prime Minister John Lyons to chair a Royal Commission into the monetary and banking systems in Australia. One of his fellow Commissioners was future Prime Minister Ben Chifley. Napier took leave of absence from the South Australian Supreme Court for 18 months from the beginning of 1936.

This was the first important contribution at a national level of a South Australian judge. The role of the Royal Commission essentially was to investigate whether the Australian banking system was responsible for some of the effects of the Depression. Even worse, some banks had gone bankrupt and depositors had lost their money. The commissioners had to inquire into the current régime and make recommendations for changes.

Over the months 200 witnesses appeared before the Royal Commission in 105 sessions held in Sydney, Melbourne, Brisbane, Adelaide, Perth, Hobart and Launceston.[38] They included economists, bankers, representatives of industry and commerce and interested members of the public. Almost 2000 pages of evidence were collected. Napier's fellow commissioners praised his talents and leadership.[39]

The central bank at this time was the Commonwealth Bank, which had opened in 1912 and taken on central roles such as note issue from 1924. The Royal Commission presented its report in July 1937 and made thirty recommendations. These included much restructuring and consolidation of the Commonwealth Bank's role to strengthen its ties with the Commonwealth government. One striking recommendation was to remove the six directors who were appointed according to their representation of special interests and replace them with six directors "selected for capacity and diversity of experience and contact".[40] A very significant recommendation was to repeal the requirement for

---

37   Letter from Mellis Napier to John Napier, 6 August 1932.
38   *Royal Commission into the Monetary and Banking Systems at present in Australia*, p. 5.
39   *ADB 1940-1980*. Sir John Thomas Mellis Napier, p. 461.
40   *Royal Commission*, cited above, p. 275.

the Commonwealth Bank to hold gold or sterling in proportion to the amount of notes in circulation.

The report became the blueprint for Australia's banking and monetary policy for the next 22 years, until the founding of the Reserve Bank in 1959, and during that time various Federal treasurers implemented its recommendations. When Robert Menzies became Attorney-General in 1939, he was so impressed by Napier's work that he offered him the Chief Judgeship of the Commonwealth Court of Conciliation and Arbitration. The vacancy had come about as a result of the death of Chief Judge Dethbridge. Napier's reply that he was "unavailable" was reported in *The Advertiser*, 9 March 1939. That same day's articles include the commissioning of Sir Langdon Bonython's portrait by Sir John Longstaff, the Lord Mayor questioning the viability of a Frome Road site for the planned Adelaide High School, and martial law being proclaimed in the Iraq Military District due to "mischief-makers". Napier may have thought he had a good chance of succeeding Murray. The Chief Justice was then seventy-six, and Angas Parsons, the senior puisne judge, sixty-seven. Napier was ten years younger than Angas Parsons.

George Murray died on 18 February 1942 and Mellis Napier was appointed Chief Justice on Wednesday 25 February 1942. Both Murray and the senior puisne judge, Angas Parsons, had been ill for the past year and Sir Mellis had been unofficially filling in as Chief.

Napier was also appointed Lieutenant-Governor following the tradition dating back to Way's predecessor, Sir Richard Hanson. But for the time being he was not appointed Chancellor of the University of Adelaide, as had been Murray in 1916. Instead, the appointment went to Murray's Vice-Chancellor, Sir William Mitchell. Justice Angas Parsons became Vice-Chancellor, remaining three years until his death in 1945.

One of the early Acts that Napier had to sign as Lieutenant-Governor just before Christmas 1944 amended the Supreme Court Act. This amendment introduced compulsory retirement for judges at seventy years of age, with superannuation.[41] Contributions to the superan-

---

41   *Acts of the Parliament of South Australia*, 1944. No 38. An Act to amend the Supreme Court Act, 1935-1936, so as to prescribe a retiring age and provide for pensions for judges of the Supreme Court, p. 178.

nuation would be eighty pounds a year (4 per cent). All judges yet to be appointed would retire at seventy, and those already on the bench could decide either to retire at seventy with superannuation, or retain their life appointments without it. Once they turned seventy, they lost that option and were bound to their life appointment. If they were already seventy or more at the time (and Angas Parsons and Richards were), they had the option to retire within the next twelve months with superannuation, or stay on but lose the superannuation offer.

In a letter that Napier wrote to his son John a week and a half before signing the Act, he had not yet made up his mind about what he would do:

> Our Parliament is giving me a problem to consider. They have passed a Judges Retiring Bill, to provide a retiring age and pensions for judges. Retiring age is 70 and pension is half salary, but to get that 80 pounds p.a. is deducted from the stipend. This Act does not apply to present occupants unless they elect to come in. That is, if I like to stay out, I am enabled to go on until I drop but I have no right to the pension. If I elect for pension I have to retire at 70 whether I want to or not. What would you do? I suppose that you would say come in, but of course I am nearer to 70 than you are. I shall have to decide one way or another before very long. One thing about it is that L.G. [Lieutenant Governor] sticks even if C.J. [Chief Justice] goes. I should still have a job of sorts.[42]

There were five judges. Herbert Angas Parsons was seventy-two and Frederick Richards was seventy-five. Angas Parsons was the first judge to retire with the new pension, in June 1945, though he died in November. Richards retired in December and lived until 1957. Napier was sixty-two and Herbert Mayo fifty-nine. They elected to retain their life appointments. Only Geoffrey Reed elected to take superannuated retirement. The legislation that Napier signed as Lieutenant-Governor had the effect that judges appointed over the next twenty years who were increasingly younger than him, would retire first.

Napier was knighted in 1943, and further elevated to KCMG (Knight Commander of the Most Distinguished Order of Saint Michael

---

42   Letter from Mellis Napier to John Napier, Monday 4 December 1944.

and Saint George) in the New Year's Honours List of 1945. He had come a long way from the day he arrived in Adelaide almost half a century earlier to find his father ostracised. But the hour when his achievements reached a zenith was tempered by news that was to weigh heavily on the family for over a year. Keith had joined the RAAF in 1941. Three years later, he was flying a coastal command in Italy in 1944:

> (21 April 1944)
> My dear Johnny,
>
> It hurts me to write what it will hurt you to read, that on 15 April Keith went out in a Boston which failed to return to base.
>
> This is all that is known according to the telegram which I received yesterday after 5pm. It followed me to G.H. [Government House] where your mother and I were at a party. I meant to take her home before I said anything to her, and I rang up Judith to be there. But on the way up she put the direct question to me. Had I heard anything? and I had to tell her.

There would never be any further news of the endlessly energetic and enthusiastic Keith, and he was eventually declared killed in action. John and Robert were also in military service. Robert did not need to leave Australia. John served as a pilot in the air force from 1940 until the end of the war. He was awarded the Distinguished Flying Cross, 1939-45 Star, Pacific Star, was "eligible for Returned from Active Service badge", and, decades later, a post-mortem Oak Leaf Cluster in recognition of his service with the Americans.

The Supreme Court under Napier changed little from where Murray left it. Napier relaxed a few of Murray's severe controls. The judges no longer were obliged to appear in public in top hat, frock coat and silver-topped cane, they could smoke in public and get their hair cut where they liked. Napier continued the tradition of lunch at the Adelaide Club to discuss cases. The result of this was that until Roderic Chamberlain joined the bench in 1959 appeals to the Full Court rarely if ever resulted in reversals, and in these, Napier never found himself in dissent.

The judges at the beginning of the 1950s were all members of the Adelaide Club and in 1953, of the then six judges on the bench, only Sir Herbert Mayo had not been, or would not be, Grand Master of the Freemasons of South Australia. There appear to have been only two Full Court appeals between 1950 and 1959 in which a judge dissented, and on both occasions this was Mayo.[43]

Until 1954, when Albert James Hannan QC, a Catholic, was appointed an acting judge, all of the 31 Supreme Court judges appointed since 1836 were protestants. By contrast, there had always been at least one Catholic judge on the High Court bench since its establishment in 1903.[44] The number of Catholics in South Australia has always been small, only a little over 12 per cent of the population in the 1950s.[45] Hannan's appointment, even if temporary, was the first sign of broadening the Supreme Court's membership in almost 120 years. At the time of this appointment, Hannan had been retired for two years from the position of Crown Solicitor he had held from 1927 to 1952. He was on the council of the University of Adelaide and a member of the Adelaide Club.

Chief Justice ca. 1954. (Courtesy Napier family)

The appointment caused tension between Napier and Playford, and according to Stewart Cockburn, was only achieved through some sort of "deal", though if there was such a deal, the details of it are not recorded. Napier's resistance to Hannan's appointment, even acting, seems more likely to have been as a result of concern over Playford's view of a Supreme Court appointment as a reward for service:

> For example, in 1946, he had wished to kick his then Attorney-General, Charles Abbott, upstairs. Abbott had not been a

---

43 *Warnecke v Pope* [1950] SASR 113 and *O'Sullivan v Truth and Sportsman Limited* [1956] SASR 58.

44 Graham Loughlin, *South Australian Queen's Counsel*, p. 66.

45 *Wakefield Companion to South Australian History*, p. 96.

particularly outstanding lawyer before he went into Parliament and some members of the Supreme Court resented his promotion to their ranks. It hardened Napier's resistance to Hannan's proposed appointment.[46]

Hannan was never appointed permanently, and the first Roman Catholic judge was James Francis Brazel, appointed 16 November 1959. A second Catholic judge, John Leo Travers, was appointed 25 January 1962.

Even more disturbing to the homogenous membership of the South Australian judiciary was the appointment of not only a third Roman Catholic judge, but also a female, Roma Mitchell. This was a radical move, not just in South Australia, but also across the nation. Mitchell was the first Australian woman appointed to Queen's Counsel, in 1962, and on 23 September 1965, the first woman Supreme Court judge in Australia. Napier had been on the bench just over forty years at this stage, and was almost 83 years old:

> Her appointment seems to have taken him by surprise. His first reaction was that all members of the court must be addressed to and referred to without distinction and she must therefore be known as 'Mr Justice Mitchell'. The absurdity of this was soon pointed out to him and he thereupon directed that all members of the court be known as 'Justice' without a prefix. This eminently sensible direction seems to have been received with ill-grace by at least some of the male members of the court. The direction remained in force, however, until Sir Mellis retired, whereupon the male members of the court reverted to "Mr Justice", the female member remaining as "Justice".[47]

This remained the case until Len King became Chief Justice in 1978 and again removed the 'Mr' so that there was no distinction based on gender.[48] King points out that, despite the shock that a female appointment might have initially given Sir Mellis, "Justice Mitchell always

---

46   Stewart Cockburn, *Playford : Benevolent Despot*, p. 222.
47   Len King. "The Judicial Career of Dame Roma Mitchell", *Dame Roma: Glimpses of a Glorious Life*, p. 66.
48   In Canada, the gender distinction with Supreme Court judges is dealt with by addressing female judges as "Madam Justice".

asserted that he received her with kindness and treated her with courtesy and the respect due to a judge of his court."

Sir Mellis as Chancellor of the University of Adelaide ca. 1954 conferring degrees in Bonython Hall. (Courtesy Napier family)

In 1948 the tradition established by Samuel Way of the Chief Justice being Chancellor of the University of Adelaide was restored. Sir William Mitchell retired and Sir Mellis replaced him. In May 1948 a new Vice-Chancellor arrived from England, A P Rowe. The university was on the cusp of a period of great change. Rowe was the university's first paid and full-time Vice-Chancellor, on a commencing salary of two thousand pounds a year, the same then as a puisne judge.

When he arrived from England in 1948 Rowe found that the University of Adelaide was not so much in a state of crisis as stasis. It had drifted away from the days when it produced people like Mawson, Bragg and Florey. The principal attributable cause of its deteriorated reputation was that Sir William Mitchell had dominated it for too long:

But by far the chief factor in bringing about the present state of affairs, one perhaps unique to Adelaide, is that the university has been governed by a dictator for decades. The late Chancellor was obviously a wise and benevolent dictator, but still a dictator. The price to be paid for having a dictatorship is that other men lose the habit of taking responsibility and thinking of higher policy or are not trained to do these things.[49]

Mitchell was also so parsimonious that he never even allowed himself an office, and during his period as vice-chancellor from 1916 to 1942 always shared the desk of the registrar. But this well-meant control over spending left Adelaide way behind in the State Government grants that then were the chief funding source for universities across the country. In *If the Gown Fits* Rowe compares the increase in grants of all the State funded universities in the ten years prior to his appointment – 1938-1948:

Melbourne	330 per cent
Tasmania	310 per cent
Queensland	258 per cent
Western Australia	171 per cent
Sydney	28 per cent
Adelaide	20 per cent

This tiny increase also suited the man who had been Premier all that time, Thomas Playford. His vision of South Australia was far-reaching but never included universities or the arts. Aside from official functions, Playford apparently never set foot inside a university until 1956.

Rowe wanted to increase salaries across the range of professors and lecturers, increase their numbers, and invest in equipment. He also wanted to introduce study leave to counteract Adelaide's isolation so that lecturers could take time off to go interstate and overseas and keep up to date with international developments in their field. All this required money from a State government which did not value universities.

Nevertheless, before the end of his first year as vice-chancellor, Rowe had obtained an increase in the State annual grant of 150

---

49   A P Rowe, *If the Gown Fits*, p.37.

per cent, from fifty-six thousand pounds in 1948 to one hundred and fifty-six thousand pounds in 1949. By his last year as Vice-Chancellor – 1958 – he had increased the State grant to over eight hundred thousand pounds a year. Rowe reveals the secret of his unprecedented success with Playford:

> Not once during my decade in Adelaide did I succeed in capturing his heart and it was an accident in 1948 I stumbled upon the royal road to the treasury chest. All that was needed was to convince the Premier that we were falling behind the standard of universities in other states. Possessing a state-consciousness almost frightening in one of the leaders of a small nation on the borders of Asia, it was this that to him was unthinkable.[50]

Student numbers were increasing substantially around Rowe's period. In 1944 a total of 2,728 students attended the University of Adelaide, by 1954 there were 4,115, and 8,634 enrolled for 1964.

Rowe's decade as the university's first paid Vice-Chancellor was a stormy one, and he published *If the Gown Fits* to provide a permanent record of his version of the events. He had met a lot of resistance to the changes he proposed, not least complacency. In the preface to the book, he singled out one person, apart from his wife and his secretary: "Sir Mellis Napier, Chancellor of the University of Adelaide and Chief Justice of the Supreme Court of South Australia, who never failed to support me in times of conflict with the state government and, in the end, with some members of the staff."[51] The two remained friends after Rowe's departure in 1958.

The 1950s was a decade of unprecedented prosperity. A larger proportion of the general population of South Australia than ever in the State's history was living in relative comfort. Home ownership had increased to near 70 per cent and the proportion of the population living in new government housing had increased to nine per cent.[52] But there was also a lot of change:

---

50   Rowe, p. 42.
51   Rowe, pp. IX-X.
52   Graeme Hugo, *Playford's South Australia: Essays on the History of South Australia, 1933-1968*, p. 32.

The growing urbanisation of the population, the increased proletarianisation of the workforce, a greater ethnic diversity, and a range of changes in family structure and functioning, the role of women, and education levels, all created a groundswell for the social legislation which Playford eschewed.[53]

Free of the economic shackles that had historically kept many of them at survival level, people were increasingly becoming aware and resentful of the social restrictions imposed on them. It is interesting to note how many of the crimes overburdening the courts then are no longer crimes: liquor sales after 6pm, homosexual acts, gaming, and abortion. The fact that these activities were later either completely legalised or freed up is a sure sign of the tension that must have been simmering in that time.

Although Don Dunstan – who first set up his legal practice in a corner of Patricia Hackett's chambers – was beginning to agitate for social changes as early as 1952, real wide-spread change could only come from a mini-revolution at the grass roots level. No-one would have predicted that a major catalyst for this upheaval would be the rape and murder of a nine-year-old girl five days before Christmas 1958 near a dusty town 800 kilometres from Adelaide. The resulting public backlash over the trial, the appeals and a Royal Commission caught both Napier and Playford by surprise. Napier, after thirty-five years on the bench, was singled out by the local press as the villain.

The conviction of Rupert Max Stuart for the murder of Mary Hattam, and the subsequent appeals and Royal Commission, remain to this day the most-discussed case in South Australian history, and one of the most discussed in the history of Australia. Three full-length books have been dedicated to the affair. The first appearing in 1962, was Ken Inglis's *The Stuart Case*, which was republished in 2002 with updated sections. The second was Sir Roderic Chamberlain's *The Stuart Affair*, published in 1973. Thomas Dixon's *The Wizard of Alice* eventually countered Chamberlain's haughty pro-establishment account in 1986. In 2002 a full-length feature film, *Black and White*, took on the story with British actors Robert Carlyle and Charles Dance playing the lead

---

53   Hugo, p. 45.

roles. In between, there have been chapters and sections on the case in other books such as Don Dunstan's *Felicia*, Gough Whitlam's *Abiding Interests*, Alex Castles and Michael Harris's *Lawmakers and Wayward Whigs*, Stewart Cockburn's *Playford*, Sir Walter Crocker's *Sir Thomas Playford* and Jack Elliott's *Memoirs of a Barrister*. In 2003 High Court judge Michael Kirby gave a speech about the case and published an article. In 2006 the Stuart case was the topic of a day-long seminar at the University of Adelaide.

To set the scene for this defining episode in Sir Mellis Napier's life and career, here is an outline of the main events:

19 December 1958: Rupert Max Stuart arrives in Ceduna with a travelling fun fair.

20 December 1958 (Saturday): Mary Olive Hattam, aged nine, found that night raped and murdered in a cave on the beach between Ceduna and Thevenard.

22 December 1958: Rupert Max Stuart arrested, questioned by six police officers. A detailed confession produced in educated English.

20 April 1959: Stuart arraigned before Justice Geoffrey Reed and a jury.

24 April 1959: Trial ends; guilty verdict. Stuart sentenced to hang.

4 May 1959: Notice given of appeal to the Court of Criminal Appeal.

6 May 1959: Appeal heard before Chief Justice Napier and Justices Herbert Mayo and Charles Abbott. Appeal dismissed.

1 and 2 June 1959: Application for special leave to appeal to the High Court before Chief Justice Owen Dixon and Justices McTiernan, Fullagar, Taylor and Windeyer.

19 June 1959: Judgment handed down: Application dismissed.

27 July 1959: Father Dixon locates the fun fair in Atherton, North Queensland.

28 July 1959: Appeal to the Privy Council in London. Fails.

29 July 1959: *The News* headline: "Stuart has perfect alibi: Three give affidavits on Stuart: Murder case bombshell". New evidence indicates Stuart was at work when the murder seemed to have been done.

30 July 1959: Playford announces Royal Commission into the trial and conviction.

17 August 1959: Royal Commission opens with Napier (who sat on Full Court appeal), Reed (trial judge) and Ross.

20 August 1959: Dorothy Napier collapses from a stroke and hospitalised. Later that day, Napier interrupts Shand's cross-examination of Phin.

21 August 1959 (Friday): Shand walks out. *The News's* headlines: "Shand quits: 'You won't give Stuart a fair go'"; "Commission breaks up: Shand blasts Napier"; "Mr Shand QC indicts Sir Mellis Napier. 'These Commissioners cannot do the job'".

24 August 1959: Dorothy Napier dies.

4 September 1959: Royal Commission resumes without representation for Stuart.

16 September 1959: John Starke QC represents Stuart.

5 October 1959: Stuart's death sentence commuted to life imprisonment.

3 December 1959: Royal Commission's report received in parliament: no reason to reverse the guilty verdict.

Over the course of this period in 1959 Stuart was reprieved seven times from being hanged, on one occasion within hours of it – 19 June, 7 July, 20 July, 4 August, 31 August, 7 September, 30 September.

The published literature provides ample details of the various stages of the process from Stuart's initial arrest for the murder until the report of the Royal Commission. The case did not stop there. Playford decided to prosecute the editor of *The News*, Rohan Rivett, for the headlines in his paper on the day Jack Shand walked out of the Royal Commission. That event is discussed more fully in the next chapter, as John Bray represented Rohan Rivett.

The question remains why the Stuart case provoked so much criticism of the courts and the Playford government. Why was Napier singled out? Even Playford, when discussing the case in August 1977 with Sir Walter Crocker, regretted acting on the Chief Justice's advice:

> One decision I made in 1959 gave me considerable cause for concern. I consulted the Chief Justice about certain procedures. That was wrong of me. It would have been much better if the Chief Justice had not been involved. He should not have been my adviser.[54]

The Premier was of course ultimately responsible for any decisions he made, not the person who advised him. According to Cockburn, this particular piece of advice was over the appointment of Geoffrey Reed, the trial judge, as a Royal Commissioner. This was indeed a mistake – even though Reed was a judge of unquestioned integrity. It was not wise practice for a trial judge to sit on a review of his own trial. Likewise, Napier had been on the Court of Criminal Appeal. As a Royal Commissioner, he would also be reviewing his own decision.

The factor that Napier seemed to have forgotten was that justice must not only be done, but be seen to be done. The "seen to be done" refers to the relationship between the judicial system and the community it serves. Alex Castles suggested in *Lawmakers and Wayward Whigs* that the Napier Court believed itself "both unchallengeable and omnipotent".[55]

Jack Elliott observed early in his career that the Court of Criminal Appeal almost never reversed a decision by a trial judge. It may well be that all those judgments were correct. But the feeling among sections of the criminal bar was that this was not true. This feeling was simmering for decades before the Stuart affair. But there was more than just the feeling that the courts were out of touch that fuelled the Stuart affair. It was the entire forensic process. There was a litany of errors and flaws right from the beginning:

1.   The doctor who inspected Mary Hattam was vague about the time of death. She estimated it first at around 9.30

---

54   Cockburn, p. 300.
55   Castles and Harris, cited above, p. 350. Castles was present at the meeting held at Dr Charles Duguid's home on 27 June 1959, which led to a petition and the involvement of the Law School in the affair.

Saturday night, when Stuart was in the Ceduna lock-up for being drunk and disorderly. She later estimated the time of death at between 2.30 and 8pm. According to the Giesemens, Stuart was at work between 2 and 4 pm. Mary Hattam was last seen at 3.30 pm.

2.   Under the Aboriginal welfare laws a welfare officer was legally obliged to be present when an Aboriginal was giving a statement. The Welfare Officer was not present. Under Northern Territory law at the time, this absence would have rendered the confession inadmissible.

3.   The confession was written not just in a style of English of which Stuart would have been incapable, but also included descriptive details beyond his ability.

4.   Apart from the assertions of two Aboriginal trackers that footprints near the cave matched Stuart's, this confession was the only piece of evidence linking Stuart to the crime.

5.   Lawyer David O'Sullivan, although earnest and doing the whole case without one penny of payment, refused a leader and as a result, the defence argument was never adequately developed and pursued. One crucial failure was not to seek an interpreter, when T G H Strehlow, an expert in Stuart's own language – Arunta – was based a few streets away at the University of Adelaide.

6.   At the trial Crown Solicitor Roderic Chamberlain insisted pedantically on Stuart's legal obligation to read his unsworn statement himself. Although strictly correct, this requirement clearly did not allow for people without sufficient fluency and literacy in English. Justice Reed should have allowed Stuart's counsel, in his role of advocate, to read it. As a consequence, the jury never heard Stuart's version.

7.   Chamberlain knowingly broke procedural rules for High Court appeals by sending a letter informing the appeal judges that he had evidence that Stuart's English was better than what the defence claimed. The judges rebuked him for this in their judgment.

All these errors or flaws contributed to the perceived injustice being dealt out to Rupert Max Stuart. In addition, the juries were selected entirely differently in 1959:

A jury panel was summoned from the roll of electors for the state's Legislative Council – a roll composed, broadly speaking, of those heads of households who chose to be on it.[56]

Until 1965, juries were all male. In other words, twelve white male property-owners would judge an itinerant Aboriginal.[57] Stuart's Aboriginality is obviously crucial to the case. An example of the way Stuart would have been treated by police officers is illustrated only too well by Detective Sergeant Phin. He offered this opinion on Aboriginals, under oath, in the Royal Commission:

> Most of them, I believe, have the mentality of an uneducated child (…). I know some of their language or should I say gibberish; they have a different monkey gibberish for every tribe (…) When I was told that a little child's body had been found foully murdered, and that the head had been battered in (…), I did not for a moment consider that outrage the work of a white man. I immediately thought it was the work of a darky.[58]

Phin was the Whyalla police officer who first nominated Stuart a suspect. The fun fair had made its way over the weekend from Ceduna to Whyalla and Phin visited it in the course of his duty. He spoke to the owner, Norman Gieseman, and to one of his employees, Allan Moir. It was Moir's information that led to Sergeant Phin contacting Ceduna police, yet Moir during the Royal Commission showed himself to be an entirely unreliable witness.[59] The very first step in the entire process – choosing Rupert Max Stuart as the most likely suspect – was flawed. Why was Moir never a suspect? He appears to have been very lucky that Sergeant Phin automatically concluded that the killer was black.

Phin's comments were made during his cross-examination by Shand on the fateful Thursday 20 August 1959, that Lady Napier had been rushed to hospital. A little later in Shand's questioning of Phin, Sir Mellis interrupted him. Sir Mellis quickly retracted his comment that

---

56   K S Inglis, *The Stuart Case*, p. 19.
57   T S Dixon lists the jurors at the end of his book, *The Wizard of Alice*, on page 412.
58   Inglis, p. 12, footnote.
59   Inglis, p. 252 and Dixon, cited above, pp. 191-193.

he had "heard enough of this" when he saw Shand's reaction. He said, "You are perfectly at liberty to continue and you can stay here as long as it suits you." Shand quit as Stuart's counsel the next day. That afternoon *The News* published its inflammatory headlines - "Shand quits: 'You won't give Stuart a fair go'"; "Commission breaks up: Shand blasts Napier"; "Mr Shand QC indicts Sir Mellis Napier. 'These Commissioners cannot do the job'". They omitted to report that Napier had wanted Shand to continue.

Over the next few days the case received front page treatment across the country in *The Sydney Morning Herald*, *The Daily Telegraph*, and two Melbourne dailies, *The Herald* and *The Sun*. Adelaide's morning paper, *The Advertiser*, never dramatised the case in the way that *The News* did. Nearly a fortnight later, on Wednesday 2 September 1959, the coverage of Shand's departure in *The News* headlines was discussed in Parliament. Playford was furious about the reporting of Shand's opinion of the Commissioners:

> These words were never spoken, yet they are put in inverted commas, and that is the sort of thing that has been used to try and drag our judges down. These words, or anything like them, were never spoken. They are the gravest libel ever made against any judge in this state.

After a question from Frank Walsh, a Labor member, Playford threatened to take legal action against *The News* and continued:

> I believe this House should carry a resolution of commendation to Sir Mellis Napier, who, in one of the most tragic times of his life, has been subject to the vilest abuse yet has carried on his duties manfully and, I believe, with great dignity.[60]

The following day *The News* ran an apologetic editorial supposedly written by Rohan Rivett, the editor:

> Well, the Premier is right. And we were wrong. Mr Shand did not use these words, and the headline should never have been published and we regret that it was.

---

60   Inglis, pp. 162-163 for these quotes.

Also Mr Shand did not single out Sir Mellis Napier in his attack, and a poster which read "Shand blasts Napier" should not have seen the light of day, and again we regret that it did. It should have read "Shand attacks Commission".

What the editorial did not mention is that Rupert Murdoch – owner of *The News* and still in his twenties – wrote that poster, and also the editorial itself.[61] At this stage Stuart was still under the shadow of hanging. Murdoch's editorial concluded:

> We have never claimed that Stuart is innocent – merely that he must be shown to be guilty beyond all doubt before being hanged.
> *The News* sees it as its duty to fight always not only for justice to be done, but for justice to appear to be done.
> We maintain this stand, and will continue, with pride, to fight for this ideal.[62]

One other important fact about the walk-out that should not be overlooked is that Shand died of cancer a little over eight weeks later. The brief exchange that caused such a tide of headlines, letters to the editor, and parliamentary debates, took place between a Chief Justice whose wife had been rushed to hospital before he left for work, and a man in the final stages of cancer whose patience was being gnawed away by pain. Ordinarily, neither of the two would have allowed outside factors, no matter the gravity, to invade their work. A moment of mutually aggravated distraction was enough to provoke a few words that opened a Pandora's box of public dissatisfaction with not just the Stuart case, but the entire system of which it was the product.

As Chief Justice and the personification of justice, Sir Mellis had to take some of the blame for the Royal Commission, even if much of it had nothing to do with him. Sir Mellis would certainly have meant well, and obviously considered himself and Justice Reed the best qualified to sit on it. He is responsible, however, for forgetting the relationship between the justice system and the community, for not taking into account the consequences of recommending himself and Justice Reed.

---

61   Dixon, pp. 406-407, from an interview with Rohan Rivett.
62   Inglis, p. 165.

He could cite other instances of judges sitting in review of their own decisions to show that it was not unusual, but that was not the point. The point was that justice must always be seen to be done, for the reason that the system answers to the community it serves. Napier had lost the ability to gauge community feelings that he had shown in his first year on the bench in *Norley v Malthouse*.

One element of the public backlash over the Stuart case can be seen in the attitude of Sergeant Phin. He condemned and convicted Rupert Max Stuart in his mind before he had even met him, just because Stuart was Aboriginal. But the public were also aware that too many police officers also extended their prejudices to other sectors. These were the days in which police testimony alone was sufficient to convict a person of a crime in which there was no other evidence against them. Anyone who did not conform to white protestant lifestyles was likely to arouse their interest. This theme recurs in the chapter on John Bray, as he was a target.

The police were not as powerful, however, as the Crown Solicitor. Sir Roderic Chamberlain had been Crown Prosecutor from 1928 to 1949, Assistant Crown Solicitor from 1949 to 1952, and then Crown Solicitor after Albert Hannan's retirement. Jack Elliott makes frequent references to Chamberlain's prejudice against accused persons in his *Memoirs*, but it is not necessary to rely on Jack Elliott's opinion. Chamberlain revealed his prejudice in his own book, *The Stuart Affair*:

> Rupert Max Stuart was known already to the police, in Ceduna and in other parts of Australia.[63]

Stuart had indeed been convicted of previous offences which included an assault on a young girl. He had also used at least six aliases. But they have nothing to do with his guilt or innocence over the murder of Mary Hattam. The fact that Chamberlain opened the third chapter of his book with this sentence shows that he is attempting to prejudice the reader in just the same way he was himself. Enough people with no criminal record at all have been convicted of murders to show that prior history does not point to guilt.

---

63   Sir Roderic Chamberlain, *The Stuart Affair*, pp. 15.

The main sentiment that runs through Chamberlain's book is his blind loyalty to the institutions with which he had been involved all his working life:

> As my last brief before my elevation to the Bench, I found that I was not only defending the conviction of the murderer, I was defending the honour and integrity of the South Australian Government, its Police Force, and indeed the very institutions on which the administration of justice depends.[64]

It led him time and time again to believing anything said by an official and disbelieving anything said by someone else. One key example is that he automatically believed the court official who claimed that Stuart had spoken perfect English at a trial in Alice Springs, and sent off a letter to the High Court without investigating further. Tom Dixon explained in *The Wizard of Alice* how Stuart had been carefully coached for just that occasion by a friend.[65]

But it is Chamberlain's defiance of any criticism of legal institutions by outsiders that is even more disturbing. He rebuked several people for interfering in the case: Father Tom Dixon (p. 173), Roman Catholic priest and missionary; Professor Strehlow (p. 173), Reader in Australian Linguistics at the University of Adelaide; Dr H V Evatt (p. 40), former High Court judge, Leader of the Opposition, biographer; and Professor Norval Morris (p. 301), Dean of Law at the University of Adelaide. He commented sardonically that these last two, "university intellectuals who knew very little about the methods of the detection of crime, and still less about the facts of the Stuart case, decided that these authorities had all been misled."[66]

Sir Mellis Napier made his gravest tactical error after the Royal Commission closed. As Lieutenant-Governor he presided at the Executive Council meeting that decided to prosecute Rohan Rivett as editor of the *News* for libel. Even Sir Walter Crocker blames Sir Mellis for "re-activating public excitement" by initiating a further trial.[67] But in the capable hands of Dr John Bray QC, all the charges were successfully

---

64   Chamberlain, pp. 3-4.
65   Dixon, p. 19.
66   Chamberlain, p. 303.
67   Cockburn, p. 300.

defended. This trial only served to diminish the respect for the offices of the long-serving Premier and his equally long-serving Chief Justice.

Another error of judgment that Sir Mellis made around this time, unrelated to the Stuart affair, did not help his reputation. He recommended his son Robert to be appointed Queen's Counsel. According to a reliable source, Robert did indeed want the appointment, which was made on 5 May 1960, though his father must have quickly regretted letting family loyalty override professional judgment. His son had been a solicitor of average ability; no one in the legal profession believed that he could conduct the complex cases that require senior counsel. After his appointment Robert received little work beyond that of the ordinary solicitor.

In 1962, Napier sent out a potential appointee to silk, Eric McLaughlin, to Jack Elliott, also on the list for appointments that year, to try to obtain an agreement from him to send briefs to Robert.[68] Elliott refused, and since McLaughlin had failed to clinch the bargain, neither he nor Jack Elliott joined Roma Mitchell, Keith Sangster, Howard Zelling and Andrew Wells in the appointments to silk in September 1962. But further discussions among the judges, and in particular between Napier and Chamberlain – now on the bench – led to Elliott and McLaughlin being both appointed just six weeks later. Ten years later, in 1971, unable to meet the requirements of trust account audits, Robert Napier removed himself from the Roll of Practitioners and his Queen's Counsel commission was subsequently revoked. He had never been dishonest, he just loathed keeping records.

The reputation of the South Australian Supreme Court and the office of Chief Justice in particular was no doubt at its lowest ebb as a result of the Stuart affair. It was put under further pressure by an unprecedented sequence of deaths and retirements in quick succession, which rocked the continuity of the court. George Ligertwood retired in 1958, replaced by Frank Piper in October, who died in office eleven months later while the Stuart Royal Commission was in session. Charles Abbott retired a month after Piper's death. These two judges were replaced by James Brazel and Roderic Chamberlain in November 1959. Brazel died in office in August 1961 and was replaced by Vivian Millhouse, who himself died in office in September 1963, to be replaced by Charles Bright. Geoffrey Reed retired in March 1962 and Bruce Ross in May that year. Leo Travers was appointed

68   Elliott, pp. 210-213.

The Bench of the Supreme Court early 1962. L-R: Vivian Millhouse, Bruce Ross, Herbert Mayo, Mellis Napier, Geoffrey Reed, Roderic Chamberlain. (SCLSA)

in March to replace Justice Reed and David Hogarth to replace Justice Ross in July.

In 1962 Napier reached eighty, the age of death of his two predecessors. After the Stuart affair he must surely have wondered if he would have been wiser to have taken his retirement at seventy in 1952. Now he felt duty-bound to remain Chief Justice together with his senior puisne Herbert Mayo (born 1885), who had opted also to keep his life appointment, in order to maintain an appearance of continuity in the court.

Sir Mellis's advanced age had been mentioned in the press during the Stuart affair, not a reflection on his mental capacities, but on the era in which his original ideas were formed. He was surely, as each of us is, a product of his times. He never learned to drive a car, unlike his predecessors Way and Murray. Son Robert, who lived with Sir Mellis and his own family in, first, "Shurdington" on Summit Road at Crafers, and then "Glenwood" in Stirling, ended up driving his father to work and back, particularly after the death of Lady Napier. At home he spent most nights and weekends in his study, alternating between keeping his legal writings and detective fiction. His favourite authors included Agatha Christie and Georgette Heyer. Occasionally he would step out and chop up some firewood.

With a new generation of judges, Sir Mellis began to find himself for the first time in his career occasionally in dissent in the Full Court, or to see his judgment as a sole judge varied by a Full Court, as in *Duurland v Hagerstrom* in 1965.[69] That year, Sir Mellis showed that although he might be an octogenarian and a key member of the estab-

---

69   [1965] SASR 196.

lished order, he was still capable of rocking the boat. His dissenting judgment in a dispute over hotel licences was a catalyst for a Royal Commission
into the licensing laws:

> Speaking generally, it is no part of our function to criticise the law
> that we administer, or to suggest how it should be amended; but
> it seems to me that we should call attention to the fact that this
> legislation, which was designed to meet the needs of a "horse and
> buggy age", is hopelessly out of touch with the needs of the present
> day. (...) as the Act now stands, it is for all practical purposes no
> more than a dead letter."[70]

These words from Sir Mellis's dissenting judgment triggered the
most comprehensive reforms in South Australia's alcoholic beverage trade in
its one hundred and thirty year history. Playford and his Liberal/Country
Party government had been voted out, and Labor was in with Don Dunstan
as Attorney-General. Dunstan had been approached by the judge of the Licensing Court who, after Napier's criticism, was finding the Licensing Act increasingly unworkable.

Napier as Lieutenant-Governor leading a guard of honour ca. 1960s.
(Advertiser)

Dunstan was also working on Sir Mellis in an effort to get him to retire. Dunstan managed to retire Sir Herbert Mayo, but Napier resisted. Roma Mitchell and George Walters were appointed, bringing the number of judges on the Supreme Court to seven. Eventually Napier admitted to Don Dunstan that he could not afford to retire,[71] so Dunstan introduced a special bill in Parliament providing

---

70   *Bay Hotel v Broadway Hotel* [1965] SASR 249 at 254 and at 255.
71   Don Dunstan, pp. 114-115.

Sir Mellis with a judicial pension. The salary of the Chief Justice in 1965 had been lifted to 7600 pounds a year, and the other judges received 6850 pounds a year. The following year, after the introduction of decimal currency. the judicial salaries were amended with a slight increase to $16,600 a year for the Chief and $14,900 a year for the puisnes.

The Lieutenant-Governor making a presentation to a boy.

When Napier retired, on 28 February 1967, he had been a judge for forty-three years to the day, and Chief Justice for twenty-five of those. The state's legal profession was not yet 130 years old, and he had been a part of it for half of its history. He was the first South Australian Chief Justice to retire for 106 years – the state's first Chief Justice Sir Charles Cooper had retired in 1861. The triple office of Chief Justice-Chancellor-Lieutenant Governor that Way had established was already broken. Sir George Ligertwood had been Chancellor of the University of Adelaide since 1961.

Napier as Lieutenant-Governor laying a wreath at the War Memorial ca. 1960s. (Advertiser)

Napier kept the office of Lieutenant-Governor, as his successor John Bray believed that the executive and the judiciary should be kept apart. Napier remained the Governor's deputy until 1973. By that time he had filled in as Governor 179 times, totalling nine and a half years – surely a record, and longer than any Governor's term. He had been Grand Master of the Freemasons in South Australia twice (1928-1930 and 1935-1939), President of the St John Ambulance Association since 1942, President

of the Adelaide Club (1952-1955) and had been awarded honorary doctorates in law by the Universities of Adelaide and Melbourne.

Some speeches he made during his first year of retirement, 1968,
reveal his philosophy of life. He believed that it was absolutely essential
for people to obey the law in order to live in a civilised society. He regretted the enormous social changes that were taking place, which he saw
as encouraging people to break the laws and challenge the Bible. In a speech given to recipients of Duke of Edinburgh awards in September 1968, Sir Mellis showed his concern at the impact of scientific progress:

Sir Mellis addressing a group of young men visiting his home
at Crafers, "Shurdington". (Courtesy Napier family)

Juvenile delinquency is assuming alarming proportions, and, whereever we look, we see young people in rebellion against the established order
of things, but with no clear idea of anything to put in its place.
It seems to me that, if this goes on, our civilisation must end in
chaos. The reason for this discomfiture of the body politic is, I
think, obvious, and it comes back to this, that "a little learning
is a dangerous thing". That fact is that, in recent years, the
advance of science and the spread of knowledge have discredited
many of the traditional legends associated with the religion of
our ancestors, and with the decay of faith, we are in danger of
losing our sense of moral values. Men have eaten from the tree
of the knowledge of good and evil, but they have been unable
to digest the fruit. In the result their minds are distended with
pride and arrogance, and their souls are filled with a vague sense
of discomfort and discontent.

He also appeared to suspect universities of provoking unrest:

Your right, to do whatever you want to do, stops short when it comes into conflict with anything that someone else has a right to do. For example, we may concede that everyone has the right to express their opinions and to protest, but that does not mean that everyone has the right to smash other people's windows, or to overturn motor cars, and it is the height of absurdity to suggest that people – even university students or lecturers – have the right to sit on the roadway, if, by sitting there, they prevent other people using the highway.[72]

His opinions may have been the reaction of an old man to a cultural revolution at that time taking place across the western world. The most dramatic example that year was the May 1968 student riots in France which led to a general strike that shut down every essential service in the country for a month. *The Advertiser* published the full text of his speech, and also attracted headlines in *The Australian*. He was yet to see the demonstrations in Adelaide in 1970 organised by the leaders of the Vietnam Moratorium.

For his service as Chancellor of the University of Adelaide, the Napier building was named after him in 1961, the same year that the original university building was named after Sir William Mitchell. Napier's service as Lieutenant-Governor is remembered in his bust near the entrance to Government House. After he died at the age of 93 on 22 March 1976 in a Kingswood nursing home, he was given a state funeral at St Peter's Cathedral, attended by 300 people. Although Napier represented many of the values of an era that the Dunstan government was sweeping away, Dunstan was nevertheless aware of the sum total of Napier's contribution to the State's judicial system. A one-kilometre-long funeral cortege travelled from the Cathedral to his final resting place at Centennial Park Cemetery.

---

72   *The Advertiser*, 19 September 1968.

CHAPTER 5

John Bray (1967-1978)

RESPONDING TO SOCIAL REFORM

Had the legendary Frank Villeneuve Smith KC lived long enough, he would not have been very surprised to see John Bray appointed Chief Justice.[1] In a letter written to John Bray in 1933, the year that Bray obtained his law degree with honours, he wrote:

> I really genuinely mean it when I repeat that I expect very big things of you.[2]

Six years later, when John Bray was established in legal practice with Genders, Wilson and Pellew, his sister Rowena wrote to him:

---

1   Francis (Frank) Villeneuve Smith KC died on 15 December 1956, aged 72. He never obtained a law degree, but qualified with the Final Certificate in Law. He became in King's Counsel in 1919 at the age of 35, with a reputation as a particularly persuasive orator. See Graham Loughlin, *South Australian Queen's Counsel, 1865-1972*, p. A112; and Jack Elliott, *Memoirs of a Barrister*, pp. 2-9.

2   25 October 1933, from Springfield House, later the home of Senior Judge Neil Ligertwood. SLSA Archival Collection, PRG1098/1.

I suppose you are frightfully busy barristing and on the way to becoming one of <u>the</u> men of South Australia.[3]

John Bray's exceptional abilities had been identified early in his law career both by a senior barrister, and by one of his peers. Yet there appears to have been a moment a quarter-century later when it was feared that, despite having exceeded even the high expectations of him, he may not be considered for the Bench. Roma Mitchell, just after being appointed to the Supreme Court, ended her response to John Bray's letter of congratulations:

I can only hope that your unique talents are being reserved for a higher field.[4]

At the time of Sir Mellis Napier's retirement two years later, there were three other capable candidates, each very qualified to take over as Chief Justice. One had already been on the bench eight years, and fully expected to take over; one was at the Bar; one was a Special Magistrate. According to Don Dunstan in *Felicia*, the senior puisne judge Sir Roderick Chamberlain had been promised the Chief Justiceship by Sir Thomas Playford.[5] But Playford had since been voted out of office, and by 1967 had stepped right back to the opposition back bench. Joseph Nelligan was a Special Magistrate, and is described by Jack Elliott as the most effective defence counsel he had ever heard in his life. Nelligan and Chamberlain had each been distinguished advocates, but time was against them. Nelligan would turn sixty-seven that year, and Chamberlain, sixty-six. In addition to these two, a leading silk at that time, Keith Sangster , had been led to understand he would be considered.[6]

But Don Dunstan had already informed John Bray in 1965, unknown to Roma Mitchell, that now he was Attorney-General he was going to make three judicial appointments: Roma Mitchell and George Walters as puisne judges, and Bray to replace Napier as chief. Dunstan appointed Mitchell within a few months of Labor coming into power in April 1965, to increase the bench to seven. He persuaded Sir Herbert

3   6 December 1939, from Helensburgh, Scotland. SLSA Archival Collection, PRG1198/1. "Barristing" and underlined "the" reproduced as in the letter.
4   25 September 1965. SLSA Archival Collection, PRG1098/1/6.
5   Don Dunstan, *Felicia*. South Melbourne: Macmillan, 1981, p. 115.
6   Hon. A K Sangster QC, Unpublished diaries.

Mayo to retire in 1966 and replaced him with Walters. But because Dunstan was unable to persuade Sir Mellis to retire as quickly as he had hoped, it seemed to some people that Bray was being passed over. After Mitchell's and then Walters's appointments, he was taunted at a function: "Why won't they make you a judge, John?" Bray replied: "Because I know people like you!"

This was closer to the truth than his drinking companion would have guessed. Not everyone wanted John Bray appointed as a judge. He had acquired an adverse reputation with the police after telling a jury during an incest trial to take note of the fact that the police officers who gave evidence had committed perjury.[7]

Later, Bray discovered that he had been under surveillance since defending Rohan Rivett in the aftermath of the Stuart trial. According to Don Dunstan in *Felicia*, Police Commissioner Brigadier J G McKinna, on hearing that Bray was to be appointed Chief Justice, told Premier Frank Walsh that Bray was not a fit person as he exhibited homosexual behaviour. Dunstan immediately demanded details and quickly discovered that the Commissioner's patrol reports did not support his insinuations:

> I looked at the Commissioner in astonishment and fury. I indicated my disgust in round terms – the matters in the patrol reports indicated no action not capable of perfectly innocent explanation.[8]

There was also around this time a rumour that also incited Dunstan's annoyance: that he was appointing himself Chief Justice after Napier's retirement. He had to seek a special meeting of the Law Society to make it clear that he had no interest in being Chief Justice.[9]

Bray was not only Dunstan's choice, but also the most outstanding candidate. Bray had excelled across the complete range of jurisdictions: in criminal, matrimonial, corporate, taxation and constitutional matters. He also held a Doctor of Laws degree, having submitted his thesis by his twenty-fourth birthday. He also had the advantage of

---

7   Interview with Brian Medlin, 19 October 2002.
8   Dunstan, p. 133. Homosexual acts were a crime then in South Australia.
9   Len King, *Unpublished Memoirs*, "The Practice of the Law", p. 52.

time on his side, as he was at least ten years younger than Nelligan and Chamberlain.

Don Dunstan had also been inspired to appoint John Bray Chief Justice because of his enormous erudition outside the law. Not only had Bray achieved a significant legal reputation, he had also been the author of a book of poetry and of several plays – for one of which, *Papinian*, Don Dunstan had been the actors' representative over a decade before. Bray was a dedicated and passionate scholar of Latin and Greek literature and culture. As a result, he had a panoramic vision of history and had little time for the fashions of the day, moral as well as sartorial. His historic perspective of humanity made him tolerant of the spectrum of its shortcomings. His erudition meant that he had the capacity to look beyond the limits of his own direct personal experience. His personality was multi-faceted. Brian Medlin found that over the forty five years he knew Bray that he was a "(…) distinguished jurist, and yet larrikin; ironical, sceptical, absolutist."[10]

He became Chief Justice of South Australia during a period in which colonial attitudes still lingered, but signs of change were increasingly more apparent. One very visible example was that in 1965, Labor won power for the first time in over thirty years, and thus ended Sir Thomas Playford's record twenty-seven years as Premier. Roma Mitchell was then appointed Australia's first female Supreme Court judge. In 1966, Prime Minister Sir Robert Menzies retired after an almost parallel leadership to Playford's, and Australia exchanged the Imperial currency system for the dollar. Don Dunstan took over the Premiership from Frank Walsh in May 1967 and Steele Hall had succeeded Playford. Both men were almost thirty years younger than their predecessors. The old guard – most of whom had been born under Queen Victoria – was finally yielding to the new. Perhaps the most noticeable change that year for many South Australians to their daily lives took place on the 26 September: that was the first evening since 1915 they could drink in a hotel after 6pm.

John Bray broke a few traditions immediately on taking office. He believed that the executive and judicial arms of government were

---

10   Brian Medlin, "Papinian: Birth of a Poet", in Wilfrid Prest (ed.), *A Portrait of John Bray*, p. 143.

best kept apart, and so Sir Mellis remained Lieutenant-Governor.[11] He did not wear a hat, a startling thing to do then. He was not a member of the Adelaide Club as had been all the previous Supreme Court judges, nor a Freemason. His preferred club was the Amateur Sports Club. It was barely a hundred metres down the road from the Adelaide Club in the basement of number 175 North Terrace,[12] but miles apart in terms of its ethos. John Bray also enjoyed drinking in front bars and catching the tram or bus – in other words, public transport – down to Glenelg or Henley Beach. He would continue to do so until towards the end of his life.

So, in his own way, Bray embodied some of the changes taking place in the general community, at least in the relaxation of strict behavioural codes in public. Uniquely, he also partly embodied Adelaide's conservative ruling-class background that resisted many of these changes. A photograph published by *The News* shows him outside his home the day after he was sworn in (1 March 1967). The photograph shows the grand façade of Bray House, as it became known, which had been owned by the Bray family for three generations. His grandfather, Sir John Cox Bray, had bought it around the time he began his term as South Australia's first native-born Premier in 1881.[13]

The house had been built on an original town acre in Hutt Street – now number 60. As a cottage in 1840, it was the temporary home for Captain Grey while he was waiting to replace Governor Gawler. In 1847, the cottage was dwarfed by a new house designed by Sir George Strickland

Bray's grandfather, Sir John Cox Bray (1842-1894). (SLSA)

---

11   Although Bray did act twice as Deputy Governor in 1968. Graham Loughlin, p. A24.

12   Now part of the Myer Centre's North Terrace façade.

13   Sir John's government – from 1881 to 1884 – was the first stable government in 27 years in South Australia. In that time there had been 32 changes of government. See Colin Bond & Hamish Ramsey (eds.), *Preserving Historic Adelaide*. Adelaide:Rigby, 1978, pp. 139-147; Peter Ward, "John Bray in Adelaide", in Wilfrid Prest (ed.), *Portrait of John Bray*, Adelaide: Wakefield, 1997, p. 2.

Kingston, formerly Deputy Surveyor-General under Colonel Light. Later, Speaker of the House of Assembly, Sir George was the father of Premier Charles Kingston. Sir George had also designed Ayer's House, still

Bray House, Hutt Street ca. 1890s. (SLSA)

standing on North Terrace.

It was Sir John Cox Bray who decided to transform the newer Hutt Street house into a mansion, by adding a large, ornate front wing. His architect was Rowland Rees, who also designed the Newmarket,

Cumberland Arms and Tivoli Hotels.[14] The result is one of Adelaide's best examples of late Victorian Italianate architecture, with no expense spared on its ornate details. The interior was rich in intricately moulded architraves and ceilings, and the hall was dominated by two giant panelled doors that opened to reveal the sumptuously furnished dining room.

Sir John lived only a few years in his new Italian-inspired mansion before he and his wife, Alice, moved to London where he was Agent-

General for South Australia. Near Sri Lanka on the way home in 1894, Sir John died and was buried at sea. Alice, Lady Bray, returned to live in the house in grand style until her death in 1935. She also outlived her daughter Blanche – who would have been John Bray's aunt. Blanche married John Lavington Bonython, son of the sole owner of *The Advertiser* and was mother to his heir, John Langdon Bonython, but died in childbirth in 1908.

Alice, Lady Bray, died 1935. (SLSA)

It has been said that the greatest achievement of Sir John Cox Bray's son Harry was being the "carrier" between his high-achieving father and son. After failing medicine at the University of Melbourne, he tried a variety of occupa-

---

14   Colin Bond and Hamish Ramsey, p. 141. Rees also designed Shakespeare Chambers, the building that housed Genders, Wilson & Bray on Waymouth St.

tions with no special success, including stockbroking and fruit-growing. He and his family occupied at least four addresses in Adelaide and one in the country before Lady Alice died in 1935. John had lived with his grandmother before his family moved in.

John Bray's mother, Gertrude, had also come from one of Adelaide's early leading families, the Stows. Her grandfather, Thomas Stow, had established the one of State's first churches on North Terrace. Her uncle, Randolph Stow, was Attorney-General three times and a judge of the Supreme Court from 1875 to his death in 1878. Overseas, the Stow family extended back to the prominent Randolph and Jefferson families in Virginia, USA. John Bray could count among his ancestors both Thomas Jefferson, the third U.S. President – after whom he received his middle name – and an American Indian chief's daughter, Pocahontas.[15]

John Bray was born in Wayville on the 16 September 1912, began primary school at Glenelg, and continued it at Sevenhill in the Clare Valley, four kilometres from the family home at Penwortham. His sister Nance Rowena (Ro) was born at Glenelg in 1919 and his brother Robert (Bill) Stow, in 1923 at Penwortham. John remembered with fondness in a 1985 interview that he and Ro used to ride a pet pony while

John Bray in around 1914. (SLSA)

they were at Penwortham.[16] John's happy childhood in the country ended before that of his sister and brother. When he turned thirteen, following the tradition of Adelaide's Anglican élite, Harry Bray sent him to board at St Peter's College and commence his secondary studies.

---

15   Pocahontas lived from 1595-1617 and was the mother of one son. Nevertheless, as John Bray reported in a review of a book on her life, she has now at least two million descendants. This book review was in *The Australian Weekend Magazine*, 21-22 January 1996, p. 7.

16   Peter Ward, pp. 2-3. See also Interview with Beate Josephi, 24 May 1985. SLSA Archival Collection OH 651/3.

John was obviously hurt by this abrupt ending to his childhood, as sixty years later in a poem dedicated to a pet pigeon being delivered to a vet, he compared himself then to the helpless bird:

> But I remember being driven for the first time to boarding school,
> Stiff in blue serge, prickled by strange underwear, neck yoked in celluloid,
> Praying that God would crash my father's car.[17]

Bray's father, Harry Midwinter Bray (1879-1965). (SLSA)

Adolescence would prove a trial for John Bray as he learned the hard reality of being gifted intellectually, at the cost of having few practical skills. This was to the great disappointment of Harry Bray:

Harry did not understand his introspective son, later self-described as "physically clumsy … inept in the handling of tools and an idiot in dealing with machinery". Early in John's adolescence his father sought to "make a man of him" by way of a gift of a set of woodworking tools; they were never used and remained a sour memory. When John turned 16, Harry presented him with a motor cycle and many years later continued to recall the moment of the gift with bewilderment. His son had looked at the gleaming machine for a bare 30 seconds and then, without saying a word, had turned and gone back into the house, never again to express interest in it or driving.[18]

Life at St Peter's College was also difficult, being strongly focussed on conformity and competition, especially in sports. The first couple of years there were the hardest, while the family was still living on the orchard at Penwortham. They moved back to the city, to Col-

---

17   John Bray, "The Crested Pigeon". In *Seventy Seven*, Adelaide: Wakefield, 1990, p. 8.

18   Peter Ward, as above.

lege Park, and happily for John he no longer had to endure the college dormitories.

But it was also at St Peter's that John discovered passions that

The Bray family on the verandah of their home in College Park around 1928. Standing: Harry, John. Sitting: Bill, Rowena and Gertrude. (SLSA).

were going to drive his life: history, literature and poetry. He came to love Horace and Virgil, Scott, Shakespeare, Pope and Tennyson. He especially admired Sir Walter Scott. His school reports show that he was always among the top in his class, though never first. He had, however, been placed in a year ahead of his age, so he was always younger than his classmates. In the Lent Term ending in May 1926, the report describes his age as 13 $7/12$, against an average age of 14 $7/12$. His marks and his placing for each subject out of classes of 35 were:

Scripture	91 (%)	1st
English	78	3rd
Latin	80	4th
French	66	11th
History	64	3rd
Maths	79	2nd
Chemistry	47	13th

His final placing in this year, the equivalent to the current Year ten, was third. The Headmaster's overall comment was: "A good trier, a satisfactory place". One of his fellow students at this time was Cedric

Isaachsen, who only retired a year or two before this book was published. Another student, two years older but in the same level, was the
then Justice Napier's son, Robert.

The following term, John's Latin dropped down to 44 per cent
while his Maths peaked at 100 per cent completely belying any predictions that someone may have been tempted to make about his future.
In his final term in Leaving Honours in 1928, then aged "16 $^3/_{12}$", his
Latin still looked mediocre - 45 per cent. Nevertheless, his overall place-
ment that year was second. The Headmaster comments that: "But for
his Latin he would have been head of the school. His other literary subjects are all very good." John's marks were good enough to get a scholarship to the University of Adelaide the following year, where he would
be studying law. He would have much preferred to study literature for
a Bachelor of Arts degree, but his parents advised him that law would
provide him with a better living. Harry and Gertrude Bray lived to see
their career advice justified, financially at least. John Bray's first book of
poetry, published in 1962, produced royalties in its first full year totalling fifty three pounds. His income from Genders Wilson and Bray that
year as Queen's Counsel exceeded seven thousand pounds.[19]

By that first year at university, John Bray had probably discovered
that, while he had been born with the disadvantages of being clumsy
and seriously short-sighted, he also had talents which would enable him
to excel not only in law, but in a variety of literary endeavours and still
have ample time for a legendary social life. One important talent was
that he could read rapidly and remember what he read, including page
numbers, with photographic accuracy. The second was that he needed
very little sleep, which gave him a much longer waking day. Even during the few hours a night that he was in bed, he would frequently wake
and read.

At the end of 1929, he attended the University Concert and
went to a party after that. He drank several glasses of wine and beer
and did not get home until dawn. In his own words: "A new world was
opening before me."[20] Most importantly, he did not suffer a hangover,
and as far as Brian Medlin is aware, never did. This capacity, together
with the minimal need for sleep, meant that, as Medlin recounts, Bray
could drink on a Saturday night until two or three in the morning, and

---

19   SLSA Archival Collection, PRG1098/39.
20   Article in *The Advertiser*, 4 January 1986.

still be up at eight and "read a pile of books that most people would consider a library". The combination of all these abilities – photographic reading and memory, minimal sleep requirements and being unaffected by alcohol – permitted John Bray to lead the equivalent of two full lives at once.

During his university years in the 1930s, he developed a lifestyle that matched his abilities. He dedicated his days to the study and practice of law, and became so absorbed by it that he continued his studies to write a thesis for the Doctorate of Laws.[21] This was such as a rare thing

A club dinner in the 1930s, possibly the Double X (XX) or Savage. John Bray is seated second from left. (SLSA)

to do that when he became Chancellor of the University of Adelaide thirty years after its completion, he was still the last person to have done it. But what the doctorate really illustrates is the depth to which John Bray is led to explore when a subject intellectually stimulates him. He won the Bonython Prize for the doctorate, and he donated the money from it to a poor family – the Depression was still lingering – so their son could start his education at St Peter's College.

---

21   The title of the thesis is *Bankruptcy and the Winding-up of Companies in Private International Law*. Submitted September 1936, awarded June 1937.

Simultaneously with his study of law, he maintained his voracious reading. He preferred to read authors in their original language. Having learnt French and Latin at school, he spent six months teaching himself ancient Greek during his law studies. Later, he must have also taught himself German. If one can gauge from the translations and responses that he later published with his poetry collections, the poets and writers that he admired included Ronsard, Musset, Villon, Heine, Bergengruen, Archilocus, Alcaeus, Xenophanes, Sophocles, Plato, Virgil and Catullus.

During this period, he also discovered clubs and hotels - especially the former - since these were still the days of six o'clock closing for hotels. The club he would remain most attached to was the Amateur Sports Club of South Australia. The club was founded by a group of males, mostly under 25, on 1 January 1932 and was located for its first four years on the top floor of the LCL building, 175 North Terrace, now part of the Myer complex. From the middle of 1936, the club relocated to the basement of this building, where it remained until 1976.

John Bray also was an enthusiastic member of the XX Club, which had been founded in 1927, and described itself on its Memorandum of Association as: "being a club duly licensed and registered at the Police Court, Adelaide, and thus above the law till 11pm". Its main object, according to the Memo, was "BEER" – in capitals – and its capital was one million gallons. Its membership proposal form asked the following questions:

> Can you hold your liquor?
> If so, how much and for how long?
> Have you ever been sober?
> If so, why?[22]

This satirical treatment of South Australia's strict liquor laws at the time appealed no doubt to the larrikinism in John Bray that Brian Medlin mentions. In 1934 its president was Eustace A Genders and the

---

22   SLSA Archival Collection, PRG1098/85. The club liked themes to its dinners and in 1936, based one around motoring: "The Last Lap". The guests included "Krankcase Wilson" and "Gas O Lean Genders", both partners of the law firm to which John Bray was a partner himself. The menu listed dishes such as "throttle soup", "piston poisson" and "nuts and bolts" to finish.

secretary was Langdon Bonython.[23] Eustace Genders was a partner in the law firm where Bray worked and Langdon Bonython was his cousin, born to his aunt Blanche, Lavington Bonython's first wife, who had died in 1908.

It was through the Wilson connection that John Bray joined Genders Wilson and Pellew as an articled clerk to Keith Wilson (later Sir Keith) in 1930. Keith Wilson had married John Bray's cousin Elizabeth (daughter of Harry's sister Blanche and Lavington Bonython). The firm had been established in the 1880s and was then in Selbourne Chambers at 40 Pirie Street, which since has been demolished. Bray was admitted as a legal practitioner in 1933, and stayed with the firm until he was appointed Chief Justice.

Bray began appearing in court early in his legal career. His name first appears in the South Australian law reports in 1935. He was assisting Eustace Genders in a personal injuries case before Acting Justice Geoffrey Reed – *Deed v Liddle*.[24] The trial took place on 8 July 1935, when Bray was still only twenty-two. The result was not, however, a triumph: their client was found liable.

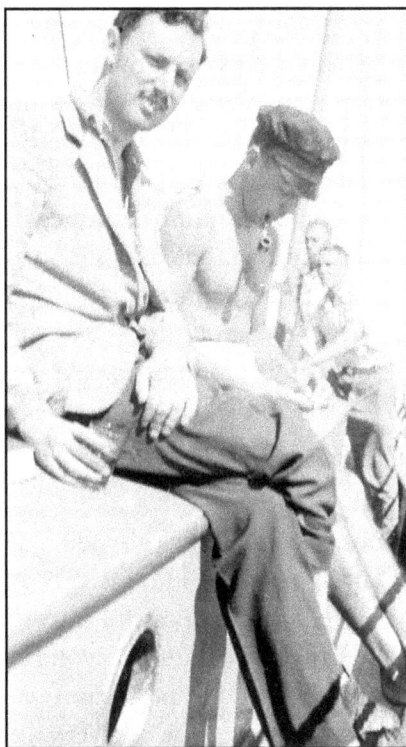

John Bray with friends on a boat. (SLSA)

The following month he appeared alone before Acting Justice Reed, representing the wife in a defended divorce.[25] The case was

---

23   John Langdon Bonython was born in 1905. His grandfather, who became the sole proprietor of Adelaide's daily paper *The Advertiser,* also had the same name and lived from 1848 to 1939. His father, John Lavington Bonython, lived from 1875 to 1960.

24   [1935] SASR 188.

25   *Hopkins v Hopkins.* [1935] SASR 295. Divorce was regulated by state laws until 1959, and was fault-based until 1976.

not clear-cut, as although the wife was suing for divorce on the basis of her husband's adultery, she did in fact admit to having herself committed adultery many times. The difference was that she had her husband's consent. This time, Bray did win and obtained the decree for divorce sought by his client. In South Australia, the law allowed for "adultery condoned", as the result of legislation passed in 1857, and so the wife's adultery was – legally at least – faultless.

During this time he had also begun the massive academic exercise of his doctoral thesis. It is entitled *Bankruptcy and the Winding Up of Companies in Private International Law* and uses its particular focus as a means of studying the broader problem of the conflict of laws between countries. This took him three years and he submitted it in September 1936. He won the Bonython prize for it and was admitted to the degree formally in June 1937. The following month, he set off on a six-month tour of Europe, given to him by his parents. Peter Ward gives more details of this, but one factor that stands out as an illustration of John Bray's family background is the cost of the fare: one hundred and forty-two pounds.[26] Ward mentions that the average wage at this time was four pounds a week. As a comparison, in 1937 the family of Bray's successor, Len King, was living on just one pound a week from his father's pension.

John Bray's life at this point appears to conform to his upper class family origins. He was very bright academically, and those around him predicted a successful career in law. But John Bray had a need for intellectual stimulation beyond even what his own deep study of the law provided. The possession of a Doctor of Laws set him apart from his peers in the practice of law, but it is more likely that John Bray did his doctoral thesis with the aim of becoming an academic rather than remaining in practice. After his return from overseas, he began to apply for university positions. In 1939 he applied for the chair in Roman Law, Jurisprudence, Constitutional Law, International Law and Conflict of Laws at Victoria University College in Wellington, New Zealand. Despite his rare qualifications – and references from the Professor of Law at the University of Adelaide Arthur Campbell, Justice Angas Parsons, Justice Mellis Napier, Keith Wilson and George Ligertwood KC – John

---

26   Peter Ward, pp. 7-8.

The Registrar,
    University of Sydney,
        SYDNEY,   N.S.W.

Dear Sir,

        I hereby make application for appointment to the
Chair of Jurisprudence and International Law in the
University of Sydney.

        My name is John Jefferson Bray.   I am 28 years of
age being born on the 12th September 1912.   I am unmarried.
I received the ordinary degree of Bachelor of Laws in the
University of Adelaide in 1932, the Honours degree in 1933
and the degree of Doctor of Laws in 1937.   This degree
was awarded for a thesis on "Bankruptcy & the Winding up
of Companies in Private International Law".   I received
the Stow Prize in 1930 and the David Murray Prize in 1931
and 1932.   In October 1933 I was admitted as a barrister
and solicitor of the Supreme Court of South Australia.
In March 1935 I became a partner in the firm of Genders,
Wilson & Pellew of Selborne Chambers, Pirie Street, Adelaide
and I have practised as a barrister and solicitor and a
partner of that firm ever since.   I am the lecturer in
Jurisprudence (including Roman Law) in the University of
Adelaide for the year 1941.

        I might add that I was rejected from the A. I. F. in
June 1940 on the ground of defective eyesight.   I was
rejected as medically unfit for the militia on the same
ground in March of this year.
        I enclose herewith testimonials obtained by me from
my partner, Senator Wilson, (now serving with the A. I. F.)
from Professor Campbell of the University of Adelaide,
Mr. G. C. Ligertwood, K. C. and their Honours Mr. Justice
Angas Parsons and Mr. Justice Napier of the Supreme Court
of South Australia at a time when I applied for the Chair
of Law at Victoria University College, Wellington, New
Zealand.

    Reference can be made to Professor Campbell or

The first page of Bray's draft application for the vacant Chair of Law at Sydney, late 1940. (SLSA)

Bray did not succeed in this application or in any other he made over the next ten years.[27]

He did, however, become a part-time lecturer at the University of Adelaide in 1942. He had been rejected by the Armed Forces in June 1940 because of his short-sightedness and was therefore able to fill in for Ralph Hague, who had gone off to war. He initially taught Hague's sub-

---

27   Roma Mitchell, "Dr John Bray and the University of Adelaide", *Portrait of John Bray*, pp 21-23.

jects – Jurisprudence and Roman Law. A few years later, in 1946, John Bray applied to teach the Criminal Law course, but the position was given to Roderic Chamberlain. Nevertheless, until he was appointed Chief Justice more than twenty years later, John Bray continued to teach Roman Law at the University of Adelaide's Law School.[28]

As well as teaching law part-time, John Bray joined the Libraries Board at the age of thirty-two in September 1944. His youth was a novelty to the other members then, but what made him a valuable person to be involved in the executive decisions of the State Library of South Australia was the fact that he probably used the library more than any other person. He was reappointed to the Board again and again and would stay almost forty-three years. The Reference Library was named after him in February 1987 when he finally retired.

The year he joined was an exciting period for the State Library as they were just preparing to introduce borrowing rights. The Board had already made the decision to open the Adelaide Lending Service a year before John Bray became a member, and it was intended that during the transition to a borrowing system, books could also be borrowed from the reference collection. Although borrowing from the reference collection was only intended to be temporary after lending began in 1946, it lasted until 1982. Over the years, John Bray would often use his ability as an expert professional advocate to ward off arguments from staff who were finding it increasingly difficult to answer queries when the books they needed were out.[29]

During the 1940s John Bray also became a regular participant on a radio programme called "Information Please", and thus became known to the general public. These were the days before television arrived in Adelaide and radio was therefore the major medium of home entertainment. "Information Please" was produced by Radio 5AD and listeners sent in questions for the participants to answer. There were also regular quiz competitions, for which John Bray would regularly supply hundreds of questions and answers. The young Dr Bray impressed his listeners with his knowledge and ability to work out problems, although, as Brian Medlin discovered later, the answers were supplied in advance.

---

28   For more details on John Bray's lecturing, see Arthur Rogerson's chapter in
       Wilfrid Prest (ed.), *Portrait of John Bray*, pp. 39-48.
29   For more details on John Bray's involvement with the Libraries Board, consult
       Jean Whyte's chapter in *Portrait of John Bray*, pp. 115-127.

John Bray's appearance on radio and his teaching jurisprudence and Roman Law were important activities in his life at this stage, but a friendship he struck up during his university years would have a pivotal effect on the course of his life. This was with Adelaide-born poet Charles Rischbieth Jury.

Jury was born in Glenelg in 1893 and had a father who recognised and encouraged his talents as a poet. Thus he was able to publish his first work of poetry at the age of thirteen in 1906: *Spring is Coming and Other Poems*. He went to St Peter's College in Adelaide and then Magdalen College, Oxford, to study Arts. While he was there, war broke out with Germany and he went to fight in France, where he was severely wounded. He obtained his degree at Oxford and from then was able to live on a private income and write poetry. He lived mainly in Greece and Sicily for the next twenty years, with a brief sojourn in Adelaide in the early 1930s. He lectured in English at the University of Adelaide during this period. By this time, he had published two other books of poetry (one jointly) and a verse play. John Bray may have met Jury then – perhaps in 1932 when he gave a lecture at the Adelaide branch of the English Association on T. S. Eliot's *The Waste Land*.[30]

Jury left again to travel through Europe and return to Greece. In 1937, he wrote to Bray in England, inviting him to Athens, but Bray was unable to go. Jury moved back to Adelaide permanently in 1938, thereby, as Peter Ward remarks, "providing John with an intellectual companionship in sharp contrast to that of the roisterers in his clubs".

The return of Jury was a turning point in John Bray's life, and would also breathe new life into Adelaide's literary culture. Jury was also responsible for the title of a poetry magazine that appeared then: *Angry Penguins*, first published by a group of students including Max Harris (1921-1995) in 1941. According to Alan Brissenden, Jury had been listening to Harris reading one of his poems where he used the term to describe drunken youths in evening suits:

> We know no mithridatum of despair
> as drunks, the angry penguins of the night,
> straddling the cobbles of the square,
> tying a shoelace by fogged lamplight.[31]

---

30   John Bray, *The Emperor's Doorkeeper*, p. 20.
31   Alan Brissenden, "Max Harris: A Life and its Legacy", in *The Age*, 4 February 1995, Books p. 8. See also Geoffrey Dutton, *Out in the Open*, p. 85.

Jury interrupted Harris: "That's exactly what you young icono-
clasts are – angry penguins!" Harris's co-editor, Donald Kerr, suddenly
knew what to call their magazine, and not only that, Charles Jury also
funded its first one or two issues. Many years later – after 1958 – Harris
would become a friend of Bray.

Another poet who would become a long-term friend of John
Bray began a poetry magazine in 1941 out in the northern South Australian country, in an Education Department house in the tiny settlement of Hammond. Flexmore Hudson began publishing his poetry
quarterly, helped by his wife, Merele Desmond. Hudson was employed
as a teacher, and he eventually moved to Adelaide. Some of his early
contributors include A. D. Hope, James McAuley and Judith Wright.
By September 1944 he was able to pay his poets, and in 1945 the magazine went international as *Poetry: an International Quarterly of Verse*. It
went all the way to gaining the second largest circulation in the Eng-
lish-speaking world, and then, in 1947, Great Britain banned the im-
portation of Australian magazines. Flexmore Hudson by this time had
become ill, most likely from the huge load of teaching, writing and
publishing, and so the magazine finished.

In 1944 *Angry Penguins* published a special autumn issue devoted to the deceased poet Ern Malley. Max Harris and his associates
at the time did not know that Ern Malley did not exist, but was the
fabrication of James McAuley and Harold Stewart. These two poets
believed that the surrealist poetry favoured by *Angry Penguins* produced
images that, while striking, were ultimately mechanical and meaning-
less. They wanted to show Harris and his supporters how easy it was
to reproduce them. Nevertheless, the hoaxers were too good as poets to
write bad poetry.

The Ern Malley affair drew an enormous amount of attention to
the fact that South Australians did actually write poetry. It was helped
as well by the fact that Max Harris, as editor, was fined five pounds
with twenty-one pounds eleven shillings costs for publishing indecent
material. The affair was news as far as America and England. It has
been the subject of at least ten books, and the Ern Malley poems have
never been out of print - ironic, given the usual fate of poems written
by "real" poets, although McAuley is not forgotten. Adelaide became
a centre of a literary and cultural renaissance at this time. Ern Malley

is listed as a poet in an anthology published forty years later, launched by John Bray.[32]   Other poets and authors who began publishing then include Geoffrey Dutton, Colin Thiele, Brian Medlin, Alister Kershaw, Nancy Cato, Ian Mudie and Brian Elliott. Eventually, John Bray would join them.

It was in this period, the 1940s, that John Bray settled into a rhythm and structure of life that he would more or less maintain for his life. He worked "rapidly and incessantly" during the week,[33] only occasionally working back late.[34] His photographic recall was a huge advantage in speeding up the pace of his work. Two or three nights a week he would be out at dinners and parties. Saturday afternoons would be spent at the South Australia Hotel and Saturday nights, at the Amateur Sports Club. On Sunday, he liked to take the tram down to Glenelg or Henley Beach or Grange (bus after 1959) with a book. Brian Medlin confirms that John Bray was a very poor swimmer, as he was "uniformly incompetent at all forms of physical activity".

At regular intervals, he would lecture at the University of Adelaide and attend Library Board meetings. His life was firmly based in the Adelaide CBD with suburban outings, and only rarely did he travel outside South Australia. After his return from Europe in 1938, he did not again leave Australia until 1974. As he said to Beate Josephi in 1985, he was a "city-urban type". Everything he liked – the public and university libraries, theatres, pubs and the courts – was within walking distance of his homes, Bray House, and later, 39 Hurtle Square.

The increasing importance of his work representing clients in the courts shows in the reported cases of the Supreme Court. At first, during the 1930s, his name appears rarely, and then from the 1940s, it appears at a steadily increasing rate. His early cases were mainly in the Family Law jurisdiction, divorces being much harder to get before 1976, when all that has been required since is a year's separation. Bray was a

---

32   Pearson, K F and Churches, Christine (eds.) *The Orange Tree: South Australian Poetry to the present day*. The title of the book is from a poem by John Bray.

33   The description later used of him by the Hon. Charles Bright QC, in "Bray in Context", *Adelaide Law Review*, Vol. 7, January 1980, No. 1 (pp. 7-18), p.14.

34   Letter from his secretary at Genders Wilson and Bray, Ms Mona Patterson, 11 January 2003.

true believer in the cab-rank rule.[35] He argued for wife or for husband; who were accusing or defending acts of adultery, desertion or cruelty.

For example, in Bray's defence of the husband in *Snelling v Snelling*,[36] his client, Mr Snelling, had been charged with habitual cruelty by his wife who was suing for divorce. The cruelty was proven, but John Bray argued that the wife had condoned the cruelty, as the couple had had sexual relations up until two days before she left him. Justice Richards did not agree with this argument and gave the wife her order for divorce. Bray's argument in this case appears insensitive to the wife, but later the same year, he represented a wife who had been the victim of repeated cruelty in *Hedges v Hedges*.[37] Mrs Hedges had been granted her divorce but was now seeking custody of the four children. The complication was that she had also assaulted her husband, throwing stones at him and striking him with a hoe. But Bray argued successfully before Justice Mayo that this behaviour was provoked by anger and disappointment in her husband, and not because she was normally prone to such outbursts of violence.

John Bray's first criminal appeal win to appear in the official reports is *Davies v O'Sullivan*, in 1948.[38] Davies had been convicted of sly grog selling by a special magistrate. The case illustrates the curious logic that used to govern Adelaide's licensing laws at this time. Bray's client, Mr Davies, had conducted his own defence before the Special Magistrate and had been convicted of selling alcoholic liquor without a licence. The Crown's case depended strongly on the evidence given by Mr Nettoon, who testified that he had bought two bottles of wine from Mr Davies. Although it does not say so in the report, it seems that the situation had been set up by the police, as Mr Davies's premises was searched immediately after the alleged purchase by two police officers who happened to be in the lane observing the sale. Nevertheless, the magistrate had not needed either their evidence nor Mr Nettoon's in order to convict Mr Davies. There were two people with Mr Davies inside and according to section 267 of the Licensing Act 1932-1945:

---

35   See Michael Abbott, "Bray as Barrister", in *Portrait of John Bray*, p.51.
36   [1944] SASR 148.
37   [1944] SASR 266.
38   [1948] SASR 9. See pp. 10 and 11 for the quotes that follow.

(…) where in any complaint it is alleged that liquor has been sold . . . on the premises specified in the complaint, the presence therein of two or more persons shall be *prima facie* evidence of such as sale.

This Act does not seem to have been drafted with any notion of the presumption of innocence. The appeal came before Chief Justice Sir Mellis Napier, who, as we will see in the following chapter, eventually would grow tired of having to interpret liquor licensing regulations and issue a judgment that would force a Royal Commission. In this case, the Chief Justice was impressed that he could rely on Bray:

(…) I am indebted to Dr Bray for an interesting argument upon the construction and application of s. 267(4). If it had been necessary to deal with all the points that were raised, I should have taken the time to consider my judgment. But the one point, upon which I think that I can dispose of the appeal, is Dr Bray's submission that s. 267(4) is inapplicable to the circumstances of this case.

Section 267 (4) applied only if the alleged sale took place "on" the premises. Bray argued that because Nettoon had not been allowed inside – possibly as he was of part-Aboriginal descent – and was handed the bottles outside in the lane, therefore the alleged sale took place "from" the premises, not "on" them. In such circumstances, the presence of two people had no bearing. Sir Mellis did not consider that the remaining testimony was reliable, as the search by the police had shown nothing to back up their allegations, most notably the existence of any wine corresponding to what Mr Nettoon claimed to have bought there.

Towards the end of 1950, a young poet called Brian Medlin arrived back in Adelaide. Medlin had grown up in the western Adelaide suburbs during the Depression, where his father worked twelve-hour shifts in a factory. After a period training as a teacher, he had left for the bush. He drove cattle, broke horses, ran brumbies, shot kangaroos – and during this time read widely and enormously, and wrote poetry.

Another young poet, Michael Taylor, introduced Brian Medlin to Charles Jury, and shortly after that brief meeting, Jury organised a dinner with Medlin and Bray. Jury was nineteen years older than Bray; Bray was fifteen years older than Medlin. The three clicked, and the dinner continued until the early hours of the following morning. Bray and Medlin found that, beyond their common appreciation of good literature, they had completely different ideas on almost everything, and took a great deal of mutual pleasure arguing about them. That night all three men forged lifetime friendships. Bray wrote a poem many years later on the topics they discussed, "To Brian Medlin", published in *Poems 1961-1971*:

To Brian Medlin (verses 2 and 5 of 7)

We talked drama, theme and plot,
Whether God exists or not,
Virgil, metrics, short and long,
The ultimate of right and wrong.

(…)

Courts, politics, academies,
Committees, personalities,
Sex and the police: then tired of this,
Fell to self-analysis.[39]

Bray's friendship with Brian Medlin would expose him to a much wider world view than he may have otherwise known. Where Charles Jury preferred only to discuss topics amicably, Medlin was fearlessly disputatious. He had grown up in a family which had encouraged passionate opinions. Bray's family had been nothing like that, but he had discovered a talent for argument in his experience as a lawyer. Medlin came from the working class and saw the world from the factory floor. Bray's family owned investment property and lived from it.

The class distinction worked like a magnetic pull: attracting both men to each other yet continually maintaining them poles apart. Medlin never believed that Bray ever really came to an understanding of

---

39   John Bray, *Poems 1961-1971*, p. 27.

the struggle of the working classes, but Bray did mitigate his inherited conservative views. If he never came properly to understand life outside his own privileged position, he understood its existence. This at least partly explains his landmark success in, as one example, the Carbone murder trial which we discuss later. It also may explain his more lenient sentencing approach in criminal trials as Chief Justice.

Bray and Medlin would frequently stay late at Charles Jury's. John Bray was very strict about not breaking any laws himself, and was deeply offended if he was presumed to be doing so. In the early fifties, Jury moved from North Terrace to Archer Street, and Brian Medlin got married and moved into the servants' quarters at the back of Bray House on Hutt Street. Often the two would go to Jury's place after work, and frequently would stay as late as three o'clock the following morning. Brian Medlin recounts how on one of these mornings, he and Bray were stopped on the way home by a patrol.

The officer in the passenger side asked, "Don't you blokes ever sleep?", to which Medlin replied: "When we feel like it." This appears to have been the sort of the response the officer was fishing for. He yelled: "Come over here! Who the fuck do you think you are? I'm talking to you bastards."

John Bray was infuriated by this unjustified intrusion. He walked up to the car and began pounding on the roof: "Who are we? I am Dr Bray, the solicitor. What right have you to molest us like this?"

"We've got every right in the world."

"You may know the law better than I do, but I doubt it."

"Well, the inspector told us…"

"What did the inspector tell you?" interrupted Bray.

"He told us to stop everyone after midnight."

Bray boomed: "Is there a curfew in this city?"

Bray continued: "I'll think about this in the morning. You may hear more of this. You'll be fortunate if you don't." He paused, a tactic often employed by the police: "On your way!" The police left, with a dramatic squealing of tyres.

Bray must surely be one of the few judges in Australian history who had personal experience of being stopped and treated in this way by police. Experiences such as these gave him an insight into the way South Australian police officers operated then. This is why he often challenged their oral evidence in court. Until then, judges had generally accepted police evidence without question. Many years later, as the result of a Vietnam war demonstration led by Brian Medlin, the Dunstan government introduced legislation in 1972 to make the Police Commissioner answerable to Cabinet.

In 1952, Brian Medlin and Charles Jury began writing verse plays, confidently inspired by the predictions of T. S. Eliot and Christopher Fry that "contemporary English verse was about to make a come-back on stage".[40] Bray's response to Jury and Medlin writing plays was: "why not me, too?", and at the age of forty-one, he began writing his verse play *Papinian*. In so doing, he finally yielded to his calling as a poet.

The dramatic substance of *Papinian* covered two of John Bray's passions: law and classical Rome. Its main character, Papinian, was an accomplished Roman jurist who had been a great friend and advisor of Emperor Severus (193-211 AD). When Severus died in Britain, his son Caracalla took over. Caracalla, who was twenty-three years old, killed his brother Geta in front of their mother to ensure he would rule alone. He demanded that his father's life-time friend, Papinian – now approaching his seventies – produce a speech justifying this murder. Papinian had to decide whether to do so or not, and this is focus of the play. In the end, Papinian refuses and he is killed, along with twenty thousand other people Caracalla believed sided with Papinian.[41]

Bray gave his completed draft of *Papinian* to Charles Jury in 1953. Jury's nine-page critique reveals his immediate recognition of Bray's poetic and dramatic talent:

> You've succeeded in making Papinian a character who is also an intellectual; and that is a thing that very few poets have done at least in English. It's hard to think of one, except Hamlet; and in that as in everything else, Hamlet is an exception.
> (...) I hope you won't mind my saying that your blank verse is an extraordinary phenomenon; I mean it as a compliment. To

---

40   Brian Medlin, "Papinian: Birth of a Poet". Cited above, p 132.
41   *Encyclopaedia Britannica*, http://www.1911encyclopedia.org/Caracalla.

find anything else like its general form one would have to go right back to the beginning of blank verse in English.[42]

Bray's *Papinian*, along with Jury's play *The Administrator* and Medlin's *Governor Bligh,* were performed at the Studio Theatre in North Adelaide in 1955. The director was Colin Ballantyne (1908-1988), who – like Charles Jury and Max Harris – was responsible for nurturing Adelaide's literary movement in that period. Ballantyne was a professional photographer and amateur theatre director who held a monthly open-house for interested writers, academics and others to meet, and read poems or plays.[43]

Graham Nerlich played Papinian, and the actors' representative on the board of Ballantyne's Company of Players was Don Dunstan – then twenty-eight years old.[44] According to Brian Medlin, who attended each performance, audience reaction varied and Bray received the better reviews. Barbara Wall reckoned the season successful for all three playwrights.[45]

Bray's success as a poet and playwright was parallel to his increasing reputation as a barrister. On 28 March 1957, he was appointed Queen's Counsel.

In the preceding two months, he had been busy with his first murder trial. His client, Mr Fredella, had been accused of killing his defacto wife and then, in February 1957, convicted by a jury before Justice Sir George Ligertwood. John Bray took Mr Fredella's appeal before the Full Court consisting of Sir Mellis Napier and Justices Sir Geoffrey Reed and Bruce Ross.[46] The appeal took place over three days in the middle of March.

There were three complications which threw doubt on the murder conviction. The first was the role that alcohol played in the tragedy:

42   Letter from Charles Jury to John Bray, 8 March 1953, SLSA Archival Collection, South Australia, PRG1098/1/36.

43   *Governor Bligh* in April; *The Administrator* in June; *Papinian* in August (4 performances) The Studio Theatre is on the corner of Tynte Street and Wellington Square, now part of the Channel Nine complex.

44   See Peter Ward, p.11-13 and Brian Medlin, same volume, pp. 130-131, for more details on Colin Ballantyne.

45   Barbara Wall, "C. R. Jury, Poet of Adelaide." *South Australiana*, vol. 5, no. 2, 1966, pp. 79-114.

46   *R v Fredella* [1957] SASR 102.

both the accused and the victim had been drunk. The second was that the victim suffered from epileptic fits and so the bruises found on her body may have been, at least to some extent, the result of falls sustained when she had them. In other words, it was difficult to prove that the accused, even though he had hit her, had actually delivered fatal blows. The third was that a key witness was Nicola Fredella, the accused's nine-year-old daughter, and being under ten, she was not allowed to swear on oath. As a result of the doubt – particularly because Fredella was drunk – Sir Mellis and his brother judges allowed a new verdict of manslaughter to replace the one for murder. This of course in 1957 meant Fredella was saved from the hangman.

While Bray's star was rising rapidly in this first year as a silk, his rich literary and philosophical life was about to be shaken up. In July 1958, Brian Medlin sailed to England to study at Oxford. On a Saturday afternoon two weeks after Medlin's departure, John Bray found himself worrying about the absence of Charles Jury from the usual eleven-thirty gathering at the South Australian Hotel after his Roman Law lectures. He walked to Jury's home at 210 Archer Street, North Adelaide, and discovered the worst: his great friend was dead.

Bray must have felt very isolated after Medlin's departure and Jury's death. It had only been in the previous twelve months that Jury had invited John Bray finally to come to his Wednesday night poetry readings. Bray took over the poetry group now and "The Poetry" met monthly at his home – Hutt Street and later Hurtle Square – from then until his own death in 1995. Another change to his literary life around this time was that he joined Colin Ballantyne's late-afternoon "school" which met in the Sturt Arcade Hotel on Grenfell Street on Saturday afternoons. Regulars included Neil Lovett, Stuart Luke, David Tippett and Peter Ward. Later, they were joined by Max Harris and his group.

The Stuart Case that was such an influence on Sir Mellis Napier's final years on the bench was also to have an impact on John Bray and his subsequent career. He was not involved formally in the defence of Rupert Max Stuart, although David O'Sullivan and Helen Devaney regularly asked his advice during the preparations for the trial and the appeals. Bray became involved later, in the aftermath of the ensuing Royal Commission after Jack Shand QC walked out.

To recapitulate, that afternoon, 21 August 1959, Adelaide's *The News* produced two posters: "Shand quits 'You won't give Stuart a fair go'"; and later: "Commission breaks up Shand blasts Napier". The headline in that afternoon's front page read: "Mr Shand QC indicts Sir Mellis Napier 'These Commissioners cannot do the job'".

In Parliament a week later, Sir Thomas Playford attacked *The News*'s and Labor's demand for a new Royal Commission – this time without the two judges who heard the appeal. Playford declared that the posters and headlines "are the greatest libel ever made against any judge in this State".[47] He threatened legal action, and on 18 January 1960, Rohan Rivett, editor-in-chief of *The News*, was charged with nine counts of libel: three for each of the two posters, and three for the headline. Each of the three items attracted one count of publishing a seditious libel; one count of publishing a seditious libel knowing it to be false; and one count of publishing a defamatory libel.[48]

John Bray researched the cases and legislation governing seditious libel and developed three main strategies. One was aimed at the concept of malice and designed to demonstrate the complete lack of prior bad motive on Rohan Rivett's part to insult the Chief Justice. Bray asked one witness: "Would you say that on or about the twenty-first of August 1959 Mr Rivett had an unbalanced mind?"; "Did you think that on that date he was seething with malice?"; "Have you ever known him to be seething with malice?"

Bray's second strategy was to show further that the sheer pressure under which the paper operated in order to meet its daily deadlines as an afternoon paper also removed the possibility of Rohan Rivett having any personal motive. He was doing nothing else than informing his readership of this event as he would any other important and newsworthy event.

Bray's third strategy was to draw the attention of the jury to the political motivation of the trial:

It had been conducted, he said, with immoderation. It was the result of a fit of pique on the part of the government. The

---

47   Don Dunstan, pp. 80-81.
48   See also Michael Abbott, "Bray as Barrister", in *Portrait of John Bray*, pp. 56-60.

Premier had said that the *The News* accused the judges of the vilest crimes. This gross exaggeration showed a mind carried away by wounded pride. Why were there *nine* counts? The fact that charges of sedition, since withdrawn, were ever included, suggested the hysteria of those behind the prosecution.[49]

The first sign of success for Bray's defence was when Justice Mayo held that there was no case to answer in respect of the three charges of seditious libel alone. The jury after five hours discussion returned and found Rivett not guilty of the three charges of seditious libel knowing it to be false, and could not agree on the third one. Playford subsequently withdrew it.

The Rivett case more than any other in Bray's career at the bar shows his fearlessness as an advocate. He had, indirectly, appeared against the most senior member of his profession – the Chief Justice – who was also the State's second-ranked citizen as Lieutenant-Governor. He could have elected to defend Rohan Rivett in a manner more likely to preserve the *status quo*. It shows his courage and fearless integrity as an advocate.

Playford's government appears to have taken Bray's dedication to justice over its own interests badly. We mentioned earlier how Police Commissioner McKinna had produced surveillance reports that he hoped would convince Premier Walsh that John Bray was not a fit and proper person to occupy the office of Chief Justice of South Australia. Don Dunstan showed John Bray these reports and Bray later wrote down his reaction to them in a document which is now in his papers held privately:

> I can only conclude from this lamentable epistle that either the police keep a dossier on everyone or everyone of any degree of prominence, or else that I have been singled out for special attention. As the charges seem to centre round a period during which I was professionally engaged in litigation which was likely to be displeasing to the government of the day, I am inclined to prefer the latter supposition.

---

49   Inglis, pp. 288-289.

If that is correct it can hardly be thought that the police would have had me watched and my activities noted on their own initiative. Equally I find it almost impossible to believe that the Commissioner of Police would have approached the Chief Secretary spontaneously. I believe that he was prompted to do this.

Who gave the order? Was it simply a police initiative out of a sense of what their superiors might find acceptable? It is certainly a fact that someone ordered police surveillance of John Bray around the time he accepted the brief to defend Rohan Rivett.

The police reports, according to Dunstan, had suggested that Bray exhibited homosexual behaviour. According to Brian Medlin, Bray was unaware of his homosexual side before his sixtieth birthday, and only after a chance encounter around 1973 did he discover that side of himself. A few years later, around 1976, his circle of friends also learned to their surprise that he had been a father for forty years. Bray's natural son was a regular at one of their clubs.[50]

From the end of the 1950s, John Bray was continuing to develop his literary activities. In 1960, he was vice-president of the South Australian branch of the Fellowship of Australian Writers, with Peter Ward as President. The Fellowship was deeply involved in the Adelaide Festival of Arts Writers' Week in 1960 and 1962. He would give poetry readings at Writers' Week at each festival until his last years. In 1964, he published his first book of poems with Cheshire, entitled simply, *Poems*. This was the first of half a dozen volumes of poetry, and was a mix of his own verse and selected translations of Latin, Greek, French and German poets.

That year he forced a change in attitudes – at least in the courts - towards South Australia's large immigrant population from Italy. Italian immigrants had come to South Australia since its settlement but only in small numbers until after World War II. After the war, the Australian Government offered them assisted passages. Large numbers left eco-nomically devastated Italy and many of these settled in South Australia. The fact that the Italians did not speak English and preferred to socialise

---

50   Bray's private life will feature in more detail in a biography being written by
      this author due to be completed in late 2007.

among themselves left them vulnerable to prejudice from some members of the Anglo-Celtic population.

On 27 July 1964 this prejudice created a tragedy when Leon Kiley attacked Giovanni Carbone, who, in the panic of defending himself, unintentionally killed his attacker.[51] Carbone was twenty-three and Kiley twenty. Kiley was unemployed, and had been drinking all afternoon. He was with a group of friends in Rundle Street (as it was then). He blocked the path of the much smaller Italian who had just left his work on a construction site in Hindley Street and provoked a fight.

More than anything else, it was their cultural differences that led to mutual misunderstanding of each other's behaviour. Kiley – as his friends testified in the trial – liked to provoke fights, but nothing more serious than bullying someone smaller. But Carbone was terrified when the group closed in, and he pulled out his pocket-knife and stabbed frantically. Kiley died and Carbone was charged with his murder.

In the trial before Justice Leo Travers, John Bray highlighted the cultural differences between not only the Italian and his assailants, but also with the police officer who could not even spell Giovanni. He succeeded in getting a policeman to admit in the court that his notes were likely to be incorrect as the result of the language barrier between himself and the accused.[52] He showed that the point was not whether Kiley had genuinely meant serious harm, but that Carbone had genuinely believed he did. Kiley's own friends testified to seeing him punch Carbone several times in the face before the victim pulled out his knife. Bray's real triumph was convincing an all-male, Anglo-Saxon jury of this cultural misunderstanding. They acquitted Carbone of both murder and the alternative, manslaughter.

That year John Bray also tried to prevent Glenn Sabre Valance from being hanged for murder, but without success. Valance became the last person hanged in South Australia, although legislation removing capital punishment was not enacted until 1976. Bray took on Valance's defence at the point of the appeal to the High Court. Until then, Rod Matheson, later appointed to the Supreme Court, represented him.[53] The case had been before Sir Mellis Napier in September 1964, and

---

51   *R v Carbone*, not reported, 1964.
52   Michael Abbott, pp. 60-61
53   Rod Matheson was appointed Queen's Counsel in 1972 and was a Justice of the Supreme Court of South Australia from 1979 until 1998.

the appeal before Justices Mayo, Chamberlain and Travers in October.[54] Rod Matheson had been arguing that his client had a history of psychiatric problems, and since he may not have known that what he was doing was wrong, he should be found not guilty by reason of insanity.

Glenn Valance had shot his former employer, Richard Strang, on 16 June 1964, and then raped his widow next to the shattered corpse. These facts were not in dispute, but his capacity to have known what he was doing was. Valance had worked for the Strangs out on their remote station near Bordertown until December 1963, when he was sacked. Strang refused to pay him his last ten days' wages. Feeling cheated, Valance took a heater, two car seat covers and some records as his own way of compensation.

That seemed to be the end of the matter, but then in June 1964, Mr Strang reported the theft. Valance – by now working on a station near Burra – was arrested. His current employer put up the one hundred pounds bail. But once back at the Burra station, Valance became depressed and tried to shoot himself. That was his third suicide attempt in a few months, and a psychiatrist had already recommended a period in hospital. A few days later, he decided to go to see Strang and frighten him into dropping the charges. Valance said in his unsworn statement that he fired accidentally when Mrs Strang woke and screamed; she said she woke up and screamed because of the gunshot.

That point of difference would have been crucial for a conviction of manslaughter instead of murder. To prove insanity the defence needed psychiatric evidence showing clearly that Valance was not aware of the quality and nature of his act The problem was that Dr Salter - called by the Crown – did believe that Valance was aware of what he was doing. John Bray was unable to convince the High Court when he went to Sydney with Rod Matheson in November and the appeal was dismissed. Glenn Sabre Valance, twenty-one years old, was hanged at Adelaide Gaol on 24 November 1964, just six months after his crime.

Bray's appointment as Chief Justice was featured on the front pages of *The Advertiser* and *The News*, and of course, the details of Commissioner McKinna's attempt at thwarting it were not mentioned. Except for Don Dunstan's allusion to it in *Felicia*, the details of the matter

---

54   *R. v Valance* [1964] SASR 361.

are published for the first time here. Stewart Cockburn's headline in *The Advertiser* on 1 March 1967 was: "A Humanist to Lead the Law". Cockburn compared Bray's persona to the French writer Honoré de Balzac, continuing:

> For SA's new Chief Justice, besides being a notable lawyer, is a poet, playwright, classical scholar – a humanist – and one of the most deeply-read professional men in the Commonwealth.

Later in the year, Max Harris's daughter Samela did a feature on John Bray in *The News*.[55] She believed that *Papinian* had brought him into the public world of theatre and literature in Adelaide. She also mentioned the scores of greetings that Bray had been getting in Hindley Street from the Italian traders who never forgot his brilliant defence of Giovanni Carbone.

Brian Medlin describes one such incident of this adulation that took place on the night of Bray's celebration of being appointed Chief Justice at the Sturt Arcade Hotel. After what Peter Ward calls a "rowdy Falstaffian feast that left publican Peter Whallin's Tap Room in great disarray the following morning",[56] Bray and Medlin ended up in the early hours at a all-night café in a lane off Hindley Street. Bray went in to buy cigarettes. After about twenty minutes Medlin got fed up with waiting:

> I went in. There were several patrons sitting around drinking coffee. John had been delayed by a woman whom I took to be the proprietess. She was saying, "You save my husband. We worship you."
> I said, "For Christ's sake come on. You've had enough worship for one night."

Medlin found that Bray often was stopped in the street or in a hotel by someone who wanted to praise him for his defence of one of their relatives.

---

55   *The News*, 28 August 1967
56   Peter Ward, p. 15.

Rohan Rivett had also maintained contact with Bray, and he wrote him a letter from Melbourne inviting him to stay at his shack at Port Willunga:

> We could have (…) a yarn about your problem of deplayfordising your unfortunate community, johnbraying the Supreme Court and otherwise giving SA a much needed facelift.[57]

Rivett's invitation reveals a general sentiment of that key period in South Australia's history. The State was ready for a change.

The first traces that Bray's influence as Chief Justice would play a key role in the changes that were to sweep South Australia over the coming decade were relatively superficial. According to Don Dunstan, as well as not wearing a hat, he also told the other judges at his first meeting with them:

> I am dyslectic, do not drive a car and when I choose, from time to time, will go by public transport. I do not propose to join the Adelaide Club. And when I wish, during lawful trading hours, to meet my friends in a public house, I shall do so. In fact (looking at his watch), I'm going there now.[58]

Bray would not ever tamper with the traditions and rituals of the court, however. Roma Mitchell, who shared the bench during all of his time, observed that: "[h]e never seemed to flinch from wearing full formal court attire, including knee breeches, ruffles, full-bottomed wig etc., whenever it was appropriate to wear it."[59]

The difference was, that although he expected officers of the court, no matter who they were, to wear the attire of their office, he did not expect members of the public to dress in a way which pleased him. This was just one of the signs of the tolerance he extended to other people. But he had hardly been on the bench four months when a disagree-

---

57   SLSA Archival Collection, PRG1098/1/6.
58   Don Dunstan, p.116.
59   Roma Mitchell and Peter Kelly, "John Bray: the Man and the Judge", in *Adelaide Law Review*, Vol. 7, January 1980, No. 1, p. 5.

ment with another judge over this very attitude ended up on the front page of *The Advertiser*.

Bray had been addressing a symposium of Justices of the Peace on the first weekend of July 1967. He told them that "courts of law were not courts of morals" and that "no court had the right to tell a defendant to get his hair cut or to go away and put on a coat or tie."[60] He continued:

> People are entitled to wear their hair down to their knees if they want to, or dress according to their fancy, short of indecent exposure.

These remarks incited a response in *The Advertiser* the following day from Justice Leo Travers, who strongly criticised Bray's dismissal of the place of morality in the courts. Justice Travers retorted that the common law in its beginning had been little else but a court of morals:

> If the learned Chief Justice's remarks are as they appear to me, to be meant to convey that people with their hair down to their knees and dressed according to their fancy have a right to thus disport themselves in court, I again must disagree. (…)
> Any people with hair down to their knees and dressed according to their fancy who wish to attend court other than in custody would, I think, do well to choose their court. If they select mine their stay is apt to be brief and possibly even somewhat unpleasant.[61]

Justice Travers's attitude was not unlike Lord Ellenborough's (1790-1871), who was offended by a bricklayer:

> "Really, witness, when you have to appear before this court, it is your bounden duty to be more clean and decent in your appearance."
> "Upon my life", replied the witness, " I am every bit as well dressed as your lordship."

---

60   *The Advertiser*, Monday 3 July 1967, front page, for the quotes from Bray.
61   *The Advertiser*, Tuesday 4 July 1967.

"How do you mean, sir?"

"Why, faith, you come here in your working clothes and I come in mine."[62]

It is important, however, to understand that Bray did not tolerate long hair just because it was in fashion at that time. He agreed with Rohan Rivett, who wrote to him from Camberwell (Melbourne) that same weekend:

> It has not occurred to the 40+ age group that anyone who had appeared with short hair in the last 1000 years before Queen Victoria would have been laughed to ridicule.[63]

This statement also illustrates the perspective from which Bray looked at the world: in relation to the entirety of its recorded history. He placed a great deal of importance on this approach, which he attributed to his traditional humanities education. He was appointed Chancellor of the University of Adelaide in 1968, and when he retired in 1983, he criticised the way the universities were focussing on topics of only contemporary relevance:

> The truth is that for the first time in five hundred years or more we are producing a generation of educated men and women almost entirely lacking in the time dimension and hence in the qualities of perspective, balance and proportion that the study of the past brings with it. I am not referring only or even principally to the history of events but also to literature, philosophy, familiarity with the anatomy and evolution of language, everything that the old curriculum was supposed to give and did give where it was successful.[64]

Bray placed a great deal of importance on what he called the time dimension. For him, this was the only way to understanding human behaviour and societies. It explains why he fearlessly used very old authorities in constructing his defences as a barrister. By trawling

---

62   Richard Fountain (ed.), *The Wit of the Wig*, p. 55.
63   SLSA Archival Collection, PRG1098/1/7.
64   John Bray, *The Emperor's Doorkeeper*, p. 185.

through cases as far back as 1640 he could convince the High Court in
R v Howe of an authority showing that when the force used in self-defence was excessive, the appropriate verdict was manslaughter and not
murder.[65]

Looking back so far also reveals his traditional side. In a way,
he was equally as conservative as his predecessors Murray and Napier,
but he would have found them too narrow for limiting themselves to
the contemporary values of their era. Bray never challenged his society's institutions; he was no revolutionary. On the other hand, being as

Farewell to Justice Travers, 1969. (L-R) Justices Hogarth, Chamberlain, Bray (CJ), Travers,
Mitchell, Bright, Walters and Zelling. (SCLSA)

widely and deeply read as he was, he knew that attitudes to morality and
censorship ebbed and flowed through different eras. He would judge
such cases during his period on the bench with what would appear to
be a fresh approach in tune with the freer morals of the day, but more
accurately, he was using the wisdom of the past.

One of Bray's early judgments – in 1968 – would come to cement his name in posterity across the Commonwealth. This was a murder in which two men had been charged with the murder of an old lady.
Mr Morley was the one who had actually killed Mrs Leggett, while Mr

---

65   (1958-59) 100 CLR 448.

Brown had been in another room. Brown and his wife were boarding with Mrs Leggett and Morley had visited one Sunday to play cards. Morley, who had a history of psychiatric problems, decided to kill Mrs Leggett, and threatened Brown that unless he helped, Morley would kill his wife and his mother.

Brown's contribution to the murder was that he left the door to the house open and later, again threatened by Morley, he coughed to hide Morley's footsteps up the passageway to Mrs Leggett's bedroom. The murder took place in August 1968 and Morley and Brown were convicted and sentenced to death in October 1968. The appeal against their convictions took place in December. Morley was appealing on the ground of insanity and Brown on the ground of duress.

The appeal judges were John Bray, Roma Mitchell and Charles Bright. Their joint judgment dismissed both appeals. Bray, however, added a separate judgment dissenting on the question of the legal effect of duress as a defence to a charge of minor participation in the murder. He challenged particularly the other judges' interpretation of two key decisions of the Privy Council:

> My brethren rely on them as authorities for the proposition that duress can never excuse either an agreement to commit murder or an active participation in murder. With unfeigned respect to them in my view the first of these cases is an authority for the converse proposition that some types of duress may excuse some types of complicity in murder. That is *Sephakela v The Queen*.[66]

Bray discusses his reasons and then continues:

> The next Privy Council decision relied on by my brethren is *Rossides v The Queen* (...) It seems to me that that case can be no authority for the proposition that duress can be no defence to lesser acts of participation in murder not including any actual killing or attempted killing of the victim.

---

66   *R v Brown & Morley* [1968] SASR 467 at 495; 496-497 for the next quote.

Whether or not it was Bray's more perspicacious interpretations of these Privy Council decisions that attracted the attention of the Privy Council itself, we shall not know. What we do know is that in 1975, Privy Councillor Lord Morris of Borth-y-Gest cited Bray's separate judgment in his own decision about a man called Anthony Barry who had been arrested as part of a group of IRA assassins in Belfast and convicted with them of the murder of a police constable.[67] Barry claimed that he was not a member of the IRA and that he acted unwillingly, convinced that he himself would be shot if he disobeyed.

One of the key principles around which the case revolved was "whether duress can avail as a defence to a charge which is presented as a charge of murder". Lord Morris believed that it could and cited the *R v Brown and Morley* case in South Australia:

> The majority of the Supreme Court in dismissing the appeal considered that duress did not excuse Brown for any acts which constituted taking part in an arrangement for the killing of the lady. The Chief Justice (Bray CJ) dissented. In a closely reasoned judgment the persuasive power of which appeals to me he held that it was wrong to say that no type of duress can ever afford a defence to any type of complicity in murder (…).

Bray naturally limited the extent to which duress could be used and Lord Morris quoted Bray directly.

The re-entry of Don Dunstan's Labor government in mid-1970 had an immediate impact in the courts in many ways, notably in its relaxed attitude to censorship. John Bray had already published an article expressing his views in 1964 in *The Australian Library Journal*.[68] In 1966, during Writers' Week in the Festival of Arts, he participated in a seminar on the topic. In both instances, he carefully analysed the meaning of words such as "indecent", "obscene", "libel", "sedition", "corrupt" and "deprave". He argued that there is "no scientific proof that alleged

---

67   *Director of Public Prosecutions for Northern Ireland v Lynch* [House of Lords]. 1975 AC 653; at 677 for the quote.

68   J J Bray, LLD, "Censorship", *The Australian Library Journal*, Vol. 13, 1964, pp. 60-70; p. 68 for the two indented quotes.

pornography has ever depraved or corrupted anyone: why aren't the censors corrupted after reading so much nasty literature?"[69]

His attitude was that each citizen had the right to read or view whatever he or she wished. His interest was more in the works of literature that had been banned up until then:

> It has fallen to my lot to discuss with a good many offenders, juvenile and adult, the reasons for their acts but I have never known any of them to ascribe his downfall to a perusal of the works of Ovid, Petronius, Chaucer, Rabelais, Joyce, D H Lawrence, Norman Lindsay, Erskine Caldwell or Henry Miller.

But at the other end of the scale of language use, Bray was just as unimpressed by claims of obscenity regarding the printing of "four-letter" words:

> It is absurd to pretend that moral harm is suffered by seeing in print words and expressions which are in common use in everyday situations in our society and which everyone hears at some time or other. If people never hear them I don't understand how they recognise them when they see them in print.

The core philosophical issue at the heart of the morality and censorship debate was how far governments should interfere in individuals' private lives. This debate had begun in the nineteenth century with John Stuart Mill's famous essay, "On Liberty", published in 1859. Mill argued that governments should only interfere in an individual's private life to the extent of preventing harm to others, but no further. A few years after this – in 1868 – the English Courts asserted the opposing view in *R v Hicklin*, which emphasised safeguarding public morality.[70] This case produced the famous "Hicklin Test", which was still in use across the Commonwealth and therefore in South Australia when John Bray became Chief Justice. The Hicklin test was an incredible example of circular logic: matter was to be judged obscene if a judge decided it could corrupt anyone who was vulnerable to being corrupted. Despite

69   "Censorship and Pornography", seminar, Writers' Week, 1966. SLSA Archival Collection, PRG1098/37/8.
70   *R v Hicklin* (1868) LR 3 QB 361.

being far from clear, it was used for over a century, including in Max Harris's conviction for publishing the Ern Malley poems in *Angry Penguins*. In fact, even the book Max Harris published in 1961 – *Ern Malley's Poems* – remained banned in South Australia at the time John Bray published the "Censorship" article in 1964.

Bray's judgments have been influential across all the jurisdictions, but it is certain that in the area of the law relating to censorship, his influence was greatest. He was never directly responsible for the evolution of the common law on obscene publications in the first part of his period on the bench, nor the legislative revolution that took place in the 1970. But as Richard Fox found:

> (…) for more than a decade, in his judgments and particularly in his extra-judicial writings, His Honour maintained a biting criticism of the deficiencies of the law which, if it did not directly shape, at least gave rational direction to the revamping that took place.[71]

Bray published two articles on morality and censorship during his term as Chief Justice, both in the *Australian Law Journal*: "Law, Liberty and Morality" in 1971, and "The Juristic Basis of the Law Relating to Offences Against Public Morality and Decency" in 1972. Both were delivered at legal conventions in Melbourne in July 1971. In "Law, Liberty and Morality", Bray listed his views. I cite just the first two of his eight points:

> 1.   The liberty of the individual and the right to privacy are values to be protected and not to be interfered with except with good cause.
> 2.   I cannot agree that the moral views generally and strongly held by society should be enforced by law simply because they are so generally and strongly held. If this is a sufficient justification for legal interference in itself there is no reason to distinguish moral views so held from religious, political, racial or social

---

71   Richard G Fox, "Depravity, Corruption and Community Standards", *Adelaide Law Review*, vol. 7, January 1980, No. 1, p. 66.

views so held, and what justifies the legal enforcement of the former would also justify the legal enforcement of the latter.[72]

These views and those in the other speeches provoked yet another public debate with a judicial colleague: Joe Nelligan QC SM declared in *The Advertiser* that "he disagreed with every word of the Chief Justice's quoted remarks on obscenity and censorship."

The use of the Hicklin test was to come to its natural end during Bray's term. Its demise in Australia was first signalled in 1968 when Justice Windeyer in the High Court declared that the test "had fostered much misunderstanding".[73] Nevertheless, the judge supported the magistrate's finding that the publication in question – *Censor* – was "indecent".

Bray wrote five reported judgments for indecency or obscenity cases in the early 1970s. In two of these, he was the sole judge. Of the three cases in which Bray shared the bench, he dissented in two of them. This is one of the factors that distinguishes Bray from his predecessors as Chief Justice; they were rarely if ever in dissent.

In the earliest of Bray's judgments on censorship matters – *Simmons v Samuels* – Mr Simmons had been sentenced to prison for importing and then exhibiting pornographic films to about fifteen of his friends. Bray – the sole judge – expressed his opinion about the Hicklin test, not without a healthy dose of irony:

I am bound by this piece of nineteenth-century philosophy and it is my duty to accept its implications loyally, whether or not in a non-judicial capacity I might think its sociology based on unproved *a priori* assumptions and its reasoning circular. [He refers to *Crowe*.] I am bound that is, to assume there are classes of persons and age groups who are liable to be depraved or corrupted by literature, films, paintings and the like, though presumably those classes do not include the customs officers,

72   J J Bray, LLD, "Law, Liberty and Morality", *Australian Law Journal*, Vol. 45, September 1971, pp. 460-461. This same article is also reproduced in John Bray, *Emperor's Doorkeeper*, cited above, and the list of views is cited in full in Andrew Ligertwood, "Bray the Jurist", *Portrait of John Bray*, cited above, pp. 76-77.

73   *Crowe v Graham* (1967-68) 121 CLR 375 at 392.

police officers, court officials, barristers, solicitors, clerks and members of the magistracy and the judiciary whose unhappy duty it may be to peruse the perilous material.[74]

Bray overturned the sentence imposed by the magistrate and replaced it with fines: $100 for the exhibiting and $1 for its delivery to the premises. His frustration was obvious.

Another case became major news and the local papers covered its progress on the front pages daily. A play called "O Calcutta" had been performed in London, Paris and Los Angeles, and also in Melbourne. Now the producer, Huber, was trying to put it on in Adelaide. He had written to Attorney-General Len King, who was unable to guarantee that he would not break the law in putting it on, even if he adapted it. Subsequently, Len King was pressured by a small group of morally anxious citizens to prevent the play from being performed. Justice David Hogarth granted an injunction. In Justice Hogarth's words, "nearly every sketch involves either dialogue concerning, or description of simulation of, sexual intercourse, masturbation, orgasm or rape (described in erotic terms); and there are touches of sadism and masochism."[75] Huber and his partners appealed to the Full Court.

Bray discussed the case through a considerable body of authorities but was unable to convince Justices Walters and Wells to agree with him. One of his major points was that at this stage, no one had committed any act which could be labelled "indecent" or "obscene". There had been no performances. The effect of the injunction was therefore to prevent any such acts which may not even have taken place. Bray reacted strongly:

> I do not think that the civil court for the first time in 600 years should now enter the new field of attempting to prevent in advance the commission of offences against public morality or decency, where no civil right or material interest of the public itself is alleged to be affected. Such matters are best left to the ordinary operation of the criminal courts with all their traditional safeguards of the rights of accused persons. It

---

74   *Simmons v Samuels* (1971) 1 SASR 397 at 400.
75   *Attorney-General v Huber* (1971) SASR 142 at 147; at 172 for the quote.

might be different if the defendant consented to the civil court deciding the matter.

He believed that it was very likely that the performance would involve indecent behaviour within the meaning of the law, but did not think it was the business of the courts to intervene unless an offence had been committed and someone had been arrested for it.

Bray's focus on procedure in *Romeyko v Samuels* was very important in revealing the strong but inconsistent prejudices that could affect trials on moral questions.[76] Mr Romeyko was a Polish immigrant who, after a bitter and unsatisfactory divorce, had begun the Divorce Law Reform Association of South Australia. He issued a newsletter in April 1971 which he sent to a number of legal and political identities, including Mr Wilson SM. This newsletter contained four-letter words and Mr Wilson SM, deeply shocked, made a formal complaint.

The case was heard by J W Nelligan QC SM, who – revealingly – convicted George Romeyko of a different set of offences than those with which he had been charged. Romeyko had been charged with having sent material through the post which was of an "indecent, obscene, blasphemous, libellous or grossly obscene character."[77] This was the first fault in the trial, as these individual offences had not been specified as separate charges. There were also other lapses in the presentation of particulars. As a result, Justice Zelling overturned the conviction at the appeal in the Supreme Court. The Crown then appealed to the Full Court and all three judges agreed that the trial in the Magistrates Court had miscarried. The appeal by the Crown was dismissed. Bray was unusually severe in criticising Mr Nelligan's conclusion:

> If the complaint was defective, I think the conviction was even more so. It fails to make it plain of what the defendant was convicted. In his remarks on sentencing the learned Special Magistrate said: "In an extemporaneous judgment on 16

---

76   *Romeyko v Samuels* (1972) 2 SASR 529.

77   Mr Romeyko has contributed to two other reported cases in the course of his fight against unfair custody decisions: *Romeyko v Wackett (No. 1)*, (1980) 24 SASR 485 and *Romeyko v Whackett (No. 2)*, (1980) 25 SASR 531. He eventually returned to Poland with his son in defiance of the custody order in favour of his wife.

July 1971, I found the complaint proved in that it has been established beyond reasonable doubt that you have been guilty of despatching a newsletter containing indecent, obscene or grossly offensive language." It is clear then that he had not found that the newsletter contained words of a blasphemous or libellous character. Yet these two words found their way into the conviction. But the defect goes deeper than that. The passage refers to "indecent, obscene or grossly offensive language", not "indecent, obscene and grossly offensive language". At the end I am left in doubt what he really meant to find.[78]

Bray made a point of not allowing a complaint of bias against Mr Nelligan, despite the Magistrate having aired his views publicly, and aimed at Bray, in *The Advertiser* the year before. Mr Nelligan's attitude may be less an individual one than an indication – no doubt more obvious with the benefit of hindsight – of the strength of the resistance at that time to changes in the moral codes.

This resistance is evident again in the other case where Bray could not convince his brother judges that Hicklin test for defining "indecent" or "obscene" or "corrupting" was unreliable. *Popow v Samuels* was an appeal from the owner of The Whisper Shop in North Adelaide for his conviction for selling material that was labelled as "indecent".[79] Bray disagreed firstly with his fellow judges that the photographs and products were pornographic. In fact, at one point he stated that he could only regard some of the sex aid products as "coarse practical jokes". Bray also emphasised that entry to the shop was restricted both physically by its design and by the warnings of the nature of the goods it sold. This meant that it was not visible to anyone who did not expressly seek it, unlike in the next case. Bray also once again strongly criticised the Magistrate for imposing his own personal moral views. Justices Walters and Zelling disagreed and Mr Popow's thirty fines had to be paid.

In *Trelford v Samuels* the situation was quite different as regards the availability of alleged pornographic material. Three delicatessen owners, one of their employees and one newsagent, were appealing against convictions for selling *Ribald*, a graphic adult magazine. In all cases the magazine was kept high up and folded over, but could be seen

---

78   *Romeyko v Samuels*, at 556.
79   (1973) 4 SASR 594.

by any adult coming into the shops. And, only adults were allowed to buy the magazine.

Bray was the sole judge in this case and he personally found that the contents of this particular publication were "gross, remorseless and ubiquitous",[80] but agreed that it was aimed at a restricted readership. By the time this case came before him, Bray was becoming increasingly frustrated with the inconsistent way in which "indecency" and its associated terms was being treated. He reiterated the argument of the appellants' lawyer, Mr Turner:

> How unjust, how absurd, he said, to create a crime which consists in the violation of community standards and then shut out evidence of what those standards are. (...) How impossible, he said, it is for a shopkeeper to know what he may safely sell within a wide and ill-defined area when all he can be told is that his liability to fine and imprisonment will depend on whether his wares are found offensive in the judgment of one man who might be anywhere between a profligate or a puritan and who is confined by the law to the guidance of the light within his own breast.[81]

Bray's judgment included, in effect, some advice to the appellants: since he was bound by legislation and the common law authorities, they needed to "seek relief from this state of things from North Terrace, not from Victoria Square". It is worth consulting the judgment to see how Bray dealt with the five appellants' convictions and fines.

Later that same year the Dunstan government provided the necessary legislative relief in the form of the Classification of Publications Act 1974 (since amended). A board of six members would now be classifying the perilous publications, and restricting their presentation for display. The classified publications could then be sold in opaque packaging with the details of their classification on the cover. Providing they were sold in this way, the vendors would not be prosecuted.

The Classification of Publications Act was a big step forward in South Australian governance as it was official recognition that adults

---

80   *Trelford v Samuels* (1974) 7 SASR 587 at 593.
81   At 596-7.

had the right to read what they chose. Four years later, the Dunstan government passed the *Police Offences Act (No. 2) 1978* which had the effect of making the Hicklin depravity and corruption test redundant in South Australian law. As Richard Fox wrote:

> By the time Bray left office, the Hicklin test had finally been abandoned as the underlying justification of the law of obscenity. What was originally perceived as a grave threat to the established moral order was, with some critical nudging from the Chief Justice, finally recognised for what it really was – a minor public nuisance.[82]

Bray outside of 37 and 39 Hurtle Square, late 1970s. (Advertiser)

Bray's contribution to the maturing of official attitudes to community standards from the judicial arm of government, and Dunstan's from the executive and legislative arms, endure to the present time. In a sense, South Australia came of age. It is all the more interesting that Bray dissented in two of the three judgments in which the Full Court heard the appeal. That Bray's opinions stand the test of time is not a slight of any kind on the capacity of the other judges. They were and are all known as judges of the highest calibre. Howard Zelling, for example, was in no way insular to general community standards. In his judgment allowing Romeyko's appeal against conviction, he quoted statistics illustrating that the average age of the population of South Australia in 1966 was 30.8 years. He made the point that in none of the law books

---

82   Richard G Fox, cited earlier, p. 78.

could he find the proposition that community standards are those held by persons over the age of fifty years – he was specifically referring to judges: "As far as the young are concerned the obscenities of this life are not four letter words. They are such things as war, racial discrimination, the imbalance of wealth and poverty, and the destruction of the ecological system. They say with Catullus, or would if they had a proper classical education":

> "Vivamus, mea Lesbia, atque amenus,
> rumoresque senum severiorum
> omnes unius aestimemus assis."
>> [My Lesbia, let us live and love
>> And not care tuppence for old men
>> Who sermonise and disapprove.][83]

Howard Zelling was one of the judges who made the Bray Court one of the strongest in South Australia's history, and like Bray he was widely read and an intellectual thinker. The factor that distinguished Bray was that he was prepared to go just that one step further than other judges to challenge convention where he believed it served no purpose beyond perpetuating itself. Michael Kirby found this in discussing Bray's exceptional influence in the High Court:

> He looked beyond legal rules to their historical origins and philosophical and social foundations. For this reason he is often cited as an authority because his analysis of legal problems tended to impart an understanding, not just of verbal formulation of the law in a wide range of subject areas, but of the rationale for the law's particular path of development. By throwing light on history and purpose, Bray was able to point with conviction and assurance to the way ahead and likely future developments of the law.[84]

83   *Romeyko v Samuels* (1971) 2 SASR 529 at 543. [Translation by John Bray, *The Emperor's Doorkeeper*, p. 46.]
84   Michael Kirby, "Bray's Impact on Australian Jurisprudence", in Wilfrid Prest (ed.), cited above, p. 100.

John Bray's private life during this time had undergone some up-heavals. Harry Bray had died in 1965, but when his mother Gertrude died in 1970, the mansion on Hutt Street had to be sold in order to pay his sister Ro her share. By the time John Bray moved out in 1972 to a house in the Darcy Lever Terrace in Hurtle Square – number 39 – he had been living at Bray House for almost forty years.

Peter Ward and Dimitri Theodoratos - two close friends from the Colin Ballantyne "school" at the Sturt Arcade Hotel - moved in next door. The three of them formed a single domestic unit across the two households, sharing facilities. Ward and Theodoratos managed the combined unit as Bray had never been able to learn those skills. The two friends increased their support in the last years when Bray's health declined with his advanced age.[85]

This domestic arrangement naturally caused concern in people unable to look beyond convention. His brother Robert's wife Betty some years later, after Bray's retirement, worried about its unusual nature, encouraged him to "regularise" his life and employ a live-in house-keeper. Bray's response is enlightening as to his general approach to his life:

> I do not want any housekeeper or warder living in the house. That would interfere with my habits and proclivities. I have no intention of regularising my life. If anything I hope it will become more irregular. I have never had much regard for decorum, respectability, bourgeois comfort or bourgeois lifestyle and I do not now have to pay lip service to them. The views of the ladies of Burnside and Stirling or the members of the Adelaide Club are of supreme indifference to me.[86]

In the year of his mother's death, Bray learnt that his close friend Brian Medlin had been beaten by the police during the Vietnam Mora-torium demonstration in September. Medlin was one of the movement's leaders and the large crowd of around 10,000 halted in the intersection of North Terrace and King William Street. The police moved in with

---

85   Letter from Peter Ward to John Emerson, 27 November 2002.
86   Letter to Bill (Robert) and Betty Bray, 18 March 1980. SLSA Archival
       Collection, PRG1098/87.

horses and as Don Dunstan describes it: "the scene became the ugliest Adelaide had seen since the beef riots of the depression years (…)."[87]

The violent confrontation led by the police, according to Dunstan, had been totally avoidable. The government had known in advance that the demonstrators were going to block an intersection. With his Chief Secretary, Bert Shard, Dunstan told Commissioner of Police Brigadier John McKinna to re-route traffic around the blocked intersection to prevent a confrontation:

> To my astonishment, he defied us. He said that it was his duty to carry out the law – the Road Traffic Act was clear, that obstruction of the traffic was an offence and it would be treated as such by the police.

At that stage, under the Police Regulation Act the Police Commissioner did not answer to government. As a result of McKinna's defiance, and of the resulting debacle, Dunstan appointed a Royal Commission, with Justice Charles Bright at its head. Justice Bright found that the Police Commissioner had been in error in rejecting the advice of the Government. In 1972, the Dunstan Government amended the Police Regulation Act to make the police subject to Executive Council, in effect meaning to Cabinet. McKinna – the same person who had attempted to thwart John Bray's appointment as Chief Justice – had retired by this time, and Don Dunstan appointed Harold Salisbury to take his place. Brian Medlin was prosecuted in the Magistrates Court; Chief Justice John Bray appeared in the witness box to testify to his good character.

But all was not bleak. In 1973, Prime Minister Gough Whitlam came to Adelaide to open the new Festival Theatre. To give an idea of the impact this had on Adelaide, more than 20,000 people visited the theatre complex during the weekend before the official opening. The smaller drama theatre – the Playhouse – was opened by Don Dunstan. He read a poem written specially for the occasion by the Chief Justice John Bray, introduced with some blank verse by Peter Ward.[88]

---

87   Don Dunstan, p. 185; also for the indented quote.
88   Don Dunstan, p. 245.

During Bray's term as Chief Justice, a number of major changes had an impact on the courts system both from within and without. The establishment of the District Criminal Court in 1970 lightened the increasing criminal trial load on the Supreme Court. The Common-

Undated ceremonial sitting in No. 1 Court: Sangster, Zelling, Mitchell, Chamberlain, Bray, Hogarth, Walters and Wells. (SCLSA)

wealth Government established the Federal and Family Courts in the mid-1970s, which released the Supreme Court from divorces and civil matters such as tax disputes.

Once Don Dunstan's government was returned in 1970, it spent the next five years overhauling old Acts and introducing a record quantity of new legislation. With more laws and regulations, the court load began to increase again, even with the support of the District Court.

Forensic science also had an impact. New technology allowed the investigation and analysis of microscopic particles – shoes, jumpers, skin, paint, pollen – in order to prove or disprove a suspect's involvement in a crime. This would have the effect of making trials longer and more complex as expert witnesses were called to explain results at length in minute detail. The van Beelen case produced eight reported trials and appeals, including one in the High Court, as the defence repeatedly challenged the prosecution's forensic evidence. The initial hearing in the Magistrates Court occupied fifty-eight days.[89]

89　　Bray CJ, *R v van Beelen*. 3 SASR 330 at 338.

John Bray's contribution to the era was in the quality of scholarship and writing of his judgments. Until he became Chief Justice, Full Court judgments were almost always joint. Over the years he pressed for judges to write their own. His brother judge Charles Bright – on the Supreme Court bench from 1963 to 1978 – notes:

> He greatly preferred to write his own judgment and not to participate in a joint judgment, for he took the view that posterity could more accurately estimate a judge who did not blur the edges of a judgment for the sake of achieving unanimity in a joint judgment.[90]

Charles Bright found as a puisne judge in the Bray court that the Chief Justice kept mainly to himself – lunching alone in his chambers and leaving promptly each evening at six-thirty to meet his own friends. He held a monthly conference of judges, but never to impose his own points of view, always to encourage a democratic discussion of issues affecting the Court. There were never any seminars on the law. Bright believed nevertheless that Bray was a true judicial leader:

> He led by example, not by precept. In the first place, his literary style was outstandingly good. (...) He used language as an instrument for expressing his views on legal matters. He was not a virtuoso performer in the florid eighteenth century tradition. His method of writing judgments was influential. It created a pattern which a perceptive judge could follow.
>
> In the second place, his clarity of style showed up the imperfections of statutes which he was considering. He applied standards of criticism that influenced the criticisms of others. He pointed out latent obscurities and perhaps induced others to do the same.
>
> In the third place, he ameliorated the application of the criminal law. Errors in summing up were mercilessly exposed, and fear of being upset in the Court of Criminal Appeal was

---

90   Charles Bright, "Bray in Context", *Adelaide Law Review*, Vol. 7, January 1980, No. 1, p. 14.

instrumental in causing greater accuracy in language by trial judges.[91]

Charles Bright also believed that Bray had been the right Chief Justice to meet the demands of the Dunstan government's reforms:

> Future historians of South Australia will, I think, look back with approval to the Dunstan-King era of social reform and to the Bray Court which gave full scope to the efforts of the Ministry. For it must not be forgotten that the labours of the judges, and in particular of the Chief Justice, are vastly increased when the Bench is confronted by a great assemblage of new statute law embodying, often in ill-chosen language, new ideas and new aspirations. It is not easy, when interpreting ill-expressed statutes, to give effect to the ideas embodied in the language but not to stretch the language further than the natural meaning of the words used. Bray's judgments demonstrate a clear understanding of the distinction.

In early 1978, Bray announced his retirement after receiving an adverse medical report on his heart condition. Dunstan at this stage was still reeling from the aftermath of sacking Harold Salisbury – successor to John McKinna – as Commissioner of Police. But Bray had, in fact, considered retiring even earlier:

> Indeed, since I received my doctorate in 1937, took silk in 1957, and was appointed Chief Justice in 1967, I thought last year that in the interests of symmetry I should retire in 1977, but my sister Mitchell then persuaded me that in this, as well as in more important legal contexts, the pursuit of symmetry can be carried too far.[92]

He left the bench on 27 May 1978 and David Hogarth acted as Chief Justice until Bray's term officially ended on 27 October, and Len King took over.

---

91   Charles Bright, pp. 14-15; p. 16 for the second quote.
92   (1978-79) 19 SASR, Bray's retirement speech at XI.

Bray remained Chancellor of the University of Adelaide until just past his seventieth birthday. He remained on the Libraries Board until February 1987. When he retired the State Library gave his name to the Reference Library in recognition of his record forty-two years of service. His life post-Chief Justice assumed the rhythm of a learned man of letters: Mondays and Tuesdays were library days; Fridays shopping on Hutt Street. Once a month he went to Friendly Street poetry readings (of which he was a foundation member in November 1975), attended meetings of the Libraries Board and of the Classical and English Associations at the University of Adelaide. On the first Wednesday of each month, he would host the Jury Poetry Group at 39 Hurtle Square.[93]

Saturdays revolved around lunch at the Sturt Arcade Hotel with Colin Ballantyne, Max Harris, Brian Medlin, Neil Lovett, Stuart Luke and David Tippett, among others, as had been the tradition since Charles Jury's death in 1958. After the Sturt Arcade Hotel closed in 1990, for a while the group had lunch over the road in Horst Salomon's restaurant. Later, as members died, remnants of the group continued to meet for Saturday lunch at the Brecknock Hotel in King William Street.

John Bray began working on the great academic work of his life after his retirement: *Gallienus: A Study in Reformist and Sexual Politics*. But despite his repeated efforts, the *magnum opus* would only be published after his death.[94] Its depth of scholarship stands alongside that of his judgments. John Bray also published a further three books of poetry: *Poems 1972-1979* (Australian National University Press, 1979); *The Bay of Salamis and Other Poems* (Friendly Street Poets, 1986); and *Seventy Seven* (Wakefield Press, 1990). There were also other volumes of selected poems and prose.

The poems offer a unique insight into John Bray's world, from his responses to ordinary day-to-day events, his surroundings in Hurtle Square, ageing – through to metaphysical musings and responses to Shakespeare or arguments with Brian Medlin. There is an abundance of humour:

Quinquennial Occasions (last verse)
Bereft of beer, of smokes, of sex,

Peter Ward's speech at John Bray's memorial service in Bonython Hall, University of Adelaide, 25 July 1995.
94   Published by Wakefield Press, Adelaide, 1997.

I only stay alive
To see what else they'll rip off me
When I turn seventy-five.[95]

But also some pessimism on the same topic:

Explanation

My verse, my friends complain, dwells too much on decay.
What else at seventy-one, I ask, is left to say?[96]

He bases many of his poems on aspects of Adelaide life, which gives a literary presence to a city that otherwise is almost invisible against the dominance of the older, more populous States. But he knits the specific details of his own geography to universal concerns:

Early Morning Reflection

Outside my room run five electric wires,
Dotted sometimes with sparrows at first light,
Clefs on a stave of music. From my bed
I watch but cannot read the changing notes.
They land and leave. Above a jet growls past,
Trailing a long polluted streak behind,
A pterodactyl struck with dysentery.
This one can merely bruise the eye and ear,
Its womb crammed with commuters chewing cake,
Not with those giant apocalyptic eggs
Which one day will be dropped to split the world.
Its rumbles fade and die. The birds return.
The last trump is not scheduled for today.[97]

Bray wrote several poems using the local bird life of Hurtle Square, and in 1994, the Adelaide City Council erected the John Bray bird bath in the square opposite his home.[98]

---

95   "Quinquennial Occasions", last verse. *Bay of Salamis and Other Poems*,
       Adelaide: Friendly Street Poets, 1986, p. 4.
96   "Explanation", entire poem. In *Bay of Salamis*.
97   "Early Morning Reflection", entire poem. In *Bay of Salamis*.
98   Full details are available in the John Bray papers, SLSA Archival Collection,
       PRG 1098/97.

In his last two or three years, John Bray began taking his friends to lunch every Monday at the Rob Roy Hotel a hundred metres around the corner down Halifax Street. The varying company included Peter Ward, Dimitri Theodoratos, Brian Medlin and Neil Lovett. In 1995, Bray would be wheeled down, emphysema gradually overcoming his resistance, but never keeping him away from a pub lunch. On Monday 26 June 1995, however, it looked as though lunch was off.[99] Peter Ward was busy, Dimitri Theodoratos had only just returned from a trip to Greece. Medlin and Lovett turned up suddenly, and the three of them went to lunch.

According to Brian Medlin, "it was the most hilarious lunch we'd had". They spoke about the past and about the old days at the Sturt Arcade. The young waitress asked Bray, as she usually did: "How are you today, Judge Bray?"

He would normally reply, gruffly: "Not very well, if you must know." Medlin often reproved him for it. On this day Bray was sicker than ever. When the waitress asked him how he was, for once he lightened his response: "Much the same."

John Bray at 80 in 1992. (Advertiser)

"That's nice", she said.

Medlin, Lovett and Bray looked at each other, realising that this time Bray was on the point of death, and laughed.

That night he died, barely ten hours from when he was last in a pub. His death was reported as far away as London. Although he had had a big party for his seventy-ninth birthday, not believing that he

---

99   This story courtesy of Brian Medlin, interview 19 October 2002.

would even make it to eighty, he had almost made it to eighty-three. Much longer than he estimated he would have lived if he had been born in his beloved classical Rome. In the 1985 interview with Beate Josephi, he said that as a sickly child born then, he most likely would have been left out to die.[100]

---

100   Interview with Beate Josephi.

CHAPTER 6

Len King (1978-1995)

REFORMING THE COURTS

By Bray's retirement, the courts were again in crisis. The Dunstan government had responded to the social revolution of the late 1960s and 1970s with a massive quantity of new legislation and government infrastructures. Together with the introduction of increasingly detailed scientific evidence, trials in both the civil and criminal jurisdictions stretched to record lengths. A backlog was again building, even after the introduction of District Courts. The question now was whether the judicial system, in its turn, would be able to adapt itself.

Speculation about Len King being appointed Chief Justice first surfaced in the press over four and a half years before his appointment, when he was approaching the end of his parliamentary career as Attorney-General. Eric Franklin's "State Politics" column in *The Advertiser* headlined that: "King of Cabinet may soon rule courts.":

> Some see Mr King as the next Chief Justice of the SA Supreme Court with the present Chief Justice (Dr J. J. Bray) elevated to a position (probably president) in a new State Appeals Court.[1]

---

1   Eric Franklin, "King of Cabinet may soon rule courts", *The Advertiser,* 16 March 1974, p. 16.

In fact, Len King joined the Bray Court as its tenth judge in June
1975 and there was no State Appeals Court. King's appointment to the
Chief Justiceship after Bray's retirement three years later probably had
little to do with those earlier rumours. Neither was it a surprise, given

The Bray Court for the last time in October 1978: Williams (AJ), King, Wells, Mitchell, Hogarth, Bray, Bright, Zelling, Jacobs, White, Legoe, Newman (AJ) (SCLSA).

his record as Attorney-General, and that Don Dunstan was still Premier.
The only protest came from the Opposition Leader, David Tonkin, and
the basis of his protest could just as easily be seen as an argument in
favour of his appointment:

> A court interprets Parliament's intentions only through the
> wording of the Acts and doesn't consult Hansard to see what
> Parliament meant. However, it will be impossible for Mr Justice
> King not to know what he meant when he was steering his
> legislation through Parliament.[2]

---

2   Quoted in Mike Quirk, "King is SA's new Chief Justice". *The News*, 30
         October 1978, See also Peter Ward, "Political Patronage – a Fine Old
         Tradition", *The Australian*, 1 November 1978 and "King new Chief Justice",
         The Advertiser, 31 October 1978, p. 3.

Up to this point we have seen that, while each Court developed a distinct personality around that of its Head, the role of the Chief Justice remained more or less the same. The Chief Justice concentrated almost exclusively on judicial matters, leaving the administration of the courts to the public service. The appointment of Len King, however, put an end to the judiciary's reliance on the executive arm of government. He believed that it was not enough for judges just to judge – they had to oversee the justice system in its totality. They had to strengthen and defend the very independence of the judiciary itself, and protect it from any interference from the other arms of government. They had to take control of their budget. They also should manage cases from their initiation to minimise delays. Under King, the office of Chief Justice in South Australia would undergo the greatest transformation in its history.

Premier Don Dunstan and the new Chief Justice 30 October 1978 (courtesy Len King).

The appointment of King as Chief Justice was in itself a sign of South Australia's continuing evolution into a more egalitarian society at that time. Len King was both a Roman Catholic and a Labor man: a double affront to the canons of conservatism that had dominated South Australia.

More than any of the Chief Justices who preceded him, Len King came to the office of Chief Justice with a philosophy of justice that would fuel the changes he would make to the organisation and structuring of the courts. This philosophy is part of a passion for a more egalitarian society, and its origins can be traced to his childhood in Norwood during the 1930s depression. Len King was the only child of Michael and Mary King, both of Irish descent. When Len was born - providentially on May Day - in 1925, Michael was fifty-five and Mary was thirty-five. Both had delayed marriage to care for their families: Michael for his aging parents on the family farm at Carrieton; and Mary, for her younger brother and sister after the death of their parents from illnesses in 1910.

Michael King introduced his son to two passions that would endure for life: the Labor movement and horse racing. Victoria Park racecourse was just a short walk down Kensington Road from their home, and Michael had an interest in horses from his days on the family farm. One of the effects that the Depression wrought on those outings was the end of the occasional visit to the grandstand, thereafter it was the free admission flat. They were often joined by Mary, who also enjoyed a day at the races. Like his father, Len's interest was not in gambling. His interest was the sport, and he remains a committed annual pilgrim to the pinnacle of the Australian track, the Melbourne Cup.

On Sunday afternoons in the early 1930s, Adelaide had a Speaker's Corner in Botanic Park, and Michael King loved to go along with his son each weekend. Among the enthusiastic crowds of people who came each week to participate – whether it was to air their views, listen or occasionally heckle – was the popular ALP ring. Budding politicians and prominent ALP members would promote the Party's policies from a stump acting as the daïs. The Lang Labor group had their own ring and so did the Communist Party.[3] Len King believes that this early exposure to this hotspot of ideas – albeit crudely expressed – had a considerable effect on his understanding of the broad Labor movement and a profound influence on the development of his own political ideas.

Ever conscious of Len being an only child, Michael King would also take his son to other events. One of these was the opening of parliament. Len King remembers his father pointing out the "august personage" of the Chief Justice, Sir George Murray, in full ceremonial dress. In his retirement speech in 1995, King said: "It would have been beyond the horizon of his [father's] wildest imaginings that his son would one day occupy the office of Chief Justice. How he would have smiled in-

---

3   In 1932 the Labor Party had split into three factions over what was known as the Premiers' Plan. The Lang Labor Party was one of these. See Dean Jaensch (ed.), *The Flinders History of South Australia: Political History*. Netley, Adelaide: Wakefield, 1986, pp. 238, 243, 382, 385.

credulously had someone forecast that his little boy would some day be in that position."[4]

The fact that he was an only child formed the foundation of Len King's later strengths. In his own words: "Being alone threw me back upon my internal resources."[5] He had to be imaginative and resourceful in order to deal with the degree of loneliness that is a large part of the experience of being an only child. He invented games, enacted battles and cricket matches. He also made friends, with two of whom he was to remain in contact for life: Mollie Pickett and John Gray, both also without brothers and sisters. It was also during this period that Len would begin reading newspapers and discover the accounts of the court cases, and grow more and more interested in the operations of the law.

The Depression dragged on throughout the entire period of Len King's schooling – firstly at St Mary's School, in Beulah Road, Norwood, and then at Marist Brothers School – and would force him to leave at the age of fourteen to help the family survive.[6] His parents lost their income for more than five years, and were forced to join the 12 per cent of the population that lived on rations tickets, worth four shillings and ten pence a week, and on whatever odd jobs they could find.[7] Michael King had originally come to Adelaide with a reasonable nest egg after having first sold the family farm near Carrieton and then being the proprietor of one of the town's hotels. With the proceeds of the sale of the hotel and a mortgage, he bought fifteen cottages around the inner suburbs with the idea of living on the rental income.

But in early 1930, the tenants became unemployed. Not only did Michael King lose his income but also his means of paying the mortgages. The mortgagees took possession and in the space of weeks the family went from modest comfort to plain poverty. Fortunately, although receiving no income, Michael King was able to retain the titles to most of the cottages and their sale after his death in 1948 realised suf-

4   Len King, *Retirement Address*, Special Sitting of the Supreme Court, 28 April
        1995, p. 2. Mortlock Library, South Australia, PRG 1163.

5   Len King, *Unpublished memoirs*, "Childhood". p. 4. [1998] I have drawn
        much of what follows from these memoirs and interviews.

6   St Ignatius Junior School now occupies the site of the former Marist Brothers
        School in Queen Street, Norwood.

7   By 1931, around 70,000 people out of the total population then of 570,000
        were receiving forms of government relief. Alex Castles and Michael Harris,
        Lawmakers and Wayward Whigs, p. 321.

ficient funds, after discharging the mortgages, to enable   to purchase a small second-hand car and, in time, to pay a deposit on his first home.

Towards the end of 1935, Michael had his sixty-fifth birthday, and so became eligible for the pension, which doubled the family's basic income to a pound a week –still very low but a considerable improvement. That was the Kings' sole support until Len left school in 1939 and was able to pay board. In 1937, to recall from the previous chapter, John Bray's parents paid 142 pounds for his overseas holiday. Chief Justice Murray was earning two thousand five hundred pounds per year and Napier, then a puisne judge, two thousand pounds per year.

But before this, the Headmaster at Marist Brothers School made a decision that showed considerable foresight, and which would open up the opportunity later for a university education – something that at the time would have seemed an impossible dream. He noticed Len's exceptional academic ability and realised that because of his family's poverty he would be certain to leave school at the then legal age of fourteen. He allowed Len to fast-track his education – jumping sixth year and then ninth year – enabling him to leave at fourteen and a half years old with matriculation level at the end of 1939.

Len's ambition was already to become a lawyer, but he saw no way of making it a reality. The family could have survived for him to do the twelfth year – then called Leaving Honours – but there was certainly no means to pay for a university education in the days before government subsidies. So Len left school and went to work as a clerk for Shell Oil. The prospects of a law career grew distant.

We can but speculate – as Len King has – about the direction his professional life would have taken, had not another event taken place on the other side of the world just a couple of months before he finished school. The outbreak of the Second World War would draw Australian troops to aid Great Britain against the invasion of Europe by Hitler's Germany, and later, Australia and her neighbours against the Japanese. In a little more than three years, Len King would leave Adelaide for the first time and go away and fight.

Long before then, during the years that Len King worked for Shell at Richmond and Mile End, he was making regular visits to the State Library to satisfy his intellectual appetite. There he would read history and philosophy books. Thinking he would never be able to study law, he decided to obtain some accounting qualifications. They would help to advance him with the Shell Company. He took night courses at Muirden's Business College and gained the top credit in the State for Leaving Honours Economics. He enrolled in a correspondence course in accounting. He was not overly enthusiastic, since it was not accounting that interested him but law. Nevertheless, by the time he enlisted for war service, he had gained not only the top result in the intermediate level examination, but found the accounting subjects more interesting than he had expected.

In between the twin demands of study and work, Len also became part of a regular group of teenage boys from the Norwood district who centred their social lives on The Parade. Len had deliberately decided to extend his friendships beyond his Roman Catholic circle, and local entertainment included going to milk bars, the cinema, dances, the football, billiard halls and even a hotel, if a barman could be persuaded. Shadowing these normal adolescent activities was the dark cloud of war. The entry of Japan with the attack on Pearl Harbour in December 1941 increased this tension and the bombing of Darwin in February 1942 brought the war to Australian shores. In Len King's words: "It had an unsettling effect on life and attitudes. The departure of the older boys into the services, the deaths, the uncertainty hanging over the future of the world, the threatened invasion of Australia, created a sometimes tense and even irresponsible atmosphere in our lives and activities."[8]

The Parade groups began to break up as the boys began enlisting. Len King could have obtained exemption from call-up as the oil industry was a reserved occupation. Although his superintendent wanted him to obtain the exemption, he made up his mind to enlist in the Royal Australian Air Force. Because of colour blindness, he could not become a pilot or a radar operator. He could however, become a radio telegraphy operator. At the age of eighteen years, Len King went to war.

He expected that, once the war was over, to return to work for Shell. But the Labor Party had come into power in 1941 under John Curtin and introduced the Commonwealth Reconstruction Training Scheme. The scheme provided for free tertiary education and a living

---

8   *Unpublished memoirs*, cited above, "The War", p. 1.

allowance, so that servicemen could build a better career back in civilian life. Len King realised that he could study law. His dream of becoming a lawyer was no longer an impossibility.

His accelerated education at Marist Brothers and the economics subjects he had done at night meant that Len King had matriculated. Thus, unlike many of the other servicemen, he could begin his law degree while still in the Air Force. The University of Adelaide law degree at that period required three Arts subjects and Len King passed the first of these, a study of the works of William Shakespeare, while he was still in New Guinea. He remembers: "The only material necessary was a volume of Shakespeare's works. That volume of Shakespeare's works, mildewed and stained through being carted around in the tropical conditions of New Guinea, remains one of my treasured possessions."[9]

King was demobilised in April 1946, just before his twenty-first birthday. He returned home to Norwood and took up full-time studies in law at the University. He found that his father had aged greatly during his absence, but his mother, twenty years younger, was working in a nearby hospital. Gradually his old friends from The Parade returned and some of the old social patterns resumed. There remained one final hurdle to a career in law, and that was obtaining Articles. The first two years of the law degree at that time required full-time study, but the final three years required students to be working in a law firm as an Articled Clerk. The problem was the impervious nature of the legal profession then. "Neither my parents nor I knew any lawyers and there was no obvious way of securing Articles. The legal profession in those days was still pretty much a closed profession and personal contacts were important."

Len King (left) at 23 years old in 1948 at Kevin Clancy's wedding. (Courtesy Len King)

---

9   *Retirement Address,* cited above, p. 6.

Michael King remembered that when he was still on the farm out near Carrieton, one of his neighbour's sons was a solicitor. He managed to rekindle the contact and Articles were arranged with Mick Kinnane, who ran his practice from the Royal Insurance Building, 13 Grenfell Street, Adelaide. This was one of the last times that Michael King was able to help his son. He died in 1948, the year that Len King went to work for the first time in a lawyer's office.

The admissions for December 1950. Len King is 4th from left, front row. (courtesy Len King)

Len King discovered very quickly the precarious nature of Mr Kinnane's practice. The solicitor, it turned out, was a confirmed alcoholic and before the year was out, the practice collapsed and he moved to Melbourne. Len King was again without Articles, although he had acquired a lot of experience in legal administration as a result of having to run the office himself with the help of Mick Kinnane's sister. In fact, the temporary hiccup proved a blessing in disguise. Before moving to Melbourne, Mick Kinnane transferred King's Articles to the firm Nelligan Mitchell and Walters, and for the first few months, he was articled to George Walters, who then left to take up a magistracy appointment.[10] He was then articled to Roma Mitchell, who remained his Principal

---

10   George Walters was 35 at the time he became a Magistrate. He was to become Master of the Supreme Court before his appointment there as a judge in 1966. He retired in August, 1984.

until his admission to practice in January 1950. Though they may not have guessed it then, all three – Walters, Mitchell and King – were destined to join each other on the Supreme Court bench and, finally, in Len King's Court.

In December, 1950, Len King graduated Bachelor of Laws and was admitted as a practitioner of the Supreme Court of South Australia. The firm could not keep him on. The senior partner, Joe Nelligan KC, summoned King and, wishing him well in his career, presented him with a copy of *Annual Practice*. Len King still had no clear idea of what direction this career would take. No one was offering any jobs. His family did not know any lawyers to whom he could go for advice.

By chance a solicitor he knew in Whyalla, Ron Reilly, called him and invited him to join his practice there. So in January, 1951, King moved to Whyalla and became a partner in Reilly and King. Ron Reilly preferred to concentrate on his business clients' legal needs and leave King the litigation work in the local Magistrate's Court. Although the cases being heard before Justices of the Peace were for minor offences or debt collection, the experience gave King an insight into advocacy, that is, appearing for a client in court. He realised very soon that this was where his interests lay.

Two months after moving to Whyalla, he also had his first experience of appearing before the Supreme Court during its circuit visit to nearby Port Augusta. To make it as difficult as possible, the March temperatures were soaring above 40 degrees Celsius, and in 1950, there was no air-conditioning. King was sharing a room at the Exchange Hotel with Clarrie Hermes who also had cases at the circuit.[11] It was so stiflingly hot at night that they were forced to leave the bay windows open and as a result, the mosquitos swarmed in. The judge and the prosecutor were no doubt suffering similarly, and the courtroom each day was an oven.

In these conditions, with everyone including the judge impatient and irritable, Len King conducted his first defended criminal trial. His client had been charged with shooting at a police officer. This was not disputed. What was disputed was whether he intended to cause grievous bodily harm, which carried a maximum sentence of life impris-

---

11   Clarrie Hermes was later Len King's best man at his wedding in 1953. He later moved to Canberra where he became a magistrate.

onment, or if he was simply intending to avoid lawful apprehension. Not yet twenty-five, in the blistering Port Augusta heat, Len King managed to obtain a verdict of guilty on the lesser charge. In addition, Reg Kearnan QC, who was prosecuting, complimented him on the way he conducted his case.

Len King knew that if he were to pursue a career as a barrister, he would have to move back to Adelaide. He asked friend Tom McGovern to keep his eye out for any openings and in fact, Tom knew of one. Hugh Martin, who ran a practice from the AMP building in King William Street, needed another lawyer. In October, 1951, Len King moved back to Adelaide and returned to live with his mother, who had been living alone – another reason he wanted to return.

As with Mick Kinnane, so with Hugh Martin: the practice was in a disastrous state. But this was for quite different reasons: Mr Martin had suffered a stroke, significantly impairing his ability to work. He died a few months later and King bought the practice, having already reorganised the administration of the office and resurrected each case that had been neglected. He managed to convince clients who were on the brink of finding another lawyer to stay with him.

But just as he was ready to establish himself in Adelaide as a sole practitioner, he discovered that the AMP would not transfer the lease to him - they wanted the space themselves and had been waiting for Hugh Martin's demise. They gave Len King three months to find somewhere else. The problem was that after the end of war, office space in the city had become impossible to find. The young lawyer found himself with a considerable debt for the purchase of the practice, and no office to run it from.

Towards the end of the three months, the situation was getting grim. By chance, on the way back from court, Len King met an old friend of Mick Kinnane's, Tom Cole, who was able to help. One of his friends had gone broke and was looking for someone to take over his office in the Norwich Union Building in Waymouth Street. Len King jumped at the opportunity and, having obtained some stability at last, looked forward finally to building his legal practice.

That year – 1951 – another young lawyer with a similar vision to Len King's of a fairer and more equitable society was also trying to establish a sole practice. This was Don Dunstan. He had been to St Peter's College and obtained his law degree in Adelaide, then returned to Fiji to begin a legal practice. Now he was back in Adelaide with the ambition of entering politics and getting the Labor party into government.[12] Len King had joined the Labor party in 1946 when he returned from the war. While at university, he assisted the campaign to win back the State seat of Norwood in the elections of 1947 and 1950.

Labor party fortunes were flagging. The Chifley government had lost the federal election in 1949 to the Liberals. In South Australia, a continuing problem for Labor was that State electorates were designated by geographical area rather than by population. The cluster of industrial areas in the Spencer Gulf and the north-western suburbs of Adelaide meant that a large number of Labor voters lived in a few, highly popu-lated electorates. On the other hand, more sparsely populated rural lands covered many electorates in which farmers lived, and they voted mainly Liberal. The consequence was that although Tom Playford had been in power since 1938, and would remain so until 1965, he did not need to have the majority of the votes, only the majority of the elector-ates.[13] This situation was an added impediment to winning elections for the Labor party.

Newly elected as vice-president of his local branch, Len King was a delegate at the ALP State Convention that endorsed Don Dun-stan for the seat of Norwood. King believed that Dunstan's arrival in Norwood offered fresh hope of securing his home seat for the party. In 1952 a new State election was called. The five Norwood sub-branches of the Labor party mounted an enthusiastic campaign to oust the sitting Liberal and Country League member, Roy Moir. Doris Taylor, Labor's campaign director, was Moir's cousin, though she was a life-long mem-ber of the ALP and one of Dunstan's most energetic supporters.[14] Don Dunstan himself had won a lot of support with the migrant communi-ties in Norwood through a successful case in the High Court for some newly-arrived Britons. He also spent all his spare time doorknocking the residents, something that Roy Moir had never done. Dunstan won

---

12   For more details on Don Dunstan's reasons for entering politics, consult Don
      Dunstan, *Felicia*, p. viii; pp. 22-32 and Don Dunstan (John Spoehr, ed.),
      Politics and Passion, 2000, 179-180.

13   For a brief summary of what was called the "Playmander", see Dean Jaensch
      (ed.) *The Flinders History of South Australia*, cited above, p. 363-364.

14   See Don Dunstan, *Felicia*, pp. 28, 33 and 35, for this paragraph.

and remained the member for Norwood until he resigned as Premier in 1979, twenty-seven years later.

After the success of Don Dunstan's election as Member for Norwood, Len King stepped back from his active political life to concentrate both on his legal career and the establishment of a family with the girl he married in January, 1953, Sheila Keane. They moved out of Norwood and for the next fifteen years, although Len King would maintain his membership with the Labor party, he restricted his direct political activity to handing out voting material at polling booths on election days. He maintained an indirect contribution to the Labor party during this period through his contact with Don Dunstan, who would come to him from time to time for advice.

Len and Sheila King on their wedding day, 24 January 1953. (Len King)

As a boy, Len King had wanted to become a lawyer so that he could defend ordinary people's rights. He had joined the Labor party for the same reasons. These twin passions were born of the same philosophy, though they remained quite separate activities. Much later, Don Dunstan, after his first short term as Premier, would offer Len King the opportunity to merge them by bringing him into the Parliament at the 1970 election and immediately appointing him Attorney-General. Until that moment, politics and law remained apart, and politics very much in the background.

He divides his legal career into three periods. The first includes the early years from admission to practice in 1950 until he took on a junior partner, James Clark, in 1957. The middle period covers the ten years until he was appointed Queen's Counsel in 1967. The final period covers the years as Senior Counsel and, from 1970, leader of the Bar as Attorney-General, until he was appointed to the Supreme Court bench in 1975. During the course of these twenty-five years, Len King would rise from journeyman lawyer in Whyalla to the Attorney-General who, to quote Andrew Parkin, enacted a period of reform "without emulation in this country."[15]

Len King inherited two important legacies when he took over Hugh Martin's practice. Both helped him gain momentum. The first was his secretary, Ruth Fisher. Apart from her secretarial skills, Ruth was able to cover for his absences from the office when in court. She acquired a range of paralegal skills and gradually took on debt collection and the administration of deceased estates. Len King acknowledges her contribution to the earlier development of his advocacy skills: "Without Ruth it would have been impossible for me to spend so much time in court and still conduct a successful general practice."[16]

The second legacy from Hugh Martin was his retainer from the Returned Services League. Referrals from RSL welfare officers for personal injury compensation cases, along with his ability to deal with them to the clients' satisfaction, gave Len King the opportunity to develop an extensive practice in this area. His practice also covered the full range of civil, criminal, matrimonial, litigious and non-litigious work. For a period, he averaged one case a week defending tenants against unscrupulous landlords impatient to evict them.

Clients during these first two periods were rarely able to afford the services of Queen's Counsel, and this is one of the reasons Len King found himself in court so often. He was able to save them money and gain himself the valuable experience he needed. But it was also during these years that Len King became keenly conscious of the important role money plays in the justice system. His clients were not usually businesses, but ordinary individuals. He saw many instances where lack of money prevented clients from obtaining justice. Without money, evidence could not be fully gathered, expert opinions could not be sought, and settlements were made out of court for less than what was due. A particularly exasperating consequence of insufficient means was when Len King could see that an erroneous decision could be corrected on appeal, but his client could not take the risk of an adverse order for costs, and so would suffer the decision. Later, he would try to broach

---

15   Andrew Parkin, "Transition, Innovation, Consolidation, Readjustment". Dean Jaensch (ed.), *The Flinders History of South Australia*, cited above, p. 302.

16   Interview with Len King 23/5/02.

the problem of financing better justice through his work with the Law Society Council and as Attorney-General.

His first reported case was for clients who could afford a QC and he enlisted the services of his former boss, Joe Nelligan QC.[17] This was a dispute over a will, and Len and Nelligan represented the plaintiffs – the trustees of the will.[18] Justice George Ligertwood heard the case.[19] An unorthodox and informal arrangement between an employer and long-term employee who went to fight in World War Two created a double-sided problem. First, the employer had died and left behind a convoluted residuary arrangement concerning his wool businesses in Adelaide and Perth. He wanted them continued for five years, to continue to employ his five employees, to divide the profits among them, and then at the end of the five years, to sell the businesses, offering them first to the employees.

Secondly, one of the employees had not worked for the employer since his return from the war, but had been both promised a job and told to consider himself an employee of Mr Tait's business until a vacancy became available. Before he went off to fight in 1942, he had worked in the Adelaide operation for twenty years. While he was waiting to go back to work for Mr Tait, he worked at Myers on Rundle Street. When Mr Tait died in May 1948, the employee had not worked for him for six years; by the time of the hearing, he had not worked in the wool businesses for over ten years.

Towards the end of the five years stipulated by Mr Tait, the problem came to a head as to whether this ex-employee was to be considered – as Mr Tait informally did consider him – an employee. The trustees had to know whether they should employ him, include him in the profit sharing, and offer him a chance to buy the wool businesses with the oth-

---

17   J W Nelligan QC graduated from the University of Adelaide with an LLB in 1921. He was appointed a Special Magistrate in 1965 and held this until his death in 1972. He chaired the Royal Commission on State Transport Services in 1966. Graham Loughlin, *South Australian Queen's Counsel*, 1865-1972.

18   *In Re Thomas Tait, Deceased; Rumsby and Another v Cowan and Others* [1953] SASR 263.

19   Sir George Coutts Ligertwood was a judge of the South Australian Supreme Court from 1945-1958. He was Associate to both Sir Samuel Way (1911-1914) and Sir George Murray (no dates available). See [1953] SASR V at X and Graham Loughlin, cited above, pp A67-A68.

er four. Justice Ligertwood decided that Mr Tait's intentions within his will were obvious: he had considered the man an employee and wanted his trustees to, and so that was what they were obliged to do.

Another area of legal practice that provided Len King with a lot of "bread and butter" cases, apart from personal injury claims and landlord-tenant disputes, were divorces and custody conflicts. One in particular illustrates a problem of the period following the second world war. Many eastern Europeans, having suffered Hitler's occupation, fled when Stalin arrived; Australia was a destination for many thousands including some who had become separated from their spouses and children. The problem was that the Stalin régime did not permit its citizens to have contact with the outside world, and so immigrants did not expect to hear from their families again.

Len King had a client who was from Lithuania. He had lost a wife and children in the rush to leave and had not heard from them since. In Australia he had met a woman and wanted to marry. What was he to do? He could not file for divorce on the grounds that his wife had committed adultery, cruelty or desertion.[20] The law also allowed for a period of seven years after which, if there was no communication from a spouse they could be presumed dead. The catch with this was that since Stalin precluded his people from contact with anyone outside his empire, the lack of communication did not necessarily signify death.

Len King argued that because a party could never expect to hear from a spouse because of totalitarianism the presumption of death should apply. The courts took this practical view and Len King's client was deemed to be a widower. Other wartime refugee migrants – mainly from Lithuania – subsequently got similar rulings so that they could begin new families.

But in 1953 Stalin died and with him the complete ban on international contacts. Len King's Lithuanian client discovered that his wife and children were alive after all and wanted to re-establish contact with him. Many immigrants from Iron Curtain countries were to make the same heart-wrenching discovery. When his client came back, asking for his advice, Len King could only tell him that the presumption of death had been made in good faith and stood, so his Australian marriage re-

---

20   The current sole grounds for divorce, separation for twelve months, came into force in 1976 with the Family Law Act.

mained valid. He would have to decide what to do himself. Len King was deeply moved by the terrible conflict of loyalty and emotion that lay ahead for this man, who had already suffered the war, the original separation from his family, and having to leave his homeland.[21]

Until the 1960s, the only way for young lawyers in South Australia to specialise early as counsel was to join the Crown Solicitor's Office. Its large volume of business offered a way of gaining experience in advocacy much more rapidly than in private practice. Many future Queen's Counsel and judges of that time acquired their early experience in this way: Roderic Chamberlain, Brian Cox, Eric Millhouse, Rod Matheson and Christopher Legoe.

Len King wanted to find a way of achieving this in private practice. Adelaide had no separate bar, although Christopher Legoe began practising solely as a barrister from September 1955.[22] Back in 1953 Len King had considered moving to Melbourne, where there were opportunities to join a separate bar.[23] In 1959, a general meeting of the Law Society decided against division of the profession into solicitors and barristers, as it had developed in the United Kingdom.

Len King could see that there would be no change in the foreseeable future. He did not have Chris Legoe's advantage of a Cambridge degree and London barrister's training. He did not yet have the Queen's Counsel appointment that allowed Jack Elliott to begin his barrister's practice in 1960. The founding of the South Australian independent bar was still four years away. King realised that an alternative solution was to create a large firm, which would allow him to specialise as counsel. This is what he would do in 1960.

---

21   There is a reported case much later which indicates how long these situations recurred, with Chief Justice John Bray handing down the judgment: *Stankus v Stankus*, (1974) 9 SASR 20.

22   See John Emerson, *History of the Independent Bar of South Australia*.

23   Victoria, like Queensland, inherited a separate bar in law upon separation from New South Wales in 1851, and in that year, the first three barristers were admitted to the Victorian Bar. Unlike Queensland, however, in 1891, an Act of Parliament amalgamated the two branches of the legal profession, although lawyers wishing to practise solely as barristers continued to do so. See John Leonard Forde, *The Story of the Victorian Bar*, pp. 113-115. See also, Arthur Dean, *A Multitude of Counsellors: A History of the Bar of Victoria*.

In the meantime, in 1957 King had taken James Clark as a junior partner so he could devote himself more completely to advocacy work. He took the most important criminal case of his legal career just after that: a murder at Port Pirie. Malcolm Howe, the accused, did not deny that he had killed the other man, but he insisted that he did it in self-defence, staving off a sexual assault. Certain details did not help his argument. The first is that he could have driven off in his car instead of taking out the loaded rifle he had underneath his seat. The second is that he took eighty pounds – equivalent to a month's wages - from the dead man's wallet. At the first trial in Port Augusta, at which Howe was defended by Dr John Bray QC and Len King, both appointed under the legal assistance scheme, the jury found him guilty of murder and Justice Bruce Ross sentenced him to hang.

Justice Ross directed the jury that whatever Howe believed about the risk of assault, if the force he used was unreasonable or excessive, then he was still guilty of murder. Bray and King disagreed. They had argued in the trial that a number of earlier cases had established a principle that even if the force used was excessive, someone defending himself or herself could only be convicted of manslaughter. The future Chief Justices decided to appeal to the Full Court consisting of Justices Herbert Mayo and Geoffrey Reed, and Acting Justice Frank Piper. Andrew Wells, Assistant Crown Prosecutor, represented the Crown.[24] The Bray-King defence was cast across over forty cases dating as far back as Henry VIII. John Bray convinced the Full Court of the possible verdict of manslaughter on the ground of excessive self-defence.[25] The three judges agreed and ordered a new trial.[26]

The Crown, however, obtained special leave to appeal to the High Court.[27] In July 1958, Len King and John Bray went to Sydney to put their arguments before a bench of five judges, including Chief Justice Sir Owen Dixon. This time, Roderic Chamberlain, the Crown Solicitor, appeared for the prosecution.[28] The High Court upheld the

---

24   Andrew Wells became a judge of the Supreme Court from 1970 until 1984. See (1984) 35 SASR V.

25   Michael Abbot talks about the Howe case in "Bray as Barrister", in Wilfrid Prest, ed., *A Portrait of John Bray*. See in particular pp. 53-56.

26   *R v Howe* [1958] SASR 95.

27   *R v Howe* (1958) 100 CLR 448.

28   Justice of the Supreme Court of SA, 1959-1971. Knighted as Sir Roderic in 1970. See [1970] SASR V.

decision of the South Australian Full Court: the murder conviction was set aside and a retrial ordered.

The retrial took place in Adelaide instead of Port Augusta before Justice Piper, who had been on the Full Court of the first appeal. But John Bray could not appear on the date set by the Crown Prosecutor, who controlled the criminal list and rejected Len King's request for a different date to suit John Bray's availability. The court had no power over this. Joe Nelligan QC took Dr Bray's place as senior counsel. Howe was found guilty of manslaughter and avoided the gallows. When Len King became Chief Justice twenty years later, he took control of the lists for the courts and set dates according to the availability of all parties. The Bray-King principle of self-defence became known as the Howe principle and was used in similar cases at least until the 1980s.[29]

The professional triumph of that year, 1958, was tempered the following year by the death of Mary King at the age of sixty-eight. She had seen her son establish a successful sole legal practice and expand this to a partnership. She had also seen two grand-children: Susan in 1953 and Michael in 1955.[30] By 1960, Len King had moved his partnership with James Clark to Cowra Chambers in Grenfell Street – now replaced by 25 Grenfell Street – and then to 24 Waymouth Street. The latter housed two other practices: a firm of four lawyers - Wallman, Palmer, hutton and Duffy - and John Mangan, a sole practitioner. Together they decided that they were well placed to merge into a single partnership, which became known as Wallman and Partners. This was the largest firm in Adelaide, and Len King was now able to practise almost entirely as a barrister. For the next ten years, until he entered Parliament and became Attorney-General, he remained with Wallmans.

Now able to devote his time more exclusively to advocacy, Len King represented the firm's clients in other areas, such as commercial and tax work, and found himself doing less criminal, matrimonial, personal injury and general common law work.

King also involved himself in several law-related activities. One was lecturing once a week in an evening course called "Law for Every Man" for the Department of Adult Education at the University of Ad-

---

29   Michael Abbott, "Bray as Barrister". Cited above, p. 53.
30   Len and Sheila King have had five children. The other three are: Catherine, 1960; Josephine, 1961; and James, 1965.

elaide. The course was aimed at people with no legal knowledge. This meant having to explain the law in clear language. Len King found that "legal jargon was useless in those situations and if I lapsed into it, there would be swift protest from the class."[31] In this way, he maintained a skill for communicating law to members of the public, something he would keep in mind later when writing judgments.

In 1960 Len King was elected to the Law Society Council and stayed a member until his appointment as a puisne judge in 1975. This is where he first had the opportunity to make his mark as a law reformer. He was a member of the Intermediate Court sub-committee from 1964 to 1969, which planned a new level of courts between the Magistrates and Supreme Courts. Roma Mitchell, by this time a Queen's Counsel, was also a member. She was in favour initially of creating a county court system similar to the one in Victoria. By the middle of 1965,

Len and Sheila King in 1966. (Courtesy Len King)

Len King had produced a detailed report that outlined an alternative if the government could not find the means of establishing an entire new court system. He provided strategies showing how the Local Court system could be extended to fulfil the function of an intermediate court. This preparatory work continued until 1969 when Robin Millhouse, as Liberal Attorney-General, introduced the Local Courts Act Amendment Bill.[32] The solution by then was to create the District Criminal Court to supplement the Local Courts, which were only for civil cases. In this way, many indictable offences could be removed from the Supreme Court, which by then was working under an increasing backlog. Much later, as we will see, when Len King was Chief Justice, the District Criminal and Local courts would merge and become the principal trial court of South Australia.

Occasionally, someone he knew in the Labor party would refer work to him. This is in a way what happened one Saturday morning in

31   Len King, *Unpublished Memoirs*, cited above, "The Practice of the Law", p 69.
32   *Acts of the Parliament of South Australia*, p.609.

early 1966, when he was at the ice machine on The Parade, Norwood. Len King was buying ice to chill the drinks that afternoon at tennis. Don Dunstan was also there for some ice. As Attorney-General, he was setting up a Royal Commission into the Licensing Laws. He had been approached by the judge of the Licensing Court who was finding the Licensing Act increasingly unworkable. One anomaly among many that had arisen since during the Playford years was that football clubs were trading in alcohol on Sundays, and they were not licensed at all. The situation had been brought to a head by the decision in the Full Court in *Bay Hotel v Broadway Hotel*. Referring to the Licensing Act 1932-1960, Chief Justice Napier denounced the existing legislation as belonging to a "horse and buggy age" and "hopelessly out of touch."[33]

Sir Mellis's judgment would trigger the most comprehensive reforms in South Australia's alcoholic beverage trade in its one hundred and thirty year history. Dunstan obtained a long list of difficulties from the Superintendent of Licensed Premises. A central issue was the trading hours that had been in force since a referendum in March 1915. The last attempt to review these, most notably the hotel closing time of six o'clock, had been in September 1938, two months before Tom Playford became Premier. But the Women's Christian Temperance Union, which had been instrumental in bringing in the closing time in the first place, was still powerful enough still to thwart efforts to change it.[34]

Dunstan had appointed Keith Sangster QC as Royal Commissioner, and now he was seeking an experienced barrister to assist him.[35] Len King accepted and would spend most of 1966 occupied by it. John Bray, also a QC by that time, with Michael White assisting,[36] represented the Hotels Association. The hotels were keen to see trading hours extended, but on the other hand, concerned about the impact on them of licensing clubs and restaurants to sell alcohol.

---

33 Quoted from Sir Mellis Napier's judgment. *Bay Hotel v Broadway Hotel* [1965] SASR 254; 255. The other two judges were Chamberlain and Bright.

34 See Eric Richards, ed., *The Flinders History of South Australia*, vol. 3: "Social History", pp. 222-224.

35 Keith Sangster was later a Justice of the Supreme Court of SA from 1971 until 1984. See (1984) 34 SASR V. Also, Graham Loughlin, *South Australian Queen's Counsel*, cited above, pp. A109-A110.

36 Later a Justice of the Supreme Court of SA from 1978 until his death in 1993.

The Royal Commission's findings were the basis of the Licensing Act 1967, which is largely the system that operates now. When the Bannon government was reviewing it in 1984, Peter Young highlighted its impact: "Most people now take for granted many results of Sangster's report that were, at the time, quite radical. It now seems quite unthinkable for example that there should be no restaurant licences or no facility, on the whole, for clubs to sell liquor, but these were just two matters that prevailed before 1966."[37] Other recommendations which were to form part of the fabric of South Australian social life were licences for sales from motels, wineries' cellar doors, and theatres and cabarets. The hotels were able at long last to stay open until ten o'clock each night. One recommendation that the Licensing Act did not bring in yet was Sunday opening.

Not long after the end of the Royal Commission into liquor licensing, Don Dunstan again came to Len King. He wanted to tackle corporate crime after a number of company frauds had deprived trusting investors of their money. The Crown Prosecutor was reluctant to prosecute these frauds because he thought a jury would get lost in the complex evidence. Dunstan decided to take up the cause himself and set up a special unit within the Attorney-General's Department. One of the first cases it took up involved a company called Davco.[38] The company had failed and many hundreds of investors lost their money. A decision was taken to prosecute the principals in the scheme for conspiracy to defraud. Dunstan engaged Len King as counsel for the prosecution. As it turned out, the case would drag on through 1967 and almost halfway into 1968. Part-way through the preliminary hearing, on June 15 1967, he was appointed a Queen's Counsel.

At least three of the men involved in Davco had a past history of setting up businesses whose primary goal was less to make money through trading than to make it through fleecing luckless investors. Two of the men had bought a disused molybdenite mine for a token sum. They joined together with their accountant and lawyer, and created Development and Vending Company – Davco. They then created some paper assets. The two mine owners sold the worthless mine to Davco for three hundred thousand pounds and then placed that money

37   P F Young, *Review of the South Australian Licensing Act 1967, and Its Administration*, pp. 30-31.
38   Don Dunstan, *Felicia*. Cited above, pp. 123-124.

back in Davco. That gave Davco now the appearance of having both the mine and the money, without, in fact, having much at all. These paper assets were then used on promotional literature to reassure potential investors that the company was safe to put money in for its new venture: American-style vending machines. High pressure salesmen lured large sums of money from vulnerable people. Then the company went broke. A corporate affairs investigator found that most of the money went to the five shareholders and their salesmen, and that vending machines had been installed in only two schools.

The catch for Don Dunstan was that the lawyer involved, Les Wright, was a personal friend. Les Wright had been a Labor candidate and now was hoping to become a magistrate. Dunstan's advisers found no evidence at this stage of his wrongdoing and so Les Wright was appointed a Special Magistrate. A few months later, when the full extent of Wright's involvement became apparent to the special unit, Dunstan was advised that if the principals were to be prosecuted for conspiracy to defraud, there was no alternative to including Wright as a defendant. Don Dunstan wept. Not only was it bad enough that he now had to suspend his friend, but his friend's wife was dying of cancer. In addition, one of the other men was suffering from advanced multiple sclerosis and was deemed not fit to stand trial.

A hearing in the Police Court and the subsequent Supreme Court trial lasted from October 1967 until April 1968. The jury found all men not guilty. Len King was up against some very skilled lawyers for the defence: Jack Elliott QC, who appeared for Les Wright; Cedric Isaachsen, for Mr Wyatt; and Bob Mohr, for Mr Salgo.[39] Jack Elliott had subpoenaed the new Chief Justice, John Bray, to give a character reference for Les Wright. Jack Elliott gives a version of the trial in *Memoirs of a Barrister*, flawed by his own friendship with Les Wright.[40] El-

---

39   Cedric Isaachsen retired in 2004 at 93 years of age; Bob Mohr became a
      Judge of the District Court of SA from 1970 until 1978, then Justice of the
      Supreme Court of SA from 1978 to 1995. Trial judge Justice Charles Bright
      was on the Supreme Court bench from 1963 until 1979.

40   See Jack Elliott, *Memoirs of a Barrister*, pp. 245-252. For example, Elliott
      claims that Les Wright had been a magistrate "for at least six years" at the
      time of his arrest (p. 245), but he was appointed in 1966, as Dunstan records.
      Elliott also says that Len King replaced Dunstan as Attorney-General in 1967
      when Dunstan became Premier (p. 248). Dunstan filled both offices until
      losing the 1968 election.

liott was certainly misinformed, though he was right in his belief in Les Wright's innocent involvement in the affair.

Two rumours in the mid-1960s may have coloured Jack Elliott's memories later. One was in 1965 that Len King would be appointed Attorney-General if Labor won office then, even though he was not even a member of parliament. He was surprised to receive phone calls congratulating him. The second came a year later. Don Dunstan was apparently going to appoint himself Chief Justice after Sir Mellis Napier retired. Dunstan attended a meeting of the Law Society Council specially called at his request to address the rumour, and Len King, as a member of the council, was present. He writes that as well as putting the rumour to rest, Dunstan, true to his style, "expressed a rather forthright opinion of those who generated rumours of that kind".[41]

Len King's last reported case before becoming Attorney-General brought him back to the place he had started in practice – Whyalla. This was a personal injury claim by a Mr Monaghan who had sustained first and second degree burns to 80 per cent of his body. Most of his skin peeled off and he suffered excruciating agony over many months. The company he worked for, Wardrop and Carroll, was building an oxygen plant for BHP at their Whyalla steelworks in November 1964. He had to do some welding in an area near liquid oxygen. The oxygen level in the air was supposed to be checked, as if the level exceeded 21 per cent - just above normal atmospheric levels – lighting a welding torch would cause combustion. No one checked and Mr Monaghan was burned. Two hours afterwards the oxygen level was checked and found to measure 50 per cent.[42]

Monaghan approached Len King directly, who took the case with John Mangan as his junior counsel. The thing that struck Len King was Monaghan's remarkable courage. He was determined to receive his full entitlement, and never lost faith in Len King's capacity to obtain it. Even when he was offered an out-of-court settlement during the trial, by which time Len King was concerned about which direction it might go, he reaffirmed his intention to get his full award. His confidence in Len King was such that during a crucial stage of the hearing, he left, saying, "we are going to win anyway, so why should I listen to all this legal talk." Len King was in fact annoyed slightly by Monaghan's

41   Len King, *Unpublished Memoirs*, "The Practice of the Law", p. 52.
42   *Monaghan v Wardrope and Carroll Pty Ltd* [1970] SASR 575.

departure at such a point. He wanted him to see the extent of the effort he had gone to in the preparation of his argument.

As Mr Monaghan never doubted, Justice Roma Mitchell found in his favour and he received the full amount of compensation. Some years later, Len King was giving a talk at an ALP sub-branch meeting in Elizabeth. He broached the dilemma that faces a client when advised by his lawyer to settle out of court. "What can the client do?" he asked rhetorically. A familiar voice responded from the back of the hall: "Get another lawyer!" Len King recognised his old client, Monaghan, grinning at the irony of his reply, for he had done just the opposite.

Meanwhile, Don Dunstan was preparing for an election. It was early 1970. When he had been in office two years before, he had remained Attorney-General after taking on the Premiership from Frank Walsh. This time, he wanted someone else – another lawyer – to take on the job of Attorney-General. It was very likely that Labor would win as it was only the gerrymandered electoral system that had caused its loss in 1968. Electorates had been redistributed more equally. At a Caucus meeting, Dunstan obtained consent to find someone who could be preselected for the new seat of Coles, and go straight into Cabinet.[43] One Sunday morning, Len King was at Dunstan's home discussing ALP policy issues. Dunstan asked him if he would be interested in being Attorney-General. There was no other lawyer in the parliamentary party. King replied: "You know what you're asking of me, don't you?" Len King had been caught completely by surprise. After the two and a half years that he had spent on the Licensing Royal Commission, the Davco case, and also a Court of Disputed Returns issue, his practice as a senior counsel had just developed momentum again. He was looking forward to challenging and lucrative work in the years to come. He was more than satisfied with the course his life was taking and very reluctant to give it up. The drop in income would be at least fifty per cent. There was also the impact that a high profile job would have on his family.

On the other hand, he was attracted very much to the potential of being in a front-line position to implement ideas he had long held on social reform, many of which had already become part of the ALP platform. He also felt indebted to the ALP for the Commonwealth

---

43   Don Dunstan, *Felicia*. Cited above, p 169.

Reconstruction Training Scheme that had given him the opportunity to study law: now the Labor movement needed those skills.

A week later, having consulted his family and found that they were quite enthusiastic, he accepted, but on the condition that he would stay no longer than two terms. In the general election that was held on 30 May 1970, Len King was elected Member for Coles. Labor won government so he consequently became Attorney-General under Don Dunstan, who was once again Premier. On 15 July, the new parliament met with Sir Mellis Napier presiding as Lieutenant-Governor. Len King was given the honour of responding to the Lieutenant-Governor's speech and thus became the first politician in South Australia to give his maiden speech from the front bench.[44] The speech is itself an historic document. In it, Len King outlined the philosophy underpinning the changes to come under Labor:

Labor Attorney-General Len King at his desk in 1972. (Courtesy Len King)

The principle which lies at the root of many derivative political principles and which determines my attitude to most of the great questions that have exercised and will exercise this house, is that of the intrinsic value of each human life. The corollary principle being that of the essential equality of all human beings. The steady contemplation of these two great and related principles leads, in my view, to the correct solution of most of the great political and social questions.

Over the following five years, most of the changes outlined in that ground-breaking maiden speech were implemented and often used as models in other States. South Australians ever since have enjoyed

---

44   *Parliamentary Debates SA,* Adelaide: First Session of the Fortieth Parliament, 1971. See pp. 51-55.

an equality before the law never imagined possible before: consumer protection, social welfare and community support, eventual abolition of corporal and capital punishment, choice of individual lifestyle through progressive erasure of sexual and racial discrimination. Len King played a central role in delivering South Australians from a closed, class-structured, sectarian society into the much more open and tolerant society that we enjoy today.

In September 1970 at Yalata Aboriginal Community. (Courtesy Len King)

Len King's five-year political career is well-documented with other achievements of the Dunstan government.[45] It is pivotal in the subsequent judicial career of Len King, as it demonstrated his ability to put his principles of reform into practice. It demonstrated that should court practices need the same overhaul that legislation did, the man to do it would be one and the same. Don Dunstan was the Premier who ap-

---

45   For example: Don Dunstan, *Felicia: The Political Memoirs of Don Dunstan*; Don Dunstan, *Politics and Passion*; Dean Jaensch, ed., *The Flinders History of South Australia*, "Political History", vol. 2; Andrew Parkin and Allan Patience, *The Dunstan Decade*.

pointed John Bray and he also appointed Len King – firstly as a puisne justice of the Supreme Court of South Australia in 1975, then in 1978 as John Bray's successor as Chief Justice.

The year 1978 was an unsettling one in South Australia's history. In January, the unthinkable happened: Don Dunstan sacked the Police Commissioner, Harold Salisbury, for misleading him over the existence of secret files kept on thousands of citizens. The federal government under Malcolm Fraser cut funding to the States, and to South Australia in particular. The Whyalla shipyard, one of the State's major employers, closed down. Thousands of newly built houses could not find buyers. South Australia's unemployment rate was the lowest in the country at the beginning of Dunstan's term; now it was the highest. Chief Justice John Bray announced his retirement due to bad health early in the year. Adele Koh, Don Dunstan's second wife, died in October, the month that Len King took over from Bray.

To make this situation even grimmer, crime rates had also risen. Len King pointed out in a speech a few years into his term as Chief Justice, that statistics collected in 1979 showed that since 1964 in South Australia, the annual murder rate had doubled from 1.7 per hundred thousand to 3.4 – 18 murders in 1964 and 44 in 1979. Serious assaults had gone up proportionately almost ten times in that period from 4.8 per hundred thousand to 37.2 – 51 in 1964 to 482 in 1979. The number of break-and-enters had risen from 4653 cases in 1964 to 23,873 by 1979 – or from 442 per hundred thousand to 1840.[46] The impact on the courts system was a growing backlog of cases and no apparent means of dealing with it.

Another change impacting on the courts was the length of trials. The increasing use of scientific evidence and expert witnesses drew them out beyond all previous records. Valance killed Strang in June 1964, was sentenced in September, lost his appeal to the Full Court that same month, lost his appeal to the High Court in November and was hanged. The whole legal process took less than three months. The complete transcript totals 152 pages. Ten years later, the van Beelen case was dragging into its fourth year and the transcript developing into several thousand pages.

---

46   Len King, "Crime and Community". Speech to the Security Institute of SA, 11/8/82. SLSA Archival Collection, PRG 1163.

In the month that King became Chief Justice, another murder trial began which would also haunt the legal system for several years and illustrate the increased complexity and length that was becoming more the standard than the exception. The legacy of *R v Splatt* was two

The new King Court 30 October 1978: Legoe, Jacobs, Wells, Mitchell, Hogarth, King, Bright, Zelling, Sangster, White, Newman (AJ) (SCLSA).

changes that would stretch the time needed for both sides to prepare for a trial for serious criminal offences.[47] Over the course of many years, Len King had been watching the increasing workload on the courts with some concern. Now that he was Chief Justice, he had the opportunity to improve the system. To do so, he was going to have to make a number of changes that might not be popular in the short term as

---

47   A note appears in (1979) 21 SASR 211 on the problems that the jury
       encountered in Splatt's trial. The Royal Commission report includes all
       details. See C R Shannon QC, *Royal Commission Report Concerning the
       Conviction of Edward Charles Splatt*. There are also the two reports that led
       to the Royal Commission: D W Bollen, *Review of Advice Given to Attorney-
       General by His Officers on Newspaper Articles Written in the Advertiser by Mr
       Stewart Cockburn About the Trial and Conviction of Edwards James Splatt*,
       and *R v Splatt: Report for the Attorney-General*. Jack Elliott, who was Splatt's
       senior counsel until his retirement, also discusses the case in *Memoirs of a
       Barrister*, cited above, pp. 319-338.

people in the system adjusted. The first change that he decided to tackle was the management of the lists of cases before the Supreme Court.

Since the establishment of South Australia with its inherited British justice system, judges had followed the tradition of delivering impartial justice in the cases that came before them and took little interest in the efficiency and organisation of the business side of the courts. Each judge functioned independently. There was a minimum of interaction and coordination between the judges. If a case collapsed or was settled out of court, no system existed to allow another case to be brought forward.

Len King's first task was the institution of a central listing procedure for the allocation of cases. This meant that for the first time in 140 years, the judges had to answer to someone else regarding their workload. This sacrifice naturally met a certain amount of resistance for a while from the judges who had been on the bench longer than Len King. But this step would just be the first in a programme of changes which would eventually unify the entire, scattered courts system into a single, streamlined administrative unit – changes that would take Len King fifteen years of determined leadership to finally get in place.

He saw interventionist management of cases by the court as the key to the efficient disposal of the court's workload and the elimination of delays. The established practice was for the pace of litigation to be in the control of the parties and their solicitors and this was seen as a major contribution to inefficiency and delay. The first step was a sustained campaign by the judges to call on and dispose of the cases in the court's civil list. This placed a great strain on the judges and the court's resources, but it was successful in eliminating the backlog. The next step was to transfer control of the progress of trials over to the court. Use was made of studies and experience elsewhere until the new system was refined to a point of maximum efficiency. Case management, as this court-controlled administration of trials became known, was introduced into the District Court and subsequently in the Magistrates Court. This process transformed the way in which litigation was managed and disposed of in the whole court system.

King was convinced that the success of the new system would depend upon the capacity of the legal profession to respond and this in turn would depend upon the way it was organised. The system could succeed only if adjournment of cases could be restricted to situations in which the interests of justice demanded it, not merely the availability of counsel. The problem was that the profession in South Australia was an amalgamated one in which the majority of lawyers practised in firms as barristers and solicitors. What was necessary was a pool of competent barristers able to take up briefs, thereby minimising the need for adjournments to suit the convenience of advocates who also had busy practices as solicitors.

There was already a small independent bar in existence and King pursued a policy of encouraging its expansion. He had to do this in the face of sustained disapproval and at times outright opposition from government as the notion, believed by King to be essential, had taken root in political circles that an independent bar was not in the public interest. Nevertheless, King believed that the public had a right to better justice from their courts and that an independent bar would be a major contribution.

The Chief Justice in 1978.
(Courtesy Len King)

To encourage more lawyers to leave firms and join the independent bar, Len King reformed the regulations governing the appointment of Queen's Counsel. Historically in South Australia, Queen's Counsel had remained in their firms practising in partnership with solicitors. King himself had remained in Wallmans for a time after being appointed silk in 1967. Although they were supposed to be the pre-eminent counsel available to conduct the heaviest and most difficult cases and to advise on complex matters, it had not been uncommon for appointments to occur not because the appointees were pre-eminent advocates, but because of the prestige and connections of the firm to which they belonged.

King was determined that a Queen's Counsel should be available to take briefs from all sections of the public and the profession free of any obligations to a firm. As Chief Justice he recommended appointments for silk to the governor. He announced in 1979 that in future the Chief Justice would not approve any application for silk unless the applicant left their firm and practised at the independent bar. This drew considerable opposition from sections of the profession and political circles, and for some years attempts were made to reverse the requirement. King firmly adhered to his policy. The result was that he saw a senior bar grow of enhanced quality and independence that performed its intended role to be available to serve the needs of all who wished to brief senior counsel, and a slipstream effect of providing a basis for others to go to the bar as juniors.[48]

In between his administrative reforms, of course, Len King was sitting as a judge himself. As Chief Justice over a much larger bench than his predecessors, he would mainly sit on appeals to the full bench, an approach that had been favoured by former Chief Justice of the High Court, Sir Owen Dixon.[49] Len King would sit on several appeals a month over his period as the Chief and regularly made *ex tempore* judgments.[50] These, like all his judgments, were intended to be clear and comprehensible, not just to people with legal training, but to litigants and anyone else.

In 1981, Len King went on an official visit to the United States, visiting Nebraska, Colorado and Idaho, three American States comparable in population to South Australia. They also had comparable courts systems – the Supreme Court at the top, a general trial court, and county and municipal courts for summary offences and minor civil claims. He wanted to examine the court administration structure in the three states, and their operation independently of their executive governments.

The South Australian courts operated quite separately from each other at this period; each answered ultimately to the Attorney-General. The Supreme Court was a separate department of government run by the Master of the court. The other courts were administered by the Law Department, which also incorporated the Crown Prosecutor's Office, the Crown Solicitor's Office and the Attorney-General's office.[51] Magistrates were public servants and did not have the statutory protection of judicial officers. All the non-judicial staff in the courts were also public servants, therefore answering ultimately to a Minister of the

---

48   See John Emerson, *History of the Independent Bar of South Australia*.
49   Garfield Barwick, *A Radical Tory*, p. 221.
50   Just one example: *Swanport Bottle Shop v Bridgeport Hotel* (1986) 47 SASR 449.
51   Hon. Leonard King AC QC, "A Judiciary-Based State Courts Administration - the South Australian Experience," *Journal of Judicial Administration* 3 (1993), pp. 133-134.

Crown. Len King had two changes in mind that he wanted to bring to the courts system and the first was to bring all the state courts under the same administrative umbrella. The second was to separate the courts from any direct link with the executive arm of government.

The problem with the existing system was firstly it conflicted with the established division of the three arms of government – Executive, Legislative and Judiciary – as to be independent of each other as far as workable. Judges had to be able to make their decisions without fear of any form of interference or retribution from a disapproving Minister of government.

It was only since Federation and its Constitution that the inconsistency had existed. Prior to then, the colonies and provinces had simply inherited their judicial models wholesale from Great Britain. In Great Britain the entire judiciary is headed by the Lord Chancellor who is also the Minister of Justice. Thus, he represents both judicial and executive arms of government.[52] The position of Lord Chancellor has its own system of checks and balances that protect the independence of the judiciary in Britain, but there has never been a counterpart in Australia of these.

When Sir Samuel Way accepted the Lieutenant-Governorship in 1894, no conflict of interest was felt. But it was by the time of Napier's retirement in 1967. John Bray did not wish to take on the ceremonial office as he believed that the executive and the judiciary should be kept apart. Len King declined for the same reason. Holding both offices led "to the incongruity of the Chief Justice in his capacity of Lieutenant-Governor signing instruments of executive government which then come up for review before the courts over which the Chief Justice presides."[53]

In 1982 Len King achieved a modest amount of change to the courts system through the establishment of the Court Services Department. The new department took over the responsibility for all the courts – Supreme, District and Local, and Magistrate. The registrar of each of the courts was made its principal administrative officer, and she or he would answer to the judicial head of the court. At this time

52   From a speech given by Len King to members of the Australian Institute of Judicial Administration, January 25, 1989.
53   Interview with Len King, May 2002.

the Victorian courts were also being reorganised to given them greater independence from the public service, and thus, from the executive arm of government. But although the establishment of the Court Services Department was a step in the right direction, it still was under the ultimate control of the Attorney-General.

After Len King returned from the United States in 1981, he had a much better idea of how an independent court system could function. The American system of government meant, however, that it would not be practical to attempt to reproduce an identical court system in South Australia. But Len King did have a model of an independent judicial administration already in operation in Australia's Westminster system. That was the High Court model. With this and his American models, he began his campaign to convince the South Australian government to establish a courts administration that was as free as possible from any direct influence from the Attorney-General.

Around this time, Len King sat on a case in which the reverse situation of what he feared was one of the issues at stake. The court was being asked to interfere in the processes of executive government and legislation. The West Lakes Development Corporation Limited had signed a contract in 1960 with the Premier and the Minister of Marine to transform the large area of swamp and low-lying land around the upper reaches of the Port River. This was enacted through Parliament as the West Lakes Development Act of 1969.

One of the contract's clauses permitted modifications to the conditions by further agreement between the development corporation and the government. This was the source of the conflict. In 1974 Football Park was built on an area leased from the developers and The South Australian National Football League wanted to allow for night sports and television coverage. This meant floodlighting the arena.

The development corporation did not want floodlighting, but in 1979 a Royal Commission recommended modifying the West Lakes Act to allow it, and to free the development corporation from any legal liability to any of the residents who may have otherwise sued it for these changes. A bill was prepared to amend the Act. Five days before the bill was due to be introduced to parliament, the West Lakes development corporation started legal proceedings for breach of contract. The statement of claim argued that the proposed amendment effectively altered the contract and therefore required the development corporation's consent.

The case was heard in the Supreme Court and produced an important judgment on the powers of parliament in relation to contracts entered into by the executive government.[54] Obviously, the Court could not alter the bill as this would have been interference with Parliament. Equally important, a private corporation had to accept that neither could it interfere with the legislative process. Some aspects of the flood-lighting legislation seem unfair *prima facie,* but written into the original contracts, indentures and Acts was the overriding condition that the contract accord with the general laws of South Australia. The court now affirmed that one of these is that there cannot be any impediment to the legislative process.

A threat to South Australia's legislative autonomy did not fire general public interest, however. Instead, headlines round the end of the 1970s and the beginning of the 1980s were made by a number of unusual murder cases. *R v Miller*[55] entered media mythology as the "Truro Murders";[56] lawyer Derrence Stevenson was found shot dead in the freezer of his strangely angled house on Greenhill Road;[57] and Neil Muir was found in the Port River chopped into pieces and floating inside a large garbage bag.

But it was another murder in which a wife had killed her husband with an axe that best illustrates Len King's compassion and impartiality. Shortly after Len King returned from his official visit to the United States, he sat on the appeal from her conviction. She had been abused and humiliated by her husband for twenty-seven years and he had sexually abused all five of their daughters. One week in April 1981 the wife – named "R" in the reported judgment – began suffering symptoms of shock. She was pale, distracted and twitched. She killed him in the middle of the night.[58]

Provocation had until this case presumed an element of suddenness, leading to a brief period of loss of self-control. This can be

---

54   *West Lakes Limited v The State of South Australia* (1980) 25 SASR 389.

55   *R v Miller* (1980) SASR 170.

56   One of the murdered girl's mothers published a book on her experience of the crimes. See Anne-Marie Mykyta, *It's a long way to Truro.*

57   *R v Szach* (1980) 23 SASR 504.

58   *R v R* (1981) 28 SASR 321.

the difference between a conviction of murder or manslaughter. At her trial under Justice Sangster, the wife was found guilty of murder and her counsel, Geoffrey Eames, appealed to the Full Court.[59]

Len King concluded that the loss of self control necessary for provocation to reduce murder to manslaughter in this case had to be considered in the light of the pressure of the years of domestic violence. He recommended a retrial. Howard Zelling was reluctant to consider the previous history but Sam Jacobs agreed.

Mr Eames had hoped for no better than a verdict of manslaughter, given the facts, it would have been unrealistic to hope for an acquittal. He urged the Full Court to substitute a verdict of manslaughter instead of ordering a new trial. In fact, the jury in the new trial found the woman not guilty of murder or manslaughter, and she was free to go.

In April 1983, Len King delivered a leading judgment in an appeal to the Full Court that would influence future decisions involving medical practitioners and their duty of disclosure to patients. A mother wanted to prevent further pregnancies and opted for a sterilisation procedure known as tubal ligation, or "tying the tubes". The doctor did this at the same time as she performed the Caesarean section for the delivery of the baby. This was in 1975. In 1976, the woman became pregnant again. Much discussion and debate followed and it was six years before the case reached the Supreme Court as *F v R*. In the trial Justice Mohr had found that the obstetrician had been negligent in not advising the woman that there was a small general risk – around one per cent – of her regaining fertility.[60]

For twenty-five years Commonwealth courts had used the Bolam principle – derived from *Bolam v Friern Hospital Management Committee* in 1957 –to determine if there was an infringement. The Bolam principle relied on the medical profession's internal codes of practice on the duty of disclosure. The principle was subsequently applied to many cases in dispute and extended to some outside of medicine.[61] This meant that the medical profession was, in effect, being allowed to make the law which defined patients' rights against doctors.

---

59   Geoff Eames was later a Justice of the Supreme Court of Victoria from 1992 to 2002, and of Victoria's Court of Appeal from 2002.

60   *F v R* (1982) 29 SASR 437.

61   [1957] 1 WLR 582. Lord Scarman restates and thus reinforces the principle in 1985 in *Sidaway v Governors of Bethlem Royal Hospital*, [1985] AC at 881.

Len King knew that in the United States and Canada, the courts did not rely on the medical profession in arriving at their judgments about the duty of disclosure. There was also the fact that the doctor had never known of a single instance of failure of tubal ligation. She had performed six hundred such operations at the time, one of her colleagues about two hundred and a second colleague two or three thousand – all without one single instance of pregnancy recurring.

What Len King and his fellow judges did in *F v R* was to establish the important principle that in cases of non-disclosure of information by doctors, the law should determine the extent of the duty to disclose, not the medical profession:

> On the facts of a particular case the answer to the question whether the defendant's conduct conformed to approved professional practice may decide the issue of negligence, and the test has been posed in such terms in a number of cases. The ultimate question, however, is not whether the defendant's conduct accords with the practices of his profession or some part of it, but whether it conforms to the standard of reasonable care demanded by the law. That is a question for the court and the duty of deciding it cannot be delegated to any profession or group in the community.[62]

This principle was subsequently used in cases in South Australia, New South Wales and the Federal Court and adopted by the High Court of Australia in 1992 in *Rogers v Whitaker*.[63]

Len King was continuing to make inroads in autonomy for the judiciary. In 1983, a new Magistrates Act removed magistrates from the public service and made them independent judicial officers, answerable ultimately to the Chief Justice. This gave impetus to regular meetings between the Chiefs of the three main courts. Sometimes the Chief Judge of the Industrial Court attended. Common policies were developed for the courts and much was done to unify procedures. Although the Chief Justice was not head of the Industrial or District Courts, he was nevertheless informally regarded as head of the whole judiciary and

---

62   *F v R* (1983) 33 SASR 189 at 194.
63   *Rogers v Whitaker* (1992) 175 CLR 479.

its spokesman.

One of the policies was that judgments be delivered promptly. Len King set up a system of returns that showed the dates on which judgments in the Supreme Court were reserved and when they were delivered. If judges fell behind, they were not allocated any cases until they cleared their arrears. Len King then circulated the returns so that judges were aware of their colleagues' progress. This of course placed considerable peer pressure on judges to keep abreast of their judgments. Similar systems were adopted in the other courts to achieve the same end: faster delivery of justice.

This was the first time in South Australia that the Chief Justice had taken such an interventionist role in the courts. Prior to that, the Chief Justice had – formally at least – been distinguished from his puisne colleagues only ceremonially. Years earlier, Justice Ligertwood had reminded the audience at his retirement speech how a judge does not serve under anybody, not the Chief Justice nor the Queen herself.[64] This would remain true for each judge's judicial integrity, but from Len King's time each judge would find that the Chief would take an interest in their efficiency.

Len King did not add this administrative burden to the role of Chief Justice to achieve some sort of power over his puisne judges. He did it because he believed that if the judiciary managed its own administration and became more efficient in the process, there would be no reason for the executive government ever to try and resume that role.

Apart from the reorganisation of the courts from within, Len King also fought to reinforce their independence ceremonially. He was alarmed at the way senior public servants had come to treat the judiciary with diminished respect, which in turn diminished its influence. He began a policy of insisting that judges of the Supreme Court be treated as equal in all respects to ministers. He reasserted the Chief Justice's precedence in being second only to the Premier and being above the other ministers. He refused to attend official functions unless this precedence was acknowledged.

One example was the opening of Parliament. In the Westminster tradition, judges attended in full judicial regalia and sat on the floor

---

64   See [1958] SASR at viii.

of the Legislative Council. In South Australia, judges had over the years been quietly pushed out to reserved seats in the gallery. It is obvious how that would have a symbolic impact on their standing. Len King insisted that the tradition be respected or the judges would be better off not attending at all. He managed to restore the judges to their traditional positions on the floor of the chamber.

He continued to campaign for a fully independent judiciary. The Court Services Department was still only a part of the way to the goal he sought: an autonomous courts administration in which all the South Australian courts answered to the Chief Justice, judicial officers and support staff alike. Speeches on the topic were one way of publicising his mission. Another was to make full use of the annual report furnished to the Attorney-General. The report had become a mere repository for statistics. Len King expanded it to do what he felt it should do: report not just the activities of the courts, but also draw attention to issues affecting their administration.

Another vehicle to increase pressure on the government was the press. The judiciary had traditionally remained aloof from all public comment, and in relation to specific cases, this would remain the case. But Len King could not see why general principles and actual day-to-day needs should not be made public if necessary. For example, at the end of 1981 he publicly expressed concern about the need for more judges and support staff in the Supreme Court. On October 7, 1981, Justice Mohr had to cancel a civil hearing for lack of staff. Dates for trials were being set up to eight months ahead. At this point there were thirteen judges. The situation was alleviated in the first part of 1982, when Justice Derek Bollen was appointed (in March) and Justice Robin Millhouse (in April). For almost six months, until the retirement of Justice Donald Williams, South Australia had fifteen Supreme Court judges. This is the highest it has ever been, having stabilised at fourteen for the following twenty years. In 2006 the number was again down to twelve and thirteen and in crisis as a result.

In July 1983, a very important event took place that would change the life of all the courts in South Australia: the Sir Samuel Way building was opened. This project had begun in January 1980 under David Tonkin's Liberal government. The cost of the project was $32 million and it provided ten criminal and seventeen civil courtrooms. The original building had been the home of Charles Moore's department store from 1916 until 1979, and was based on the design of the Galeries Lafayette department store in Paris - complete with the grand marble staircase and dome.

The opening began a new era in South Australia as it physically integrated most of the higher State courts in one central location. On the western side of Victoria Square, it was adjacent to the original Supreme Court building, which would continue to be the main venue for civil cases and for the chambers of the members of the Supreme Court bench. It would also allow the continued expansion and development of the District Court and thus, increased efficiency in the flow of cases.

That year - 1983 - was also of particular interest for the mix of the Supreme Court bench. The month before the opening of the Sir Samuel Way building, Elliott Johnston QC began his judicial tenure. For a few months, until Justice Dame Roma Mitchell's retirement in September, there would be both a Catholic woman and a Communist together with their increasingly diverse brother judges. This change to the bench of the State's superior court is highly revealing of the distance that South Australia had travelled since the end of the Playford era.

In 1987 Len King, together with brother Justices Brian Cox and John von Doussa, were faced with a murder appeal that demanded the same impartiality and compassion as *R v R* – the abusive husband killed with the axe. Len King wrote the leading judgment, supported by the other two judges.

A sixty-two year old man of unblemished reputation had killed his mentally-ill wife at her own request after thirty-six years of marriage. He was convicted on his own confession. The sentencing judge at the trial was obliged by law to set a mandatory life sentence, but given the extraordinarily tragic circumstances, had set the non-parole period at ten days. This had the effect of immediate release. The Attorney-General appealed, alarmed at the message such an apparently light punishment sent out to the public.

The murder had taken place in February 1986, and the husband was sentenced in January 1987. The Full Court published reasons for their decision in July.[65] The story behind the death has echoes twenty years later, at the time this book is being prepared. Euthanasia remains

---

65   *R v Johnstone* (1987) 45 SASR 482.

a passionately debated topic, with no hope of resolution between those who believe in choice and the morally anxious souls who do not.

The husband and wife were married happily for the first six years and became parents to a son and a daughter. Their life turned after a series of miscarriages. This became too much for the wife to bear and she fell victim to manic depressive psychosis, also known since then as bipolar disorder.

So extreme were the fluctuations between her manic and depressive states, that in 1964 she underwent a leucotomy to try and alleviate the problem. This operation – also known as a prefrontal lobotomy – did nothing but make things worse. Over the years that followed the wife became alcoholic and attempted suicide three times. She often asked her husband to help her die. During the whole time, however, he devoted himself to her care and defended any attempts to put her into an institution. He seemed able to withstand even her most unpleasant behaviour. At the same time, he managed to have a successful career in engineering and be an active member of his church.

On the fatal night, the two were drinking. The wife convinced the husband to take her life, and out of concern for her future if she continued to live, he did.

Len King observed, in his reasons:

> Cases such as this present great difficulty to the sentencing judge and to an appellate court. People cannot be permitted to take life in defiance of the law, however altruistic their personal motives may be.[66]

He could not overlook the fact that the sentencing judge had been affected by the husband's awful suffering. But King had to ask if the interests of justice and the welfare of the community required that the unfortunate offender be returned to prison. At this stage, the husband had been at liberty for six months. Len King decided to leave him there, but strongly emphasised the exceptional nature of the case, and that it was not to be used as a precedent.

---

66   Cited above, at 485.

This case also illustrates an accepted way by which the executive can challenge results in court, although some judges do view appeals from the Attorney-General with concern. The following case is an example of a different area of tension: the question of if and when the court has jurisdiction over matters discussed during parliamentary debate.

As a member of the Cabinet for five years, Len King was well equipped to sit on disputes resulting from parliamentary practice. This conflict originated in April 1987 during question time in the House of Assembly. Peter Lewis, the Liberal Member for Mallee, asked a question of the Minister for Environment and Planning that implied Steven Wright had received favourable treatment in a planning application because of his former position as secretary to Don Dunstan. Since this allegation was made under parliamentary privilege, Mr Wright could only respond with a letter denying the allegation, which was published in *The Advertiser* on May 13. Mr Lewis sued Mr Wright and Advertiser Newspapers, claiming general, aggravated and exemplary damages.

Peter Lewis could not obtain judgment in his favour in the Magistrate's Court. Two years later he did in the District Court. But Judge Lunn also sought the opinion of the Supreme Court Full Court on whether the matter was justiciable - able to be heard in a court - or whether it was a matter for parliament to sort out. At the same time Mr Wright and the *Advertiser* appealed the decision.

No legal precedent was located detailing a similar situation. The case raised fundamental issues of constitutional law and became important for its exploration of the limits of parliamentary privilege. In the Full Court, Chief Justice King and his brother judges White and Olsson each produced lengthy reasoning that unanimously allowed the appeal.[67] One of the key factors in giving the courts jurisdiction was that Mr Lewis had opened the process in the courts. He had been protected by parliamentary privilege and Mr Wright could not take him to court. Mr Wright, however, had every right to counter publicly the allegations against him if he believed them untrue, and that is what he did. If Mr Lewis then wanted to begin a legal dispute about that, he could not use parliamentary privilege to prevent Mr Wright from defending himself. Len King commented:

---

67   *Wright and Advertiser Newspapers Limited v Lewis* (1990) 53 SASR 416.

If a Member of Parliament could recover damages for true statements about his conduct in Parliament because the maker of the statement was prevented from proving their truth, public criticism of the conduct of Members of the Parliament would be effectively stifled.

Justice Olsson agreed. He also said that neither the original British 1688 Bill of Rights, which defined parliamentary privilege, nor any of the authorities cited to the court, established that the privilege was absolute:

> The express purpose of the Bill of Rights was to erect a protective shield of defence for Members of Parliament, so that they may discharge their duties without constant fear of action being taken against them. It was not enacted for the purpose of forging a sword of oppression, whereby individual Members of Parliament could, at their initiative, prosecute proceedings for civil relief against citizens in a manner which denies those citizens access to the normal defences made available to them by law.[68]

The decision continues to apply to the South Australian State Parliament and stands as a judicial protest against attempts to use parliamentary privilege in a way that causes oppression and injustice.

Since the 1960s one of the most important of the many changes that have taken place in Western society has been the growth in understanding of the particular experience of women. Countless women over the centuries found themselves silent victims of a brutal husband, condemned to stay with him for life for want of any avenue of escape. If occasionally they were driven beyond the bounds of endurance and killed the man, as was the axe murder case – they risked being condemned a further time to a prison sentence for want of an understanding of the unbalanced state of mind that long-term abuse and fear can induce.

Len King led a landmark decision in 1991 that faced up to the particular problems confronting women in oppressive domestic circumstances and as a result, greatly improved the quality of justice in South

---

68   Cited above, at 426; at 416 for the preceding quote by King CJ.

Australia - and not just for murder cases. *R v Runjanjic; R v Kontinnen* admitted for the first time in Australia the defence of what was then termed "battered woman's syndrome".[69] The details of the case are in themselves unusual, but they illustrate how the result on a woman of living in perpetual terror and being beaten regularly deprives her of her will and ability to escape her situation.

The tyrant in this case was called Hill, but he died before the trial reached court. He had two female partners – Runjanjic and Kontinnen – whom he forced to work as prostitutes, and at home to attend to his every need. The price of disobedience was a severe beating. Hill had met Runjanjic in 1981. About 1987, he added Kontinnen to his household. In 1989, Runjanjic bore a child by him. He looked upon them as his women and designated them "Number One" and "Number Two".

The three of them purchased a property at Swan Reach, a remote town next to the River Murray. They also had the use of Kontinnen's house in Adelaide. This was the source of the trouble that ended up in the courts. That house was broken into and Hill believed that one of Kontinnen's female friends was involved. He ordered Kontinnen to trick her into coming up to Swan Reach. This his fearful "Number Two" did. As soon as the woman arrived, Hill beat her savagely with a shotgun, breaking her arm.

This woman was then handcuffed to a bed and kept for days in agony at the Swan Reach house. Hill beat her again and cut her rings from her fingers. He forced her to collect firewood. Their injured prisoner made her escape when, on Hill's orders, Runjanjic was taking her to another house. The victim managed to wave down a car on the main road and get taken to a police station.

At the trial, Ranjunjic and Kontinnen were found guilty on charges of false imprisonment and intentionally causing grievous bodily harm. The trial judge had not allowed the defence to lead evidence of the "battered woman syndrome", and one of the reasons for their appeal by Kevin Borick was that the judge was wrong in not allowing that evidence.

Len King agreed. He could not find any case in Australia that had tackled the topic but he found that it had been widely accepted in the United States and Canada. The syndrome had been described in a

69   *R v Runjanjic; R v Kontinnen* (1991) 56 SASR 114.

book by Dr Lenore Walker called *The Battered Woman Syndrome* and had become an acceptable part of expert evidence during the 1980s. He ruled that the convictions be set aside and a new trial held in which "battered woman" evidence would be allowed. The other two judges, Justices Legoe and Bollen, agreed. It was a pioneering decision that led to such evidence being admitted across the Australian jurisdictions, and also led to a better understanding of the situation of victims of habitual domestic oppression and violence.[70]

Len King had never been satisfied with the establishment of the Courts Department, later the Courts Services Department, as it was ultimately controlled by the Attorney-General. By 1988 in their report to the Attorney-General and Parliament, the judges argued that "the time is ripe for further consideration of the feasibility of the establishment of a system of court administration, independent of executive government and the Public Service (...)."[71]

In the 1989 report the judges expressed their regret that there had been no response, which brought a negative one. In 1990, the judiciary-based system of court administration in the High Court of Australia was extended to the other Commonwealth courts – the Federal and Family. The 1990 judges report argued that the Commonwealth trend made the objections put forward by the South Australian government irrelevant.

Finally, Len King received a letter from State Attorney-General Chris Sumner, saying that on 17 February 1992, the government had approved in principle, "a unified non-executive-based system of courts administration". An establishment committee was set up including the chief judicial officers and the Attorney-General. He introduced the Bill into the Legislative Council and through the rest of 1992 and early 1993, it was debated.

At one point the Bill was referred to the Legislative Review Committee of both houses of parliament and Len King attended and gave evidence. It was an historic occasion as that appears to be the first time a

---

70   For example, this case was cited in the High Court of Australia in *Osland v R* (1998) 197 CLR 316.

71   King, Len, "A Judiciary-based State Courts Administration - the South Australian experience", *Journal of Judicial Administration*, Vol. 3, 1993, p. 134.

Chief Justice has given evidence before a parliamentary committee. On 25 March 1993, the Bill was passed.

The final step was to implement it. The Courts Administration Authority began operations on 1 July 1993 with a ceremony at which the Attorney-General – representing executive government – handed over the administration of the courts to the Chief Justice. This was the most triumphant day of Len King's time as Chief Justice. It represented the culminating moment of more than fifteen years of pressure on both Labor and Liberal governments to relinquish their control of the courts.

The creation of the Courts Administration Authority changed the role of Chief Justice. Now, instead of being a mainly symbolic and ceremonial title, it offered real control over the operations of all the State courts – Supreme, District, Youth, Magistrates, Drug, Coroner's, Environment Resources and Development and Industrial Relations. Moreover, since the Chief Justice now embodied a unified and structured judiciary, his symbolic status was stronger than ever before.

Len King's legacy means that since 1993 in South Australia, the courts of this state have been fully independent. The Attorney-General was not completely removed from the operations of the courts. She or he must still approve the courts' budget and remains entitled to full information about the administration of the courts. Since 1993, however, he Chief Justice was able from then on, however, to be,

The Chief Justice with the Governor in the early 1990s - his former principal at Nelligan Mitchell and Walters, when he had been an articled clerk. (Courtesy Len King)

in Len King's words, "ever in the watchtower on the lookout for any inroads which the implementation of government policy might make upon the independence of the judiciary and the system of justice".[72]

There is yet another important aspect of the legacy of South Australia's first unified and independent courts system. While the State's population increased only ten per cent during the seventeen years that Len King held the office of Chief Justice – from just under 1.3 million to 1.46 million – the size of the legal profession more than doubled, from 750 to 1600 or so. The increase was even more dramatic in the independent bar. Three sets of chambers were in existence in 1978 with around twenty barristers. By 1995, seventeen sets of chambers housed well over a hundred practising barristers. It is important that such an expanding profession has as its epicentre a solid, unified, independent courts system, that assures the South Australian populace its justice system is the best in its history.

1998: Len King in retirement. (Courtesy Len King)

At the end of April 1995, Len King became the first Chief Justice of South Australia to retire at the compulsory age of seventy, introduced more than fifty years earlier when he was still fighting the Japanese in the steamy jungles of New Guinea. Napier was already a judge when it came into effect, and Bray retired early, at sixty-six. It was the end of an era, when there was more change to the office of Chief Justice in seventeen years than in its entire history since its inception in 1856. Len King left his successor, John Doyle, in control of the whole South Australian court system, and consequently with a much greater control over the justice process itself.

---

72   Cited from his retirement address, 28 April 1995.

CHAPTER 7

Conclusion

CHIEF JUSTICES OF SOUTH AUSTRALIA
SINCE FEDERATION

How has the office of Chief Justice in South Australia changed over a hundred years?

The most significant legislative change took place on 1 July 1993 when the Chief Justice took control of the entire State courts system from the Attorney-General. On that day the functions of the office were officially widened for the first time to include administrative responsibility for the courts as a whole and as a result the judicial arm of government was finally independent of the executive. With the power enshrined in the Courts Administration Act 1993, the Chief Justice can genuinely act in the best interests of a truly independent judiciary. Her or his symbolic presence as the gate-keeper of justice is greatly strengthened.

The most significant groundroots change took place in 1960. The controversy ignited by the Stuart case was a catalyst in bringing about change to a judiciary which had grown increasingly out of touch. Napier's speeches reveal that he was attached to noble ideals but also that he believed them to be immutable. He thought perhaps that it was he who set community standards, not the community - when as Chief Justice, he embodies those standards.

Before Stuart, the representatives of law and order – police, crown prosecutors, judges – more or less expected that their authority would be unquestioned. After Stuart, their authority would be forever scrutinised. From Sergeant Phin's racist logic, to Dr Kathleen Thompson's vague forensics, to David O'Sullivan's deficient defence, to Crown Solicitor Roderic Chamberlain's disregard of the presumption of innocence and of the Evidence Act, to Justice Geoffrey Reed's refusal to hear Stuart's prepared statement, to the Full Court's and then the High Court's inability to address any of these issues – not to say the Royal Commission that followed – the South Australian system of justice was exposed as completely unable to acknowledge its own fallibility.

The Stuart case also pinpoints the beginning of the period of the media's open criticism of the courts. The papers had often attacked Way and had occasionally satirised the judges of the day, but never challenged the very system itself. Sixty years later, under young, ambitious, seemingly fearless Rupert Murdoch, *The News* took it on. Exaggerated though their coverage may have been, the owner and editor of a tabloid newspaper were the only people able to prevent the hanging of a man whose confession, together with the flimsiest of circumstantial evidence, did not at all prove beyond reasonable doubt that he had committed murder.

The press intervened in the judicial process twenty years later in the Splatt trial. Once again, the combination of police, prosecution and trial processes was unable to detect fundamental flaws that allowed a man to be convicted of a murder without sufficiently tested evidence. After the Stuart Royal Commission and the Rohan Rivett seditious libel trial that followed, Stewart Cockburn apologised to Sir Mellis Napier on behalf of Adelaide's other journalists for the way their colleagues at *The News* had treated him. With Splatt, Cockburn took on Rivett's earlier role, the journalist forcing a revision of a flawed judicial process. If not for Cockburn's efforts, Sergeant Cocks's analysis of the fibres that condemned Edward Splatt would not have been reviewed and found defective. Relying on scientific evidence continued to be an Achilles heel in the South Australian judicial system until at least 1994.

But the journalism of Rohan Rivett and Stewart Cockburn was still a journalism that shared the same interest as the courts in the search for justice and the truth, rather than sales. In the first instance the Chief Justice had lost his sense of his own fallibility, in the second the results of a nascent forensic science were too hastily accepted. In each case the ultimate source of the injustice was over-zealous, if well-meaning, police officers, and the error of the judicial system was to rely too heavily on their evidence. Len King, firstly as Attorney-General and then as Chief Justice did much to improve standards of police evidence presented in court. After Splatt, scientists took responsibility for forensic evidence from front-line investigating officers.

The Stuart Case marked the beginning of a new era in media worldwide. Rupert Murdoch left Adelaide in 1960 to build an international empire of over a thousand newspapers, magazines, publishing houses, television channels, film studios and satellite services. He perfected the profit-oriented tabloid style – not just in daily papers but also in television news and current affairs – fuelled by ratings, and his competition have followed his example or perished. The courts are an easy target for such journalism.

The Chief Justice since Len King must, in addition to the increased administrative role, also be able to manage the media hunger for sales-oriented scandal. The media have the power to shape or distort a community's image of its system of justice. The courts system is often criticised for its delays. Some delay is the insurance for the citizens it serves that all sides of a dispute or of a crime will be heard, in detail, and that contradictions will be explored and explained. In contrast, the daily media operate under the tyranny of daily deadlines and bottom-lines. The media also single out individual cases – almost exclusively criminal - and sow dissatisfaction in their readers, listeners and viewers with the way the courts deal with them. The modern Chief Justice has to manage this facile media manipulation, by the use of isolated examples, of the public's general perception of the justice system.

How well do South Australia's Chief Justices compare with their colleagues elsewhere? In *Lions under the Throne* Anthony Mockler found that while the Lord Chief Justices of the Victorian age were "a very mixed bunch", some "Lord Chief Justices of modern times have been almost totally disastrous."[1] Mockler did not include Lord Justices Parker, Widgery or Lane (who was Lord Chief Justice when the book was published in 1983), but called their six predecessors, from Webster

---

1   Anthony Mockler, *Lions under the Throne*, p. 223. Mockler at the time of the book's publishing was a barrister called at Inner Temple and a Fellow of St Antony's College Oxford.

to Goddard, an "appalling collection of judges that by their combined ineptitudes dragged the office down to absurd depths." Nevertheless, Mockler hastened to add in the next line that none of these Lord Chief Justices was corrupt or even incompetent.

In contrast, Robert J Steamer's study of the office in the United States of America, *Chief Justice: Leadership and the Supreme Court*, concludes much more favourably:

> To excel in the multiple roles of chief justice requires extraordinary talent and although none of the incumbents has performed perfectly, a few have been brilliant; several have been distinguished; all have been competent. Despite the partisan politics frequently surrounding the appointment of chief justices, the record of their service has been uncommonly free of petty partisanship, and not so much as a hint of personal or public corruption has ever tainted the office. It is a record to which the nation can point with justifiable pride.[2]

The South Australian Chief Justices obviously serve a much smaller population than the United Kingdom and the United States, yet qualitatively must meet the same essential standards expected. The first of the "appalling" British judges, Webster, was Lord Chief Justice around the time of Samuel Way. Thus all six come within the same historical period this book covers. Has South Australia fared better than her judicial progenitor?

I only found reason to be critical of one Chief Justice, Napier, and that was in relation to the Stuart case and to his role in the appointment of his son as Queen's Counsel. It seems as though, around 1960, Napier momentarily lost his sense of proportion. If he had taken the option to retire at seventy, he would have left with an otherwise unblemished record. It must not be forgotten, nevertheless, that his single most influential judgment was given well after he turned 70 – *Bay Hotel v Broadway Hotel* – and led to long overdue reforms in liquor licensing that finally saw light of day in 1967.

Samuel Way's reputation as a judge alone was reinforced by the fact that none of his decisions was reversed by the High Court, when

---

2   Robert J Steamer, *Chief Justice: Leadership and the Supreme Court*, p. 301.

from its first days it established a reputation for reversing State Supreme Court judgments. While George Murray was occasionally overturned by the High Court, one of his court's most important judgments – *Grant v Australian Knitting Mills* –was restored by the Privy Council.

Samuel Way had tried to increase the dignity of the still young South Australian Supreme Court by ensuring its sartorial standards equalled those of England. Murray, with his Cambridge education and Inner Temple training, scrupulously continued this absolute allegiance to English traditions. His judges wore top hats in the street and on circuit, were forbidden to smoke in public or socialise in public houses, and even had to have their hair cut in chambers. Napier was a traditionalist who would surely have continued these practices, but reluctantly had to recognise that the top hat was ultimately just a fashion statement and not a timeless icon of respectability. But the fact that all three judges exercised such controls beyond the bench shows how very aware they were of the need to maintain the public's overall respect for the Supreme Court. Their flaw may have been not recognising that their standards were not timeless but Victorian. On the other hand, such a flaw may have also sprung from the same source of strength in resisting passing whims in the public's conception of justice.

Bray was the scholar of the five, with judgments wrought into works of genuine literature. At the same time though, it should not be forgotten that litigants are not chasing judgments of literary interest, and those of pragmatic judges such as Way and King who aimed at clarity and economy are at least as valuable as Bray's.

Bray, let us not forget, was just as much a traditionalist when it came to robes, wigs and breeches as Way, Murray and Napier. Being well-read in classics and literature, Bray appreciated the powerful symbolism of ceremony. Bray could keep the traditions in perspective with the explosion of individual freedom taking place in the 1960s and 1970s. Without sacrificing the Supreme Court's past, he was able to reconnect it with community values, at least with his own judgments. Perhaps his well-publicised bohemian lifestyle helped.

Bray's appointment as Chief Justice also marks the beginning of a new era in which the judicial arm of government asserted its independence from the executive. Bray refused the Lieutenant-Governorship, which had been attached to the office of Chief Justice since 1890. He correctly believed that to hold both offices conflicted with the notion of judicial independence. One of Len King's major achievements was to cement that independence with the creation of an administrative structure that assured its permanence.

Bray was also a fearless defender of the right of individuals to make their own moral decisions. He spoke openly against censorship, and for civil liberties. Many of his judgments – when in a Full Court, often dissenting – take this view. Bray was also known as a poet, and the South Australian public could go and see him giving readings at Writers' Week. Bray also broke the stilted, stiff and insular image of the judiciary. His disdain for the Victorian-age conventions his predecessors cherished helped his court get in touch with the tumultuous changes taking place in South Australian society then. He became famous for taking the bus down to the beach with his towel over his shoulder.

While Bray's erudite judgments may not have always convinced a few of his judicial colleagues, he brought the Supreme Court back to the people. After Napier, more than just the court's reputation was in tatters: "The Napier Court brought the State into disrepute," in the view of former Prime Minister, Gough Whitlam.[3] Bray's first act to repair the damage was quite simple: refusing the Lieutenant-Governorship. By refusing that office Bray firmly detached the judiciary from the executive and set the direction for its complete independence 26 years later.

Don Dunstan chose both Bray and King as Chief Justice, and his vision of the evolution of South Australian jurisprudence is still to be fully appreciated. But if Bray had been born later, and had come after King instead of before, would he have made a good Chief Justice? With the need to administer not just the Supreme Court, but also the District Court, the Magistrates Court, the Industrial Relations Court, the Youth Court, the Environment, Resources and Development Court and the Coroner's Court, he may well have fled in horror. In the large system that is the Courts Administration Authority, the Chief Justice who heads it must be a good administrator and also its champion.

Bray was the last Chief Justice/Chancellor. The break with the tradition, emphasised as it was by Napier's staying on as lieutenant-governor after retiring from the bench, became its demise. Bray's successor

---

3   Letter from the Hon. E G Whitlam AC QC to John Emerson, 28 October 2003.

as chancellor was Roma Mitchell, a member of the Supreme Court, but not the Chief Justice. The office of chancellor had changed substantially since the half-century up to 1942 that it had been occupied by Way and Murray. In their time the University of Adelaide was small and the Supreme Court was small. It was possible for one person to preside over both. The vice-chancellor was also an unpaid, part-time office. The university grew and the court grew, and the demands on the time of those in charge of both grew increasingly heavy. When A P Rowe was appointed the first full-time paid Vice-Chancellor in 1948, the chancellor was no longer involved in the university's day-to-day management.

Bray had always had a strong yearning for a university career and he must have been initially delighted to have been appointed its titular head in 1968. He had already broken Way's triple crown by refusing the lieutenant-governorship; it would have quickly dawned on him that Way would have been shocked by the chancellor's powerlessness. During Bray's period in that office the university – like most others – was reducing the emphasis on academic education and focusing increasingly more on vocational training. Bray – even as Chancellor and Chief Justice – could not stand in the way of this tide, that to his point of view replaced a "panoramic vision of the past" with "individually selected peepholes".[4]

The Chief Justice remains a "first among equals" in his or her judicial capacity. There has never been an assumption that the Chief Justice should be able to unduly influence or coerce the other judges on the Supreme Court. In practice, Way, Murray and Napier did appear to expect the other judges to agree with them on joint decisions. But in practice also, if a judge really did not agree, then he could do so without fear of retribution. On occasions Gordon challenged Way, Cleland challenged Murray, and Mayo and Chamberlain challenged Napier. Since Bray, judgments dissenting from the Chief Justices have been seen more as the sign of a robust court.

It is probably more important as the courts have grown in size that the status of the Chief Justice no longer depends entirely on the office-holder being able to dominate the course of judicial decision-making as Way, Murray and Napier did. Apart from the more complex extra-judicial demands, it would in any event be impossible for anyone to do so, because of the larger numbers of the courts and judges. And

---

4   John Bray, *The Emperor's Doorkeeper*, p. 195.

(from what has gone before) the dominance of the earlier chief justices did have its downside.   But as before, and all the way throughout history, the person holding the office of Chief Justice remains the person who embodies society's ideal of justice.

Bibliography

Books - consulted and cited

Abel, Richard L. *The Legal Profession in England and Wales*. Oxford: Basil Blackwell, 1988.

Auerbach, Jerold S. *Unequal Justice: Lawyers and Social Change in Modern America*. New York: Oxford University Press, 1976.

Austin, A. G. *The Webbs' Australian Diary 1898*. Melbourne: Pitman and Sons, 1965.

Barwick, Garfield. *A Radical Tory*. Leichhardt (Sydney): Federation Press, 1995.

Bennett, J. M. *Sir William a'Beckett*. Lives of the Australian Chief Justices. Leichhardt (Sydney): Federation Press, 2001.

Bennett, J. M. *Sir James Dowling*. Lives of the Australian Chief Justices. Leichhardt (Sydney): Federation Press, 2001.

Bennett, J. M. *Sir Francis Forbes*. Lives of the Australian Chief Justices. Leichhardt (Sydney): Federation Press, 2001.

Blewitt, Neil and Jaensch, Dean. *Playford to Dunstan: The Politics of Transition*. Melbourne: Cheshire, 1971.

Bond, Colin and Ramsay, Hamish. *Preserving Historic Adelaide*. Adelaide: Rigby, 1978.

Bundey, W. H. *Conviction of Innocent Men*. Adelaide: Wigg, 1900.

Campbell, Enid and Lee, H. P. *The Australian Judiciary*. Cambridge, Cambridge University Press, 2001.

Campbell, John. *The Lives of the Chief Justices of England*. London: John Murray, 1849 (4 vols.).

Cardozo, Benjamin N. *The Nature of the Judicial Process*. New Haven and London: Yale University Press, 1921.

Chisholm, Richard and Nettheim, Garth. *Understanding Law*. Revised Edition. Sydney: Butterworths, 1978.

Castles, Alex. *An Australian Legal History*. Sydney: Law Book Co., 1982.

Castles, Alex; Ligertwood, Andrew and Kelly, Peter. *Law on North Terrace*. Adelaide: Faculty of Law, University of Adelaide, 1983.

Castles, Alex and Harris, Michael. *Wayward Whigs and Lawmakers*. Adelaide: Wakefield Press, 1987.

Chamberlain, Sir Roderic. *The Stuart Affair*. Adelaide: Rigby, 1973.

Cockburn, Stewart. *Playford : Benevolent Despot*. Kent Town (Adelaide): Axiom, 1991.

Dixon, Thomas Sidney. *The Wizard of Alice*. Morwell (Victoria): Alella Books, 1987.

Duncan, W.G.K. and Leonard, Roger Ashley. *The University of Adelaide, 1874-1974*. Adelaide: Rigby, 1973.

Dunstan, Don. *Felicia, the Political Memoirs of Don Dunstan*. South Melbourne: Macmillan, 1981.

Dunstan, Don. *Politics and Passion*. Unley (Adelaide): Bookend Books, 2000.

Elliott, Jack. *Memoirs of a Barrister*. Adelaide: Wakefield Press, 2000.

Emerson, John. *History of the Independent Bar of South Australia*. Adelaide: University of Adelaide Barr Smith Press, 2006.

Estcourt Hughes, J. *History of the Royal Adelaide Hospital*. Adelaide: Royal Adelaide Hospital, 1967.

Evan, William M. (ed.) *The Sociology of Law*. New York: The Free Press (a division of Macmillan), 1980.

Fish, Peter. *The Office of Chief Justice*. Charlottesville: University of Virginia, 1984.

Forde, John Leonard. *The Story of the Bar of Victoria, 1839-1891*. Melbourne: Whitcombe and Tombs, c1908.

Fountain, Richard (ed.). *The Wit of the Wig*. London: Leslie Frewin, 1968.

Frick, Graham. *Judges of the High Court*. Hawthorn, Victoria: Hutchinson, 1986.

Friedman, Leon et al. (eds.) *The Justices of the United States Supreme Court 1789-1969*. 4 vol. New York: Chelsea, 1969.

Gibbs, R. M. A *History of South Australia: From Colonial Days to the Present*. Blackwood (Adelaide): Southern Heritage, 1990.

Giblin, L F. *The Growth of a Central Bank: The Development of the Commonwealth of Australia 1924-1945*. Melbourne: MUP, 1951.

Glass, Margaret. *Charles Cameron Kingston*. Melbourne: Melbourne University Press, 1997.

Hague, R. M. *Sir John Jeffcott: Portrait of a Colonial Judge*. Melbourne: Melbourne University Press, 1963.

Hague, R.M. (Ralph). *Hague's History of the Law in South Australia, 1837-1867.* Adelaide: University of Adelaide Barr Smith Press, 2005.

Hannan, A. J. *Sir Samuel Way.* Sydney: Angus and Robertson, 1960.

William Harcus (ed.). *South Australia: its history, resources and productions.* London: Sampson Low, Marston, Searle, and Rivington, 1876.

Healey, John (ed.). *S.A.'s Greats: The Men and Women of the North Terrace Plaques.* Adelaide: Historical Society of South Australia, 2001.

Hocking, Jenny. *Lionel Murphy: A Political Biography.* Cambridge: Cambridge University Press, 1997.

Holdsworth, Sir William. *A History of English Law.* London: Methuen, 1903. Fourth Edition, 1936.

Inglis, K.S. *The Stuart Case.* Melbourne: Black Inc., 2002.

Jaensch, Dean (ed.). *The Flinders History of South Australia.* Vol. II, Political History. Adelaide: Wakefield Press, 1986.

Kwan, Elizabeth. *Living in South Australia.* Vol. 2: "After 1914". Netley (SA): SA Government Printer, 1987.

Lee, Simon F. *Judging Judges.* London: Faber, 1988.

Linden, Allen (ed.). *The Canadian Judiciary.* Toronto: Osgoode Hall Law School, 1976.

Marr, David. *Barwick.* North Sydney: Allen and Unwin, 1980.

Mockler, Anthony. *Lions Under The Throne.* London: Frederick Muller, 1983.

Montesquieu, Charles de Secondat, baron de. *The Spirit of the Laws.* Tr. Thomas Nugent. New York: Hafner Publishing, 1949. [1748]

Morgan, E.J.R. *The Adelaide Club 1863-1963.* Adelaide : Adelaide Club, 1963.

Morris, Gwen et al. *Laying Down the Law.* Sydney: Butterworths, 1996.

O'Neill, Bernard; Raftery, Judith and Round, Kerrie. *Playford's South Australia: Essays on the History of South Australia, 1933-1968.* Adelaide: Association of Professional Historians, 1996.

Parkin, Andrew and Patience, Allan. *The Bannon Decade: the Politics of Restraint in South Australia.* St Leonards, NSW: Allen and Unwin, 1992.

Pascoe, J. J. (ed.) *History of Adelaide and Vicinity.* Adelaide: Hussey and Gillingham, 1901.

Pike, Douglas. *Paradise of Dissent: South Australia 1829-1857.* Melbourne: Melbourne University Press, 1967.

Prest, Wilfrid (ed.). *A Portrait of John Bray.* Adelaide: Wakefield Press/ John Bray Law Chapter of the University of Adelaide, 1997.

Prest, Wilfrid et al. (ed.). *The Wakefield Companion to South Australian History.* Kent Town (Adelaide): Wakefield Press/ John Bray Chapter of the University of Adelaide Alumni Association, 2001.

Richards, Eric (ed.). *The Flinders History of South Australia.* Vol. III, Social History. Adelaide: Wakefield Press, 1986.

Robertson, Geoffrey. *The Justice Game.* London: Chatto and Windus, 1998.

Rowe, A.P. *If the Gown Fits.* Melbourne: Melbourne University Press, 1960.

Royal Commission on Law Reform (The Jury System), First Progress Report. Adelaide, 1923.

Royal Commission into the Monetary and Banking Systems at present in Australia. Canberra: Commonwealth Government Printer, 1937.

Savvas, A. and Becker, A. (eds.) *Sixty-nine years of events from the pages of The News.* College Park (SA): A. Savvas, 1992.

Selway, Bradley M. *Constitution of South Australia.* Sydney: Federation Press, 1997.

Steamer, R. *Chief Justice: Leadership and the Supreme Court.* Columbia, S C: University of South Carolina Press, 1986.

Trollope, Anthony. *Australia and New Zealand.* London: Chapman and Hall, 1873. The edition consulted, edited by P. R. Edwards and R. B. Joyce. Australia. St Lucia: University of Queensland Press, 1967.

Mark Twain. *Following the Equator.* New York: American Publishing Company, 1897. The edition consulted includes only the Australian and New Zealand section: *Mark Twain in Australia and New Zealand.* Ringwood: Penguin, 1973.

Umbreit, Kenneth Bernard. *Our Eleven Chief Justices.* New York: Harper, 1938.

Whitelock, Derek. *Adelaide, 1836-1976: a History of Difference.* St Lucia (Melbourne), Qld: University of Queensland Press, 1977.

Woodruff, Philip. *Two Million South Australians.* Kent Town (Adelaide): Peacock Publications, 1984.

Periodicals consulted

Adelaide Law Review. Vol. 7, No. 1. January 1980. Adelaide: University of Adelaide Law Review Association.

Australian Law Journal. Sydney: The Law Book Co., Vol. 27, No. 3, July 30, 1953. "The Eighth Legal Convention of the Law Council of Australia", pp. 133-224.

Law Calendar. South Australian Attorney-General's Department. Adelaide: Government Printer, 1889-.

South Australian Year Book. Adelaide: Commonwealth Bureau of Statistics, South Australian Office, 1966-. (Formerly *Official Year Book of South Australia* and now *Australian Bureau of Statistics*)

Articles and cited

Bray, J. J. "Law, Liberty and Morality", *Australian Law Journal*, Vol. 45, September 1971.

Charles Bright, "Bray in Context", *Adelaide Law Review.* Vol. 7, January 1980, No. 1.

Castles, Alex. "Sir Mellis Napier", *The Adelaide Law Review.* Vol. 3, No. 1, June 1967, pp. 1-6.

Cadzow, Jane. "The Wayward Ways of Christopher Pearson", *Good Weekend*, March 30, 1996, pp. 27-31.

Edgar, Suzanne. "The King of the West End", *National Times*, May 2-8, 1982, p. 14.

Edgeloe, V.A. "Sir George Murray (1863-1942): His Public Community Career", *Journal of the Historical Society of South Australia.* No. 19, 1991, pp. 173-182.

Richard G. Fox. "Depravity, Corruption and Community Standards", *Adelaide Law Review*. Vol. 7, January 1980, No. 1.

Heerey, Hon. Justice Peter. "Storytelling, Postmodernism and the Law", *Australian Law Journal*, Vol. 74, No. 10, pp. 681-691.

King, Len. "A Judiciary-based State Courts Administration - the South Australian experience", *Journal of Judicial Administration*, Vol. 3, 1993, pp. 133-142.

Kirby, the Hon. Justice Michael AC CMG. "The Five Queensland Justices of the High Court", *Australian Bar Review*, Vol. 15, No. 1, December 1996, pp. 61-72.

Lavers, Anthony. "Murray House", *New Outlook*, March 1994, p. 33.

Graham Loughlin. "Paris Nesbit, Q.C.", *Journal of the Historical Society of South Australia*, vol. 3, 1977, pp. 55-61.

Parkinson, Andrew. "The Regret of Samuel Way", *Australian Journal of Legal History*, vol. 1, 1995, pp 239-257.

Archival Material in Public Collections

Bray, the Honourable Dr John Jefferson AC QC. Papers. Mortlock Collection, State Library of South Australia. PRG 1098.

King, the Honourable Leonard James AC QC. Speeches and other papers. Mortlock Collection, State Library of South Australia. PRG 1163.

King, the Honourable Leonard James AC QC. *Retirement Address*, Special Sitting of the Supreme Court, 28 April 1995. Mortlock Collection, PRG 1163.

Murray, Sir George. Papers. Mortlock Collection, State Library of
    South Australia. PRG 269.

Way, Sir Samuel. Papers. Mortlock Collection, State Library of South
    Australia. PRG 30.

Archival Material in Private Collections

King, the Honourable Leonard James AC QC. Various papers, press
    clippings, personal memoirs.

Napier, Sir Mellis. Various papers, press clippings, correspondence.

Reports and Reviews for Government

Bollen Q C, D. W. *Review of Advice Given to Attorney-General By His
    Officers on Newspaper Articles Written in* The Advertiser *by Mr
    Stewart Cockburn About the Trial and Conviction of Edward James
    Splatt.* Adelaide: Hanson Chambers, 26 June 1981.

R v Splatt: Report for the Attorney General. [1981]

Shannon Q. C., Carl Reginald. *Royal Commission Report Concerning
    the Conviction of Edward Charles Splatt.* Adelaide: Government
    Printer, 1984.

Unpublished works - consulted and cited

Hon. Clyde R Cameron AO. "The King of West End". Unpublished
    article, 25/5/2003, p. 3.

Edgeloe, V.A. *The Establishment and the Elite.* Typescript, 1981. Barr Smith Library Special Collections.

Edgeloe, V.A. *The University of Adelaide: The Murray-Mitchell Era.* Unpublished, Appendix 3.

Hague, R. M. *The Judicial Career of Benjamin Boothby.* Adelaide, 1992.

Hague, R. M. *Henry Jickling.* Adelaide, 1993.

Hague, R. M. *Mr Justice Crawford: Judge of the Supreme Court of South Australia, 1850-1852.* Adelaide, 1995.

Hannan, A.J. *History of the University.* Unpublished, 1964. Accessible Barr Smith Special Collections Library of the University of Adelaide.

Heaney, M. A. *The Adelaide Hospital Dispute (1894-1902)*, BA Honours Thesis, unpublished. University of Adelaide, 1980.

Loughlin, Graham. *South Australian Queen's Counsel, 1865-1972.* BA Honours Thesis, University of Adelaide, 1974.

Poetry

Bray, John. *Poems.* Melbourne: Cheshire, 1962.

Bray, John. *Poems, 1961-1971.* Brisbane: Jacaranda Press, 1972.

Bray, John. *The Bay of Salamis and Other Poems.* Unley (Adelaide): Friendly Street Poets, 1986.

Bray, John. *Seventy Seven.* Adelaide: Wakefield Press, 1990.

Index

This is an index primarily of the people who have featured in the book, followed by major events, major institutions and any other entity that had a prominent role. Titles are omitted, except aristocratic ones. It is not exhaustive, but readers are welcome to request an electronic copy of the book from the publisher in PDF format for more detailed searching. The electronic version is free for buyers, and is available by emailing: inquiries@papinian.com.au

Pocahontas 165
Poems 1972-1979 211
Poole, Thomas 91, 96, 122, 125, 127
Portus, G. V. 88, 89, 92
Prince Alfred's College 91
Privy Council 11, 23, 25, 32, 35, 37, 38, 39, 40, 54, 78, 101, 103, 104, 124, 125, 143, 195, 196, 267
Public Library 11, 32

R

Reed, Geoffrey 135, 143, 145, 152, 153, 171, 183, 264
Reilly, Ron 224
Richards, Frederick 44, 86, 135,
Rivett, Rohan 144, 148, 149, 151, 161, 185, 186, 187, 191, 193, 264
Ross, Bruce 144, 152, 153
Rowe A.P. 139, 140, 141

S

Salisbury, Harold 207, 210, 242
Salmond, John 76
Sangster, Keith 152, 160, 235
Seventy Seven 166, 211
Shakespeare, William 167, 211, 222
Shand, Jack 144, 147, 148, 149, 184, 185
Shebbear 17, 18, 53
Shell Oil 220
Short, Bishop 7, 28, 30, 32, 34, 35
Simms, William 77, 78
Smith, Ramsay 115
Snow, Francis 93, 95
Sparks, Henry 15
Splatt, Charles 243, 264
Starke, John 144
Steamer, Robert J. 266
Stevenson, Derrence 249
George Stevenson 15
St Peter's Cathedral 157
St Peter's College 69, 91, 131, 166, 167
Strehlow, Thomas 146, 151
Stuart, John McDouall 65
Stuart, Ruper Max 3, 9, 142, 143, 144, 145, 146, 147, 148, 149, 150, 151, 152, 153, 161, 184, 185, 197, 211, 263, 264, 265, 266
Sturt Arcade Hotel 184, 190, 206, 211
Sumner, Chris 259
Symon, Josiah 16, 76, 77, 83, 96, 97

T

John Emerson owned and operated small businesses while publishing the odd article and working in a radio station until taking on a series of degrees in the 1990s. He specialised in French and Australian cinema history, completing a postgraduate degree at the Sorbonne Nouvelle in Paris and a PhD at the University of Adelaide. His thesis compared the way contemporary French and Australian cinema represented their colonial pasts. Since 2002 he has been working on books on the history of Adelaide's legal profession with the John Bray Law Chapter of the University of Adelaide's Alumni Association. He is currently working on a literary biography of poet and influential Chief Justice John Jefferson Bray.

www.ingramcontent.com/pod-product-compliance
Lightning Source LLC
Chambersburg PA
CBHW062010090426

42811CB00005B/814